Investigation into the King's Cross Underground Fire

Presented to Parliament by the Secretary of State for Transport
by Command of Her Majesty November 1988

THE DEPARTMENT
OF TRANSPORT

LONDON
HER MAJESTY'S STATIONERY OFFICE

Cm 499   £19·50 net

Plate 1   View of the scene at King's Cross on the evening of 18 November 1987 from Euston Road looking up Pancras Road

Investigation
into the King's Cross
Underground Fire

Inspector:
Mr Desmond Fennell OBE QC

Department of Transport
2 Marsham Street
London SW1P 3EB

21 October 1988

The Rt Hon. Paul Channon MP
Secretary of State for Transport
Department of Transport
2 Marsham Street
London SW1P 3EB

Dear Secretary of State,

King's Cross Underground Fire Investigation

I was appointed by you on 23 November 1987 to hold a formal Investigation into the circumstances of the King's Cross Underground fire. I have completed the Investigation and enclose my Report.

Yours sincerely,

Desmond Fennell

Desmond Fennell

Contents

List of Plates

Acknowledgements

Plates reproduced by courtesy of:
BRITISH TRANSPORT POLICE: (Plate 3)
DAILY EXPRESS: (Plate 1)
HARWELL: (Plate 27)
HEALTH AND SAFETY EXECUTIVE: (Plates 6–9, 13, 17, 21–26 and 28–31)
LONDON FIRE AND CIVIL DEFENCE AUTHORITY: (Plates 5, 14–16 and 18–20)
METROPOLITAN POLICE: (Plates 4 and 12)
PHILIP I. POWELL, BSc(Eng), MIMechE, MIEE: (Plate 2)
TUCKER ROBINSON: (Plates 10 and 11)

COVER PICTURE: ASSOCIATED PRESS

List of Appendices

List of Figures

Synopsis

passenger unable to be evacuated by Midland City subway — arrival of London Fire Brigade senior officers — arrival of London Underground senior managers — Midland City gates unlocked — evacuation of Metropolitan side staff — evacuation of tube side staff — attempts at fire-fighting — discovery of station plans — arrival of London Underground Incident Officer — fire crews reach lower level — two station staff discovered in messroom and released — fire surrounded and damped down — search and salvage operations.

CHAPTER 10 THE RESPONSE OF LONDON UNDERGROUND STAFF

Background of inadequate training, no evacuation plan, poor communication and no effective supervision — staff instruction and attitude to dealing with fire — the response of tube side operating staff considered — staff absent from duty — the response of Metropolitan side operating staff considered — role of the booking office staff — conclusions — performance of HQ and line controllers — failures of communication — senior managers on scene — Duty Incident Officer — no effective control or communication or liaison with emergency services.

CHAPTER 11 THE RESPONSE OF THE EMERGENCY SERVICES

London Fire Brigade — particular problems at King's Cross — the London Fire and Civil Defence Authority — first call — London Underground procedure for calling London Fire Brigade — predetermined attendance plan — logging of calls — arrival of first appliances — Station Officer Townsley — no rendezvous point or meeting by London Underground — initial assessment of fire — flashover — heroism of Station Officer Townsley — Station Officer Osborne and Mr Bates — Temporary Sub-Officer Bell directing passengers — location of London Underground hose — crews on the surface driven back — Assistant Divisional Officer Shore and Midland City entrance — Divisional Officer Johnson — Deputy Assistant Chief Officer Wilson — discovery of station plans — no strategic appraisal or reconnaissance of alternative entrance — Assistant Chief Officer Kennedy — rendezvous with fire officers below — fire surrounded — background to evaluation of performance assessment — lessons to be learned — recommendations — courage and devotion to duty.

British Transport Police — chance presence of British Transport Police officers — organisation of British Transport Police — L Division — basic training — B Division mobile unit on the scene — emergency radio call — meeting of fire brigade — diversion of passengers — call for trains not to stop — arrival of more officers — evacuation of passengers — the flashover and courageous actions of P.C. Hanson and P.C. Bebbington — assistance to passengers and fire-fighters — conclusions — after the flashover — W.P. Sgt. O'Neill and Metropolitan side — Inspector Wilkinson and attendance of other officers — failure of liaison — recommendations.

Metropolitan Police — supporting role — Inspector Coleman — establishment of rendezvous point — deployment of traffic units — central casualty bureau — conclusion and recommendations.

London Ambulance Service — less detailed evidence heard — ban on overtime and staff shortage — first call — ambulances on alert — points of concern — attendance of senior officers — recommendations.

CHAPTER 12 THE DEVELOPMENT OF THE FIRE — EYEWITNESS ACCOUNTS AND SCIENTIFIC INVESTIGATION

Unprecedented development of escalator fire — apparently small fire minutes before flashover — need to explain flashover — initiation of the fire beneath the escalator at about 19:25 — possible causes considered — first obsevation of the fire and its development — observations of the fire above the escalator — observations of smoke in the ticket hall and adjoining subways — observations of the flashover and development of the fire in the ticket hall — experiences of passengers and of station inspectors beneath escalator.

Review of scientific investigations — mass of material burnt in fire — ignition tests on samples of grease and detritus — likelihood of ignition by lighted match — tests on Prodorite paint.

Opinions put forward and examined in Part One — Moodie — Eisner — Tucker — no consensus — theories examined in Part Two — computer modelling of flow and temperature of gases — unexpected phenomenon of the 'trench effect' — one-tenth model fire tests — Duggan — Rasbash — Moodie — divergence of views over role of paint — further submissions allowed.

Post Part Two investigations — computer modelling of effect of air movements — the piston effect of train movements — one-third model fire test — Drysdale further fire tests — agreement about 'trench effect' and separation of flow — remaining areas of uncertainty.

Conclusions — ignition by smokers' materials — fire on right-hand side escalator running track — its spread phenomenon of the 'trench effect' — separation into two streams — eruption of lower stream of flame into ticket hall — black smoke — ignition of ticket hall ceiling — role of the paint — recommendations.

CHAPTER 13 THE MANAGEMENT OF SAFETY

Scope of judgement made on London Underground safety management — relative safety of travel by Underground — London Underground's responsibility for passenger safety — safety enshrined in operating ethos — priorities — occupational safety — misunderstanding of health and safety statutory responsibilities — approach to passenger safety reactive not pro-active — lessons from earlier fires — failure to carry through recommendations of inquiries — directors would not have acted differently — corporate view of London Regional Transport about fires — unqualified assumptions — RoSPA Director General's view on the evidence — London Underground's actions since the disaster — a proper approach to safety management — absence of accidents not a safe indicator — fire not an occupational hazard — need for hazard analysis and a managed safety programme — recommendations.

CHAPTER 14 THE AUDITING OF SAFETY

Chairman of London Regional Transport's view of the role of the holding company — statutory position — proper discharge of duty by holding company — safety of operation to be subject of audit — London Regional Transport to set corporate safety objectives — appointment to Board of London Underground of non-executive member responsible for safety — safety audit the yardstick by which safety is measured.

CHAPTER 15 STATION STAFFING AND TRAINING

Investigation of system in place, not the conduct of individuals — overall response uncoordinated — inadequate training and instruction — new station staffing proposals — responsibilities of station 'landlord' — use of relief staff — deployment of medically restricted staff — cultural change required — 'management by memo' — failure in organisation, delegation, communication — need for clearer accountability, more exchange of information, outside recruitment, a structured safety regime.

Evidence of inadequate training — quality of training before 1987 — new training programmes — need for professional advice — training in station evacuation — 'safety procedure' for each station — instruction to staff and rule book — recommendations — professional advice — London Underground response to the Health and Safety Executive APAU report and consultants' report on fire safety training: view of Director General of RoSPA — recommendations.

Emergency services training — importance of joint exercises — London Fire Brigade and British Transport Police training by London Underground — recommendations.

CHAPTER 16 COMMUNICATIONS SYSTEMS

Importance of communications — HQ and line controllers — telephone systems — British Transport Police information room — ordering of trains not to stop — logging of calls — public address systems — passenger inquiry points and public telephones — closed circuit television — radio in stations (London Underground, British Transport Police, London Fire Brigade) — train communications — training and practice in use of equipment — recommendations.

CHAPTER 17 FIRE CERTIFICATION

Main legislative provisions governing fire safety — 1903 Paris Metro fire and aftermath — Fire Precautions Act 1971 and Health and Safety at Work etc. Act 1974 — application of 'railway premises' — Opinion of Counsel to the Court — response of Railway Inspectorate and London Underground — the correct view — Fire Precautions Act set a standard for good practice — London Underground relied upon short visits by London Fire Brigade — fire certificate requires adequate means of escape not available at King's Cross before flashover — Midland City exit locked — absence of adequately trained London Underground staff — dangers of smoke known from earlier fires — need for rolling programme of station improvements — identification of possible escape routes following Oxford Circus fire — nearest and best escape route at King's Cross not recognised — subject of certification has wide ramifications — recommendations.

CHAPTER 18 ROLE OF THE RAILWAY INSPECTORATE

Railway Inspectorate's role under railways legislation — inspection of new or altered railway works — agency role under health and safety at work legislation — the Inspectorate's understanding of its responsiblities considered — need for more active role to reflect responsiblity for public safety — drew comfort from London Fire Brigade inspections — decision to stop receiving London Fire Brigade inspection reports — problem of escalator fires identified by Inspectorate in 1973 — the Inspectorate's approach to London Underground considered — inspections of machine rooms in 1987 — adequacy of existing powers — proposed actions — more vigorous use of enforcement powers — improved liaison with London Fire Brigade — recommendations.

CHAPTER 19 MATTERS FOR FURTHER CONSIDERATION

Financing of London Regional Transport — climate of budgetary constraints — allocation of resources — investment criteria — capital underspending — staffing levels — Underground ticketing system — congestion relief at King's Cross — monitoring of congestion and remedial action — crime — smoking and littering byelaws — a passenger safety inspectorate — publication of fire inspection reports — publicity for safety improvements — staff consultation and trade unions — safety representatives and safety committees — taking charge and coordination of emergencies — national disaster planning — identification and handling of bodies — coroner's inquests — not in public interest to have two public inquiries — implementation of recommendations and progress reporting.

CHAPTER 20 RECOMMENDATIONS

Actions taken by London Underground — recommendations made by represented parties — level of priority to attach to Report recommendations — recommendations grouped under Chapter headings — implementation of recommendations — table of cross-references by Chapter, action number and represented parties' recommendations number.

CHAPTER 21 CONCLUSION

Chapter 1

Executive Summary

1. At the heart of this Investigation lie three questions:
   (i) How did the fire start?
   (ii) Why was there a flashover?
   (iii) Why did 31 people die?

How did the fire start?

2. It is clear from the evidence that people continued to smoke in the Underground in spite of the ban in February 1985 following the fire at Oxford Circus station. They did so in particular by lighting up on the escalator as they prepared to leave the station. The Court was provided with detailed information of 46 escalator fires between 1956 and 1988 and in 32 instances the cause was attributed to smokers' materials.

3. About two weeks before the disaster, gaps were observed between the treads and the skirting board on the Piccadilly Line escalator 4 at King's Cross. They were caused by the crabbing movement of the escalator. Thus there were gaps through which a lighted match could pass. Moreover 30 per cent of fire cleats were missing, making it easier for a match to fall through the gap and for a fire to flourish.

4. Beneath each side of the treads lay the running tracks of the escalator. Those running tracks should have been cleaned and lubricated properly. They were not. There was an accumulation of grease and detritus (dust, fibre and debris) on the tracks which constituted a seed bed for a fire and it was into that bed that the match fell. When the forensic scientist inspected the scene after the disaster he recovered several matches from the running track underneath the lower part of the escalator.

5. When the skirting board of the escalator was examined it was clear from the burn marks that fires had started on many previous occasions. Happily, they had gone out. On 18 November 1987 the fire bed ignited and the grease on the right-hand running track began to melt. The fire had started.

Why was there a flashover?

6. A detailed investigation into the fire dynamics was carried out by the Scientific Committee. I set out the details and my findings in Chapter 12 'The Development of the Fire: Eyewitness Accounts and Scientific Investigation', but for the purposes of this summary I can put the matter this way. The fire began at about 19:25 probably in the vicinity of step 48. Since the escalator was running, the fire was carried up to other sites nearer the top and involved the left-hand side of the escalator by flame spread beneath the treads where there was grease and detritus.

7. The fire beneath the escalator produced significant pre-heating of the balustrades and decking which made them more susceptible to ignition and spread of fire. The fire on the running track ignited the dry plywood skirting board, which was impregnated with oil and grease, thus providing a path for the fire beneath the escalator to spread to the top side. The flames passing between the treads and skirting board were the source of ignition of the rubber dressguard, the balustrades coated with yacht varnish and the treads and risers.

8. The sudden change in conditions between 19:43 and 19:45, when a modest escalator fire was transformed into the flashover which erupted into the tube lines ticket hall, proved immensely difficult for the Scientific Committee to explain. But I am now satisfied that what has been identified and become known as the 'trench effect' is the proper scientific explanation. In essence, when the fire is burning on one balustrade only the flames behave in a conventional manner and rise more or less vertically out of the escalator trench into the main air stream. When both balustrades and the floor of the escalator trench become involved, air can no longer entrain into the uphill side of the flames and a switch in regime occurs. The flames lie down in the escalator trench, the hot gases are mainly constrained to follow in the trench; pre-heating of the wood ahead of the flame becomes very much more intense and the flames begin to extend very rapidly up the escalator trench. In addition, the flames burn more cleanly and smoke emission may fall even though the fire is burning more rapidly. Nearer the top of the escalator, part of the trench flow circulates up over the facia boards, advertisements and ceiling, involving the ceiling paint and producing thick black smoke. In the result the fire was transformed in character by the trench effect causing it to erupt into the tube lines ticket hall at about 19:45 preceded or accompanied by thick black smoke. Without the application of water or fire extinguishers there was nothing to restrain it.

Why did 31 people die?

9. The alarm was raised by a passenger at about 19:30. Following the procedure in the rule book one of the staff went to inspect. But he was not based at King's Cross and he had received no fire training: he informed neither the station manager nor the line controller. London Underground had no evacuation plan. By chance two police officers were present and as their radios did not work below ground, one ran to the surface to call the London Fire Brigade. It was 19:34. Thereafter the police decided to evacuate passengers from the lower levels of the station by way of the Victoria Line escalator and through the tube lines ticket hall. They did not know the geography of the station and believed they had chosen the quickest and only way for passengers to reach the surface in safety. They could not have anticipated the flashover or the immense amount of dense black smoke.

10. The first London Fire Brigade personnel reached the tube lines ticket hall about 19:43 only two minutes before the flashover. It was too late for them to do anything. Between 19:30 and 19:45 not one single drop of water had been applied to the fire which erupted into the tube lines ticket hall causing horrendous injuries and killing 31 people.

The Report

11. In the following chapter I set out my appointment and the background to the Investigation. In Chapter 3, I discuss the relationship between London Regional Transport and London Underground from which it is clear that London Regional Transport believed that all operational matters including safety were a matter for the operating company, London Underground. The Chairman of London Regional Transport, Sir Keith Bright, told me that whereas financial matters were strictly monitored, safety was not strictly monitored by London Regional Transport. In my view he was mistaken as to his responsibility and I propose later that a Safety Audit shall be introduced which will be the yardstick by which safety is measured (Chapter 14). Only with such a management tool can the Board of London Regional Transport and hence the general public through you, be satisfied that all aspects of safety are maintained at the proper level.

12. Thereafter I examine the ethos of London Underground (Chapter 4) and its organisation and management (Chapter 5). It is clear from what I heard that London Underground was struggling to shake off the rather blinkered approach which had characterised its earlier history and was in the middle of what Dr Ridley, the Chairman and Managing Director, described as a change of culture and style. But in spite of that change the management remained of the view that fires were inevitable on the oldest and most extensive underground system in the world. In my view they were fundamentally in error in their approach.

13. Having considered the history of escalators in the Underground (Chapter 7) and set out a timetable of events for Wednesday 18 November 1987 (Chapter 9), I examine the response of the London Underground operating staff (Chapter 10) followed by that of the emergency services (Chapter 11).

14. The evidence on the fire dynamics occupied a great deal of time and was the principal concern of the Scientific Committee. Since the Investigation has extended the boundaries of scientific knowledge I thought it right to set out in detail the eyewitness and technical evidence which has provided the explanation for the flashover (Chapter 12). The mechanics by which the fire developed were unknown until established by this Investigation, although it is important to note that

the circumstances in which the fire could develop all arose from the condition of the escalator on that night. Thus it is my view that a disaster was foreseeable.

15. I have devoted a chapter to the management of safety (Chapter 13), because the principal lesson to be learned from this tragedy is the right approach to safety. London Underground rightly prided themselves on their reputation as professional railwaymen; unhappily they were lulled into a false sense of security by the fact that no previous escalator fire had caused a death.

16. In Chapter 13 I consider London Underground's approach to passenger safetyoth before and after the King's Cross fire. That approach was particularly important in the light of London Regional Transport's view that safety was principally a matter for the operating company, London Underground. Although I accept that London Underground believed that safety was enshirined in the ethos of railway operation, it became clear that they had a blind spot over the hazard of fire on escalators in stations. In my judgement Dr Ridley was correct to say that London Underground at its highest level may not have have given as high a priority to passenger safety in stations as it should have done.

17. I believe this arose because no one person was charged with overall responsibility for safety. Each director believed he was responsible for safety in his divsion, but that it covered principally the safety of staff. The operations director, who was responsible for the safe operation of the system, did not believe he was responsible for the safety of lifts and escalators which came within the engineering director's department. Specialist safety staff were mainly in junior positions and concerned solely with safety of staff.

18. London Underground did not guard against the unpredictability of fire. Since no one had been killed in the earlier fires they genuinely believed that with passengers and staff acting as fire detectors there would be sufficient time to evacuate passengers safely. But they had no system to train staff in fire drill or evacuation and their attitude towards fire (which they insisted should be called 'smouldering' and regarded as an occuptional hazard) gave the staff a false sense of security. They failed to appreciate the particular problems of smoke.

19. Accordingly I recommend that a managed safety programme shall be instituted which will enable hazards to be identified and eliminated. No passenger transport system can be allowed to have a fire policy which is based on fire precaution. It must be based upon fire prevention.

20. To underline the Court's view about the importance of safety, I outline in Chapter 14 a system that should be put in place for a Safety Audit. If the financial state of a company can be gauged by a financial audit then the state of safety can be similarly established by a Safety Audit.

21. I then undertake a consideration of station staff and training, for that is a fundamental part of safety management. Your invitation to say what lessons should be learned made it essential that I should examine the system in place on 18 November 1987 and consider the system of management, supervision and training of the staff. I devote Chapter 15 to those subjects. My object has been to concentrate upon the system in place, which allowed the disaster to take place, rather than seeking to make personal judgement on those involved.

22. It was clear that there was no efficient control by London Underground supervisors or staff at any time before the disaster occurred. The response of the staff was uncoordinated, haphazard and untrained. London Underground now recognises the need for better training of staff. Similarly, a cultural change in the management is required. What is needed is clear accountability for job performance, an open approach to the exchange of information and an injection of outside talent both permanently and in the form of professional advice.

23. Good communications are at the heart of a modern system of mass transportation and I examine the position at King's Cross in Chapter 16, together with the wider position in London Underground. The control room at any Underground station must be the nerve centre of communication and it was a material deficiency on the night of the disaster that there was no member of London Underground in the room and much of the equipment was out of order. Neither was the public address system used at any time. I go on to consider the position of radio in stations and train communications.

24. I discuss the problem of fire certification in Chapter 17 and, having concluded that the position in law is ambiguous, suggest that you should take steps to resolve the issue.

25. In Chapter 18 I discuss the role of the Railway Inspectorate and conclude that it misunderstood its responsibilities under the Health and Safety at Work etc. Act 1974. I was driven to the conclusion that its relationship with London Underground was too informal and that there was no proper liaison with the London Fire Brigade regarding their respective interests in safety on the London Underground.

26. I turn finally to other matters raised during the Investigation and conclude my Report with 157 recommendations.

Chapter 2

Introduction and Scope of the Investigation

1. Shortly after the evening rush hour had passed its peak on Wednesday 18 November 1987 a fire of catastrophic proportions in the King's Cross Underground station claimed the lives of 30 people and injured many more. A further person was to die in hospital making the final death toll 31. I set out at Appendix D the names of those who died.

2. On Monday 23 November 1987 I was appointed by you to hold a formal investigation under section 7 of the Regulation of Railways Act 1871 into the causes and the circumstances of the King's Cross Underground fire.

3. On Wednesday 25 November 1987 you appointed four assessors to assist me in my task:

    Professor Bernard Crossland CBE DSc FRS FEng
    — Pro-Vice-Chancellor of The Queen's University, Belfast 1978–82.
    — President of the Institute of Mechanical Engineers 1986–87.

    Sir Peter Darby CBE CStJ QFSM CBIM FIFireE
    — lately H.M. Chief Inspector of Fire Services for England and Wales.

    Major Anthony King BSc
    — an Inspecting Officer of Railways in the Department of Transport's Railway Inspectorate.

    Dr Alan Roberts DSc MIChemE CEng
    — Director of the Explosion and Flame Laboratory, the Health and Safety Executive, Buxton.

    The function of the assessors was to give me their advice on technical matters. In the context of this Investigation that has been a matter of particular importance since the scientific problems to be solved occupied a great deal of time. Happily those problems were solved, and I am particularly grateful to my assessors for all their help, without which this Investigation could never have reached a satisfactory and speedy conclusion. But in the end it is I alone who must accept the responsibility for this Report.

4. The terms of section 7 required me to have regard to three particular matters:
    (i) the causes of the accident;
    (ii) the circumstances attending the accident;
    (iii) any observations or recommendations arising out of the Investigation.

5. I made it clear at the outset that this was to be an investigation and not litigation: it was not a law suit in which one party wins and another party loses. It was quite different from the ordinary criminal process which is accusatorial in character. This Investigation was inquisitorial. It was an exercise designed to establish the cause of the disaster and to make recommendations which will make a recurrence less likely. Those who died deserve nothing less.

6. To assist the Investigation in its task of finding out what happened and whether there were any lessons to be learned, Mr Roger Henderson Q.C. was appointed by the Attorney General as Counsel to the Court. He was assisted by Mr Robert Jay and Mr Ian Burnett. They were instructed by the Treasury Solicitor. I would like to express the Court's gratitude to each of them.

7. Between our appointment and the opening of the formal hearings of the Investigation, the following steps were taken:
    (i) I held two preliminary meetings to give directions as to representation and procedure;
    (ii) the task of assembling the evidence for presentation at the hearing was undertaken by the Treasury Solicitor;
    (iii) Messrs. Cremer and Warner, Consulting Engineers, were appointed at my request as consultants to the Court and instructed to advise the Treasury Solicitor on all technical matters; and
    (iv) a Scientific Committee was set up, chaired by Professor Crossland, to try and clarify the technical problems and, where no agreement was possible, to arrange a programme of research to narrow the issue.

8. The Investigation was held in open court with evidence taken on oath. Part One of the hearings opened at the Methodist Central Hall on 1 February 1988 and was devoted principally to eyewitness evidence, both oral and written. It concluded with expert evidence as to the mechanics of the flashover. Part Two of the Investigation began immediately after Easter on 6 April 1988 and was devoted principally to the human and physical state of affairs in place at King's Cross on the night of the disaster. There was also extensive further scientific evidence.

9. At the outset of Part Two, I was invited to make rulings on the scope of the evidence to be received during the remainder of the Investigation. The Association of London Authorities submitted that the Court should consider the funding of London Underground. I ruled that such

a question was *ultra vires* the Investigation which was concerned with what happened at King's Cross on the night of 18 November 1987 and why it happened. I went on to make it clear that I would allow proper questions directed to the underlying philosophy of the management towards safety and how decisions were made, together with the basis upon which they were made, insofar as they related to what happened in the disaster.

10. The Court moved to Church House, Westminster on 3 May 1988, and the public hearings concluded on 24 June 1988 after 91 days. There was still no agreement about why the flashover happened and so I invited the Scientific Committee to continue work until 31 July 1988. I later extended the deadline to 31 August 1988 to enable further experimental work to be undertaken and to allow the parties sufficient time to make their final submission on technical matters.

11. A Procedural History, which gives a fully account of the preliminary and formal hearings and the Scientific Committee, is at Appendix B.

12. I am grateful to the very many members of the general public who wrote to me or my Secretariat at the Deparment of Transport making comments, observations and suggestions as to the cause of the fire and the flashover. The letters were all considered by the Court and I have taken them into account whenever appropriate.

13. This introduction would not be complete without a special word of thanks to the Secretariat who served me so well. Initially it was thought that the Investigation might last three months, but when London Underground produced documents which exceeded 80,000 in number and the scientific evidence became vigorously contested it was clear that we could not achieve that target. Nonetheless a small team consisting of Keith Forrest, Cameron Jones, and Alexandra Tucker led by my private secretary, Mrs Susan Rooke, coped with exemplary efficiency and wonderful good humour. The graceful tribute paid to them by Sir John Drinkwater QC at the end of the Investigation was richly deserved. There are two others to whom I owe a real debt of gratitude. Joyce Fallconi, who by herself has borne the heat and burden of the typing and whose cheerfulness, patience and skill have been remarkable. There remains Richard Bennett who joined the team after the Investigation opened and who has acted as rapporteur, to which post he has brought the twin virtues of the English civil service, intelligence and hard work. I am very grateful to them all.

14. This Investigation had only one goal: to ascertain the cause of the tragedy and to try and ensure that it will never happen again.

Chapter 3

London Regional Transport and London Underground Limited

1. London Regional Transport was created by the London Regional Transport Act 1984 and came into being on 29 June 1984. It is a statutory corporation charged with the general duty of providing public transport for Greater London. Its predecessors had been responsible to central Government at different times and, between 1970 and 1984, to the Greater London Council.

2. The responsibilities and powers of London Regional Transport are laid down in the 1984 Act. Section 2 requires London Regional Transport "in conjunction with the Railways Board to provide or secure the provision of public passenger transport services for Greater London." In carrying out that duty London Regional Transport is required by section 2(2)b to have due regard to "efficiency, economy, and safety of operation".

3. London Regional Transport provides passenger services, mainly but not exclusively, through two wholly owned subsidiary companies, London Underground Limited and London Buses Limited, which were incorporated on 29 March 1985. These two companies are answerable to the holding company, London Regional Transport, which, in its turn, must satisfy financial and other objectives set by the Secretary of State for Transport. The Chairman of London Underground Limited and London Buses Limited are also executive members of the Board of London Regional Transport. The directors of London Regional Transport and London Underground in November 1987 are shown in the chart at Figure 11.

4. Before 1984 the London Transport Executive (LTE) was a centralised organisation run directly by the Chairman and Chief Executive through his colleagues. The executive centre of LTE was an Executive Committee to which all decisions of any consequence were referred. When London Regional Transport was established the Secretary of State for Transport determined various objectives to supplement its statutory and financial duties. In a letter of 20 July 1984 to the Chairman of London Regional Transport the Secretary of State set out four tasks:

    (i) to improve bus and underground services . . . within the resources available, and to make the service more attractive to the public;

    (ii) to reduce costs, including fraud, and the call on taxpayers' and ratepayers' money, and generally secure better value for the community;

    (iii) to involve the private sector in the provision of services where that is more efficient and to make better use of publicly-owned assets . . .;

    (iv) to promote better management through smaller and more efficient units with clear goals and measurable objectives.

5. London Regional Transport is responsible for identifying the public passenger transport needs of London and procuring the provision of services from, amongst others, London Underground. London Regional Transport also makes grants to London Underground to enable it to provide services. It agrees financial targets with London Underground and approves all capital items over £1 million. Every four weeks the Chairman and Managing Director of London Underground presents to the Board of London Regional Transport a report containing information on operating and engineering matters and financial performance, with any additional information he feels should be brought to the Board.

6. In its turn London Regional Transport provides London Underground (and its other subsidiary companies) with objectives which comply with those set for the corporation by the Secretary of State. These corporate aims of London Underground are laid down in standing orders and directives issued by London Regional Transport. The first aim is:

    "to provide consistent with safety, the best value for money rail services within the resources made available, by the pursuit of service quality, unit cost reduction and effective marketing."

    This is the only specific reference to safety in either the Secretary of State's objectives for London Regional Transport or in those of London Regional Transport for London Underground.

7. In his evidence to the Investigation the Chairman of London Regional Transport, Sir Keith Bright, said that London Regional Transport did not interfere in the day-to-day operation of the railway, believing that the proper people to make decisions about operations were the professional railwaymen employed by London Underground. He said that London Regional Transport believed safety was enshrined in the railway operating ethos. London Regional Transport's position of leaving operational matters to London Underground was underlined at every stage during Sir Keith's evidence. He drew the Court's attention to the fact that Dr. Ridley, the Chairman of London Underground, and also a member of the Board of London Regional Transport was able to keep London Regional Transport abreast of matters in relation to safety. He went on to say that the Board of London Regional Transport became involved in safety matters when projects were presented for approval and it did, from time to time, change the course of a project for safety reasons. Sir Keith's position was that London Regional Transport and its predecessors have always regarded the safety aspect of their activity as paramount and that London Regional Transport has never knowingly compromised safety for financial or other reasons.

8. It is apparent from the evidence given by the Chairman that whereas financial matters, namely productivity and budgeting, were strictly monitored safety was not strictly monitored. I asked Sir Keith:

> Q. *If you were able to set independent guidelines by which you could judge economy and efficiency, was there any difficulty about setting such independent guidelines which would enable you to judge whether the safety aspects were being properly considered?*
>
> A. *If I may pause a moment and try and give you the best answer I can . . . (after a pause) I think the answer is that we did not approach it like that.*
>
> Q. *Was there any reason why you should not have approached it in the same way as you approached economy and efficiency?*
>
> A. *Yes. We felt that safety in the subsidiaries was something that was special to those subsidiary companies. Bearing in mind the history of the organisation and the custom and practice elsewhere we felt that we should not tamper with that. In addition to that, the formation of London Underground especially as a separate company brought it within the various Railway Acts which have safety connotations. We felt that one should not try to mix the two, if you like, legal positions on the Underground company. Therefore, we decided to stand back from it, bearing in mind that it is very much an operational matter, and having the feeling that the way the traditions had always been with the engineering side being responsible for the apparatus and the operations side being responsible for organisation of passenger transport. Bearing in mind there were, I think, well over 100 people in the Underground company on the safety side, we felt that was a matter to be left with the London Underground Limited Board. We felt that we would be informed as to what went on by the fact that Dr Ridley was on the Board of LRT and by the fact that we had two LRT directors on the Underground Board. We felt that that was the right thing to do. We were heavily influenced, I believe, by what went on elsewhere, and I very much personally looked to the continental way in which things operated. In America it is rather different. They tend to have holding company Boards without any Board member from the operating business on it at all. We felt that was not what we would be doing. Therefore, we more or less endorsed what the custom and practice was in the past and copied to a certain extent what went on on the Continent.*

9. I shall consider further London Regional Transport's approach to safety in Chapter 14 'The Auditing of Safety'.

Chapter 4

The Ethos of London Underground

1. A recurrent theme in the evidence given to the Court by London Underground witnesses, and in particular by its senior managers, was the changing ethos of the organisation in recent years. An understanding of the way in which the actions of London Underground and its predecessors have been conditioned by the management style and nature of the organisation, and the way in which they are likely to be so in future, goes to the heart of this Investigation and the lessons to be learned.

2. The situation was described most clearly and frankly in the evidence given by Dr Ridley. Upon his appointment to the London Transport Executive as Managing Director (Railways) in 1980 he found that the Underground railway was in effect run, as it had been for decades, by the engineers who had built, developed and maintained it. The Chief Civil Engineer, Chief Signal Engineer, Chief Electrical Engineer and Chief Mechanical Engineer were the 'four barons' who had a proprietorial interest in the railway, which was operated on their behalf by an operating department seen as being staffed by worthy but less accomplished people. Furthermore, until the late 1970's the post of Chief Operating Manager had for many years been held by professional engineers.

Engineering Directorate

3. There was a clear demarcation between each of the four disciplines within the Engineering Directorate, and Mr Lawrence, the Engineering Director in post at the time of the Investigation, described his main task over nine years as that of breaking down the boundaries between the different engineering disciplines. Moreover there was little cross-fertilisation between Engineering and Operating Directorates and even at the highest level one director was unlikely to trespass on the territory of another. Thus, the Engineering Director did not concern himself with whether the operating staff were properly trained in fire safety and evacuation procedures because he considered those matters to be the province of the Operations Directorate. However such matters clearly had a bearing on the safety of passengers in stations for which he shared corporate responsibility, and the security and maintance of the assets for which he was directly responsible.

4. Mr Lawrence testified that as his predecessors and senior managers had been satisfied with the processes in place, he would have found it very difficult to say that the system in place was inadequate. Yet a series of reports from within London Underground and from outside had repeatedly drawn attention both to the lack of training in emergency procedures and to the fire hazards on the system.

Operations Directorate

5. Mr Clarke, the Operations Director in post at the time of the Investigation, for his part did not concern himself with the state of the escalator machinery and machine rooms, or decisions concerning the replacement of wooden components on escalators or re-siting of water fog controls. These were seen as being in the province of the Engineering Directorate.

6. Dr Ridley, as Chairman and Managing Director of London Underground, did not go deeply into the manner in which the railway was operated or staff were trained since, as he told the Court, the holders of the post of Operations Director after he joined the organisation were staff of very long service and recognised as being capable managers. Although he and others had recognised that major changes in direction were needed to carry through the modernization programme and new objections had to be set for the company, the Operations Department was run very much as it had been for decades until Mr Clarke was appointed as Operations Director in April 1986 in order—in Dr Ridley's words—to look at the whole Department with new eyes.

7. In both the Operations and the Engineering Directorates there had been a tradition of very long service. Many of the witnesses from London Underground had spent their entire working lives with the company and been promoted through the ranks largely on the basis of seniority. Very few staff failed the training course which qualified them for promotion after a given length of service. Conversely, there was no means for anyone who was talented and ambitious to be promoted before his qualifying period. Few junior staff held professional or public examination qualifications. Indeed the Operations Director accepted that it was likely that there was nobody who had a nationally recognised qualification at King's Cross station on 18 November 1987, when they were responsible for perhaps £40 million worth of assets and a quarter of a million passengers.

8. Only 5% of management level posts were advertised externally, and appointments from outside the organisation were rare. In the specialised areas of the Engineering Directorate, Mr Lawrence argued that there were unlikely to be better resources available outside London Underground. He did accept that weaknesses in staff skill levels had been identified in 1987 in the Lift and Escalator Department and that improved training was still required. The opportunities for further education to allow staff to gain professional qualifications remained very limited.

9. This long-established and deeply rooted approach to staffing and training also had its effect on the ethos of London Underground. Staff

tended to have narrow horizons and would instinctively look inside the organisation for advice and the solution to problems. Compartmental organisation resulted in little exchange of information or ideas between Departments, and still less cross-fertilisation with other industries and outside organisations. While on the one hand this inward-looking approach may have allowed London Underground to become pre-eminent in certain technical fields such as signal engineering, it undoubtedly led to a dangerous, blinkered self-sufficiency which included a general unwillingness to take advice or accept criticism from outside bodies. The Court heard, for example, about advice from the London Fire Brigade regarding the importance and procedure for calling them which went unheeded (see Chapter 11 'The Response of the Emergency Services: London Fire Brigade'); and criticism of the quality of data and staff resources relating to occupational health and safety by the Health and Safety Executive's Accident Prevention Advisory Unit, upon which no action was taken.

10. Dr Ridley spoke eloquently about the change in the culture and the style of the organisation which he and his managers expect to bring about. New approaches to staffing, training and accountability are being made which will allow the operators to provide the service to the public and the engineers to act more as service departments, and with responsiblity for safety in stations resting clearly with the 'landlord' operating staff. He also expected to see an increasing proportion of management positions being filled by external appointment. I return to the new staffing proposal in Chapter 15 'Station Staffing and Training'.

11. These proposals for change, many of which were in progress before the disaster, are far-reaching and I do not doubt the commitment of Dr Ridley in seeing them through. But changes in staffing structure alone will not improve London Underground's ability to improve safety and prevent disasters. A much more searching and outward-looking approach to safety management is required, which will demand a willingness to embrace new ideas. The old idea of the engineers running a railway must be replaced with a recognition at all levels of the responsibility of providing a mass passenger transport service for the public.

12. It was, therefore, a matter of some concern to me that the directors of London Underground should still subscribe to the received wisdom that fires were an occupational hazard on the Underground. Dr Ridley did not feel able to agree with the Court that fire should be regarded as an unacceptable hazard to be eliminated, since it was considered that fires were a part of the nature of the oldest, most extensive underground railway in the world. It was seen as unrealistic to believe that any increased effort by London Underground could get to a

position where there would be no fires on escalators. Dr Ridley saw London Underground's key task as to minimise the risk of fires becoming a danger to passengers by a better control procedure and by removing materials which posed the greatest fire hazard. In effect he was advocating fire precaution rather than fire prevention.

13. It is my belief that this approach is seriously flawed because it fails to recognise the unpredictable nature of fire. A mass passenger transport service cannot tolerate the concept of an acceptable level of fire hazard. In my view what is needed from London Underground is an entirely new pro-active approach to safety management. This should involve quantified and monitored objectives to reduce the incidence of fires.

14. I discuss the proper approach to safety in more detail in Chapter 13 'The Management of Safety'.

Chapter 5

London Underground Organisation and Management

1. London Underground owns and operates the oldest, most extensive and most complex undergound railway system in the world. The railway dates from 1863, and some 80% of the system is more than seventy years old. Today there are nine separate lines running over 260 miles of track to 270 stations, 130 of which are below ground. Each weekday the system carries some 2.6 million passengers on about 450 trains. In 1987/88 trains ran 31.8 million miles and carried 800 million passengers. The company employs some 19,000 people.

2. London Underground Limited is a wholly-owned subsidiary of London Regional Transport. It has a Chairman and Managing Director and a Board which is wholly accountable to the Board of London Regional Transport. In November 1987 Dr Ridley was Chairman and Managing Director and before that from 1980 had been Managing Director (Railways) of the London Transport Executive. He is also an executive member of the Board of London Regional Transport. His fellow directors of London Underground were:

Mr J Allen	— Finance Director and Company Secretary
Mr W Clarke	— Operations Director
Mr L Lawrence	— Engineering Director
Mr R Straker	— Personnel Director
Dr H Fitzhugh	— Marketing and Development Director

   In addition there were four non-executive directors, Mr B Dale, Mr R Dorey, Mr B Hooper and Mr D Turner. Mr Dale was also Finance Director of London Regional Transport and an executive member of their Board, and Mr Hooper was also London Regional Transport's Commercial Director. The organisation of London Regional Transport and London Underground Limited at Director level is shown in Figure 11.

3. Simplified organsiation charts for the rest of London Undergound are shown thus:

   (i) the Operations Directorate in November 1987 (Figure 12)

   (ii) the staff rostered for duty at 19:30 at King's Cross on the night of the fire (Figure 13)

   (iii) the Engineering Directorate in November 1987 (Figure 15).

   Those officers who gave evidence to the Court are identified in red type.

4. It is worthy of note that these charts had to be expressly prepared for the Investigation. Witnesses from London Underground generally only knew about the organisation of their own deparment or division.

It may be an indication of the compartmental approach to management within London Undergound that no up-to-date or complete chart showing the level of responsibility at which decisions were being taken was available. Such a management tool was, in my view, essential for senior managers to identify properly where decisions were being taken and where gaps in responsibility could occur.

5. The Operations Directorate is responsible for all aspects of the day-to-day running of the underground railway. It can be seen from Figure 12 that the nine railway lines were organised into four operating divisions: the Metropolitan and Circle and Jubilee Lines; the Central and Bakerloo Lines; the Northern and Victoria Lines; and the District and Piccadilly Lines. In November 1987, the first two divisions were the responsibility of a General Manager (Operations) 'A', who was located at Baker Street, and the second two divisions were the responsibility of a General Manager (Operations) 'B', who was located at 55 Broadway.

6. Thus, both General Managers (Operations) had responsibility for different lines and areas of a complex station such as King's Cross. London Underground overcame this managerial difficulty by allocating each station to a particular operating division. In the case of King's Cross, the division chosen was that of the Metropolitan Line and not the tube lines.

7. The station staff, group manager, area manager and traffic manager directly responsible for King's Cross station thus reported through the Divisional Operations Manager (Metropolitan and Jubilee) to the General Manager (Operations) 'A'. Within each operating division there were three or four operating areas, each under the control of an area manager. King's Cross was within the Edgware Road area stretching between Hammersmith, Baker Street and Aldgate. Each group of between four and ten stations (depending on size and complexity) was the responsibility of a group manager. The group manager who had responsibility for King's Cross in November 1987 also had Aldgate, Liverpool Street, Moorgate, Barbican and Farringdon stations under his control.

8. The other divisions of the Operations Directorate of particular relevance to the Investigation were those of the General Manager (Station Development), to whom the Traffic Superintendent and Chief Fire Inspector reported; and of the Senior Personnel Manager, to whom the Training Manager and Safety Manager reported.

9. It can be seen from Figure 15 that the Engineering Directorate was in the process of being divided into 'client' and 'contractor' groupings. Section 6(1) of the London Regional Transport Act 1984 places London

Regional Transport under a general duty to invite competitive tenders to carry on those of their activities they determine to be appropriate. To prepare the Engineering Department for competitive tendering London Underground divided the organisation into 'client' and 'contractor' groupings. The 'client' would then specify the work to be undertaken and the 'contractor' would be among those invited to submit a tender. In May 1986, the lift and esclator manager's work-force was first operated as a maintenance unit at arm's length from the lift and escalator engineer's division. In April 1988 the separation was extended further when the lift and escalator engineer's division became part of the newly-formed Engineering Operations Directorate.

10. Mr Styles, who was the lift and escalator engineer from 1973 to 1987, told the Court that his staff were much occupied during 1985 and 1986 with getting the new management system running. Until 1984, his division had been part of the Operations Department and, after the move to the Engineering Department, informal contact with operating staff had largely ceased and there was some confusion over areas of responsibility. In addition, from 1986 there was some uncertainty about responsibilities between the engineering client and the contractor. Recommendations for action involving escalators made in internal inquiry reports of accidents did not always reach the Engineering Department. The client/contractor split was not properly established at the time of the King's Cross fire, and the lift and escalator engineer said that he did not succeed in monitoring escalator cleaning standards to his satisfaction or have enough staff to do so.

11. The lift and escalator maintenance manager, Mr Izienicki, for his part, said that the effect of the organisational changes had been to delay improvements in the arrangements for escalator cleaning until October 1987.

12. Thus, the organisation of London Underground at the time of the fire was such that management responsibility for the operation of King's Cross station fell to the division which included the Metropolitan Line and not the division with responsibility for the tube lines on which the disaster occurred. It may also be seen that the Engineering Directorate had undergone and was still undergoing organisational changes which served to weaken its liaison with the operational side. Finally, the new system for escalator maintenance and cleaning was not properly established.

13. I discuss the consequences of these organisational shortcomings in Chapter 13 'The Management of Safety'.

Chapter 6

King's Cross Station

1. King's Cross is one of the country's great travel gateways. The area around the station was originally known as Battle Bridge and tradition has it that it was here that Queen Boadicea routed the Roman legions before putting Roman London to the fire and sword. Battle Bridge became King's Cross when in 1830 a tall octagonal building surmounted by a statue of George IV was erected in the area. The building was demolished in 1845, but King's Cross remained as the name of the area and the new terminus for the Great Northern Railway took the name when it was opened in 1852. To this day the British Rail station at King's Cross is famous as the start of the east coast route to Scotland and the North of England. The overground railway also serves parts of England nearer to London and to the east.

2. The underground railway first came to King's Cross in 1863 when the Metropolitan Railway line was opened between Farringdon and Paddington, linking the terminals of the Great Northern at King's Cross, the London and North Western at Euston and the Great Western at Paddington. The Great Northern, Piccadilly and Brompton Railway, running between Finsbury Park and Hammersmith (which now forms part of the Piccadilly Line) reached King's Cross in 1906. The following year a separate station was opened to accommodate a second tube railway, the City and South London Railway, which now forms the City branch of the Northern Line. The Victoria Line was linked to King's Cross in 1968.

3. As well as the main line at King's Cross station, two other British Rail stations are served by the Underground station. These are St. Pancras, for the East Midlands main line services, and King's Cross Midland City, now known as Thameslink, principally for commuter destinations between London and Bedford.

4. King's Cross Underground station is a labyrinth of passages, shafts and tunnels where five lines meet—the Metropolitan and Circle, Piccadilly, Northern and Victoria. Figure 1 is the familiar London Underground map showing the five Underground lines and the British Rail Thameslink (formerly Midland City) line passing through King's Cross. Figure 2 shows the streets in the King's Cross area and the access to the Underground system. Figure 3 shows the location of the Underground concourse beneath street level. Figure 4 is a more detailed plan of the tube lines ticket hall and surrounding area. Figure 5 is a simplified plan showing the Underground lines in relation to the tube lines ticket hall and station exits.

5. The underground station is unique in being built at five different levels below ground and is connected by passageways, staircases and escalators. This is shown in the three-dimensional view of the station in Figure 6. The layout of the tube lines ticket hall and the connections to the Metropolitan and Circle Lines may also be seen in the photographs of the station model at Plates 12–14.

6. Of the five lines serving the station, the Metropolitan and Circle Lines, using the same tracks, were built in the main on the cut and cover principle. They are relatively close to the surface. The trains are driven in the conventional manner and are equipped with radio and a public address system, although there is no guard. The other three lines are deep bored tubes as shown in Figure 6. For the sake of clarity this diagram does not show the other features such as sewers and cable ducts woven between them.

7. On the Piccadilly Line the trains are operated by a driver: there is no guard but each train has a radio and a public address system. On the Northern Line the train crew comprises a driver and a guard. Each train has a radio. The Victoria Line was the first tube line in the United Kingdom on which the trains were designed to be operated by the driver alone. Trains are operated automatically, but there is a facility for the operator to take manual control. The operator is able to speak to the line controller and there is a public address system.

8. In 1987 King's Cross was the busiest station on the Underground network. On an average weekday over 250,000 passengers used the station with 100,000 or so passing through in each peak period—between 07:30 and 10:00, and 16:00 and 18:30.

9. There are various entrances to King's Cross Underground station: from Pancras Road, the north and south sides of Euston Road, and from the concourses of King's Cross and St. Pancras British Rail stations. Connecting passages lead from these staircases to the perimeter subway, or outer circular concourse, and a short stretch of passageway, known to London Underground staff and others as the 'Khyber Pass'. This subway is set at a slightly higher level than the tube lines ticket hall and is connected to it by four entrances with steps and handrails at the sides and the centre. There are Bostwick gates (the "concertina" type of gates as illustrated in Plate 9) at the foot of each set of steps. In the passageway leading to Pancras Road there are public lavatories owned by the London Borough of Camden. There are four shop units in the outer wall of the perimeter subway which at the time of the fire were used as a shoe repairers (heel bar), a newsagent, a bureau de change and a builder's store. Certain of these shops were protected by an automatic sprinkler system. Where the Khyber Pass meets the perimeter subway there are a number of rooms which were given over to the booking office staff. In the area between the tube lines ticket hall and the perimeter subway opposite the escalator shaft was further staff accommodation and a travel information office. There are other mess rooms, a kitchen and staff lavatories off the subway leading to St. Pancras station. These may be seen on the detailed plan in Figure 4.

10. The Metropolitan and Circle Lines platforms are reached by a flight of steps from the passageway which runs immediately underneath the Euston Road. There is a long and broad concourse between the eastbound and westbound platforms with the ticket office at the near end and the station manager's temporary office and staff accommodation at the far end, as shown in Figure 5.

11. The tube lines ticket hall has a central booking office of the 'island' type, flanked by seven ticket collectors' boxes which are linked by barriers with hinged gates. On either side of the booking office was a group of three automatic ticket vending machines. Access between the tube lines ticket hall and the platforms is gained by two banks of escalators, the Piccadilly Line escalators which are escalators 4, 5 and 6, and the Victoria Line escalators which are escalators 7 and 9 with a fixed stairway between them. There is a third set of escalators leading down to the Northern Line platforms from a small concourse adjoining the foot of the Piccadilly Line escalators.

12. It is also possible for people to move around the tube lines side of the Underground without using the main escalators, as may be seen from Figure 6. Passengers can walk from the Northern Line platforms to the Piccadilly Line platform concourse and then to the Victoria Line platform concourse without using the escalators. Access from the Northern Line is by way of stairs and a passageway which emerges in the concourse between the Piccadilly Line platforms. By walking to the Piccadilly Line escalator concourse it is then possible to gain access to the Victoria Line platform concourse by walking up several flights of stairs. There is then a short distance to walk to the bottom of the Victoria Line escalators. Finally, it is possible to leave the Underground from either the Piccadilly Line platforms or the Victoria Line platforms by walking along the subway which links the two lines and then emerges by way of the Midland City British Rail station in Pentonville Road. There were three sets of Bostwick gates in this subway which were locked in the evening, the first two at the Victoria Line and Piccadilly Line end owned by London Underground, and the other at the entrance to the Midland City station owned by British Rail. I refer to this subway throughout the Report as the Midland City exit, shown in Figure 2.

13. At the time of the fire, a temporary wooden hoarding had been erected in the tube lines ticket hall which sealed off the northern part of the hall nearest to King Cross's British Rail station. The hoarding ran from the top of escalator 6 on the Piccadilly Line escalators to one of four sets of stairs leading from the perimeter subway into the tube lines ticket hall as shown in Figure 5. It blocked off access to the fourth set of stairs and concealed both the fire hydrant and hose and one of the London Fire Brigade plan boxes. This hoarding consisted of softwood studding and was faced on the passenger side with plywood coated with

intumescent and fire-retardant paint. It had been erected to enable the demolition of a station operations room and other work connected with the installation of the Underground Ticketing System (UTS) to be carried out without inconvenience to passengers.

14. There was a temporary station operations room in the tube lines ticket hall next to the Victoria Line escalators. It had a one-way window commanding a view of the area of the tube lines ticket hall at the head of the Victoria Line and Piccadilly Line escalators, and was of a similar construction to the wooden hoarding on the opposite side of the hall.

15. The station manager and the two station inspectors, who constituted the supervisory staff on duty that night, each had separate offices. Contrary to his wishes, the station manager's office had been moved from the tube lines ticket hall to a temporary site at the western end of the Metropolitan and Circle Lines platforms, before the installation of the Underground Ticketing System (UTS) gates. The tube lines inspector had his office at the far end of the Victoria Line platform concourse with the staff accommodation between the Victoria Line platforms. The Metropolitan and Circle Lines station inspector had his office beside the stairs which led down to the Metropolitan and Circle Lines platforms running under Euston Road.

16. There was a number of telephones in offices and staff accommodation on the station which were all connected to the London Underground automatic telephone network. There was an emergency connection to the information room of L Division of the British Transport Police. The other communications equipment in the Underground, including closed circuit television and public address equipment, is described in greater detail in Chapter 16 'Communications Systems'.

17. The location of the main fire equipment in the tube lines ticket hall and surrounding area is shown in red on the plan at Figure 4. In addition, on the platforms of each tube line there was a cupboard containing a fire hydrant and hose with a nozzle and adaptor to allow London Fire Brigade equipment to be attached to the hydrant. All platforms had fire extinguishers and sand buckets and there were fire extinguishers at the top and bottom of each set of escalators and in the machine rooms. The upper machine room of the Piccadilly Line and Victoria Lines escalators also contained a hose reel.

18. The ventilation of the station is achieved during the day mainly by the movement of trains. A description of this system and of the tunnel cooling fans is given in Appendix I.

Chapter 7

Escalators on the Underground

1. Escalators were developed in America towards the end of the last century, and were first exhibited in Europe at the Paris Exhibition of 1900 by the Otis Elevator Company. Otis also provided the first escalators to be installed in the London Underground at Earl's Court station in 1911, which transported passengers between the Piccadilly Line and District Line platforms. These machines were known as the 'Seeburger' or 'A' type escalator, and a total of 22 were installed at ten Underground stations between 1911 and 1915. These escalators had flat steps and shunt ends, which forced passengers to step off sideways at the top or bottom landings. They were designed for vertical rises of between 8.5 and 16.5 metres, and they operated at 27.5 metres per minute.

2. Between 1924 and 1929 a total of 65 'LH.D' type escalators were installed in the Underground. The earliest of these machines were similar to the 'A' type, with flat steps and shunt landings. In December 1924 the first escalators to be fitted with cleated steps and combs were installed, which made it possible to step straight off at the landings. Subsequently all the old machines were modified to the cleat step and comb arrangements. These machines, which were reversible, were designed for rises of up to 18 metres and a speed of 30 metres per minute which could be reduced to 15 metres per minute when they were not carrying passengers.

3. In 1963 the programme of modernising these LH.D machines began, and the modernised machines were known as 'LH.D-M' type escalators. They were of all-metal construction with aluminium balustrades, decking and side panels or skirting boards, with closely spaced aluminium cleated steps. The speed was increased to 33.5 metres per minute or 36.5 metres per minute if new gearboxes and motors were fitted.

4. From 1931 to 1961 a total of 108 'M' series escalators were installed. The MH type machines, designed for rises of up to 27.5 metres were the type installed to serve the Piccadilly Line at King's Cross station. The M, MX and MY types were designed for rises of up to 12 metres. They were designed for speeds between 30 and 35 metres per minute. All these machines, except for the MY type, were similar in appearance, with wooden balustrading, decking, side panels, cleated steps and risers. Many of these machines are still in service.

5. The three MH escalators at King's Cross between the Piccadilly Line and the tube lines ticket hall were installed in 1939. These machines were inclined at 30 degrees and rose through 17.2 metres. MH escalators are special purpose machines for high rises and heavy traffic conditions. Plate 2 shows a photograph of the Piccadilly line escalators at King's Cross before the disaster.

6. To prevent access to the escalator, chains were originally provided at the top and bottom with hooks adjacent to the control panels on the newel posts. The chains were later replaced by black and yellow woven plastic straps housed in a container and pulled out against a tensioning spring. At the top and bottom of the decking between escalators 4 and 5, and escalators 5 and 6 are rectangular metal boxes which house the emergency stop diamonds. Holes in the vertical sides of the boxes are covered with red paper seals which must be broken before the switch can be operated.

7. Figure 7 shows a longitudinal section of the escalator in its shaft including the upper and lower machine rooms. The entrance to the upper machine room is a door adjacent to the top of escalator 4 in the tube lines ticket hall, as shown in Figure 4. The upper machine room houses the electric driving motors, the worm reduction gears and the chain drives to the drive shaft for each of the escalators. It also houses the associated electrical control gear and the circuit breakers which connect the motors to the mains supply. Access to the lower machine room is via a trap door and vertical ladder on the right-hand side of the Piccadilly Line escalator concourse, which can just be seen on the bottom right of Plate 3. The lower machine room houses the lower carriages of the three escalators. These carriages carry the idler sprocket wheels over which the escalator steps pass, and the chain drives to the handrail newel wheels. There are tensioning weights to apply tension to the step chains. Also in the lower machine room there is a sump pump.

8. Figure 7 also shows a cross-section through the escalator shaft, while Figure 8 provides a more detailed view. It will be seen that there is a narrow staircase between escalators 4 and 5 and another between 5 and 6, but there is a less restricted staircase directly below escalator 5. The escalator tracks and components are supported on a steel truss carried on the supporting walls. The supporting walls for escalator 5 are on each side of the staircase with periodic gaps through which a person on the central staircase can get a very restricted view of the undersides of escalators 4 and 6.

9. Figure 9 gives a three-dimensional view of part of an MH escalator. Each step assembly is supported on two pairs of wheels, which are supported on running tracks each side of the escalator. It will be seen that one pair of wheels, the chain wheels, run on the outboard side of the two tracks, while the other pair of wheels, the trailer wheels, are on the inboard side. This leaves a 15 cm wide gap on the track between the two sets of wheels where grease and detritus can accumulate, as can be seen in Figure 10 and Plate 20.

10. The accumulation of grease and detritus actually found on the Piccadilly Line escalators at King's Cross can be seen in the photographs at Plates 12 and 13. The lift and escalator maintenance manager Mr Izienicki explained that cleaning of the running track was done by hand, and that the running track was virtually impossible to reach without dismantling the escalator. It had never been the practice in London Underground to remove the steps of MH escalators for cleaning. The lift and escalator maintenance manager said that to the best of his knowledge the running tracks of the Piccadilly Line escalators at King's Cross had never been cleaned completely.

11. The detailed construction of the MH escalator can be seen in the cross section in Figure 10. The steps are metal-backed 17 mm plywood board with maple wood cleats, with a metal fire cleat at each side of the step to prevent cigarette ends and matches falling down the clearance between the steps and the skirting board. The risers are made of shaped oak fastened to sheet metal which forms part of the step. At either side of the step there is a 7 ply (21 mm) plywood skirting board, which is in sections running the full length of the escalator and is backed by a steel angle section. The clearance between the step and the skirting board varies with the adjustment of the running chains, but it can be as much as 15 mm. Immediately above the skirting board is a rubber dressguard. Balustrades and decking are made of 6 ply (11 mm) plywood with a 28 swg (standard wire guage) galvanised steel backing sheet, and there is a 6 ply (8 mm) plywood facia board with 28 swg steel sheet backing on the walls of the escalator shaft adjoining escalators 4 and 6. Framed advertisements are attached to the facia boards.

12. The handrails are made of fabric bonded rubber with steel tape inserts and vulcanized joints run on a metal handrail guide, which is supported above the decking by wooden distance pieces. Both the trailer and chain wheels are made of plastic. The original wheels were black and made of phenolic resin and canvas, but the replacement wheels were of a brown plastic produced by Texolex. The wheels have metal bushes and are secured on axles. The wheels are lubricated by forcing grease between the wheel and axle and into the chain links. Fixed bearings are lubricated by a chain-driven oil pump.

13. On 24 December 1944 there was a particularly severe fire in the Bakerloo Line escalators at Paddington which were completely gutted. A review of escalator fires at about this time stated that there had been 77 fires on escalators in the period 1939–44 and that the MH, MA and M type escalators were particularly prone to fire. These fires were mainly attributed to the ignition by smokers' material of accumulated dirt under escalators.

14. As a result of the Paddington fire the frequency of escalator cleaning was increased, and water fog equipment was fitted experimentally to two escalators. By 1948 water fog equipment had been fitted to a further nineteen escalators including the three Piccadilly Line escalators at King's Cross. Subsequently, water fog equipment was fitted to most MH and M type escalators in the Underground. Water fog equipment consists of water sprinkler heads fed from the fire main, and arranged in pairs at spacings of about two metres along the whole escalator as shown in the diagrammatic plan in Figure 7. The sprinkler heads are located each side of the centre line of the escalator, as shown in Figure 8, with one of each pair pointing upwards towards the underside of the steps and one downwards on the returning idle steps. The application of the water fog for about a minute is sufficient to wet all parts of the machinery within reach of these sprinkler heads. The handrail driving gear is sprayed at the top of the escalator by a separately operated system. The operating valves for the water fog and handrail driving gear sprays are normally located just inside the door to the upper machine room. Plate 11 shows these control valves.

15. It was originally intended that the water fog equipment should be operated for a short time every night, with the object of dampening down any smouldering there might be. However, experience showed that this practice caused excessive and unacceptable corrosion of the machine, although at the same time it was noted that some of the more inflammable fluff was removed. As a compromise it became the practice to apply the water fog about once a fortnight. In recent years however the water fog equipment has not been operated regularly. Nevertheless, the equipment has been available for use in the event of a fire. It was generally believed that the water fog would only extinguish a fire in its early stages; for a more developed fire it would only delay the spread.

16. The automatic operation of water fog equipment was envisaged as early as 1948. Essentially the problem was to find a detection system for smoke or heat which would cover the entire escalator system and be sufficiently sensitive to detect a fire early enough for the water fog to be able to extinguish it. An initial trial of smoke detection equipment on an escalator at Tottenham Court Road in 1954 was followed by a second stage in 1964 when equipment was installed on two escalators at Baker Street and a further two at Paddington. These did not automatically operate the water fog equipment but did incorporate an alarm system. Over the next ten years there were numerous proposals to install smoke detection equipment on other escalators, including the Northern Line and Piccadilly Line escalators at King's Cross. However, no action was taken because, on one occasion, the proposal was inadvertently left out of the budget, and subsequently the proposal was rejected on the grounds that the M series escalators did not have

enough life left in them to justify the expenditure. It was also said that the detection equipment gave more false alarms than real ones. In fact some of the M series escalators were expected to remain in service into the next century.

17. In 1976 smoke detection systems were fitted on a trial basis to the new escalators installed at Baker Street and the existing escalators at Monument. They were considered to be unreliable and were not adopted more generally on the system. In 1986 a more suitable smoke detection system involving an air sampling tube went on trial in the upper machine room of the escalators at Euston station.

18. Statistics for fires on escalators between 1958 and 1987 were presented to the Investigation by London Underground. Records were held of over 400 fires and so-called smoulderings, some of which were serious enough to cause the evacuation of stations, serious delays and considerable damage to the escalators involved. Until 1985 the only source of such statistics was the fire and fusing reports returned by station staff; the fuller record from station logs was available only from 1985. The position on the keeping and analysis of statistics on fires by London Underground was quite unsatisfactory.

19. Until 18 November 1987 there had been no fatalities as a result of escalator fires, although some people had suffered smoke inhalation, serious enough to be taken to hospital. The statistics indicate that 45% of these fires and smoulderings occurred on MH escalators, which were particularly prone to fires on their running tracks. The cause of these fires had usually been attributed to smokers' materials falling down between the treads and the skirting board and igniting the grease and detritus on the running track. That accumulation of dirt formed a seed bed for fire.

20. A review of recent serious escalator fires and the Oxford Circus station fire, with the recommendations made in reports or by the internal inquiries into these fires, is given at Appendix J. The analysis shows that of the 46 serious escalator fires recorded over the last three decades, the cause of over two-thirds had been attributed to smokers' materials.

21. Among the recommendations I make in Chapter 20 are proposals for more effective cleaning and lubrication, monitoring, alarm and sprinkler systems, and improved methods of securing access to escalators and machine rooms.

Chapter 8

Staff on Duty at King's Cross on 18 November 1987

London Underground Staff

1. King's Cross Underground station had a resident complement of 58 staff in November 1987. They worked different rostered duty times and were supplemented by rest day cover or relief staff to provide the varying numbers of staff required at different times. On the evening of 18 November 1987 at 19:30 when the alarm was first raised, there were 23 staff rostered for duty (of whom three were absent) and an additional relief station manager. Two further London Underground employees, an automatic equipment technician and a part-time cleaner, were also present.

2. The chart at Figure 13 shows the names and grades of the staff rostered for duty that evening and their deployment between the tube lines side of the station and the Metropolitan and Circle Lines side. It will be seen that there were on duty a total of five booking clerks, two of them on the Metropolitan side, who provided the ticket office window service and maintained ticket machines. There was one supervisory booking clerk. There were three railmen, all on the tube side, who provided attendance on platforms, helped passengers with information, despatched trains and assisted with crowd control. There were eight leading railmen, four of them on the tube side, four on the Metropolitan side, who collected and checked tickets at "way in" and "way out" barriers and assisted passengers with inquiries.

3. There was one station inspector supervising the Metropolitan side and one relief station inspector supervising the tube side of the station. Their duties included ensuring that ticket selling and collection were working properly, checking equipment and dealing with equipment failures, handling lost property, maintaining passenger safety, manning the station operations room as necessary, and taking part in the response to any operating incidents.

4. The station manager was responsible for ensuring that the station was operated safely and efficiently, for deploying staff and making regular station patrols and inspections. At King's Cross it had recently become the practice, because of an increase in the numbers of passengers, for a relief station manager also to be on duty at peak times. His main responsibility was to assist with crowd control in the Khyber Pass area which was liable to become extremely congested. I return to the general question of congestion in Chapter 19 'Matters for Further Consideration'.

5. The disposition of the staff around the station at the time the alarm was first raised is shown on the plan at Figure 14. From this it may be seen that 11 members of London Underground staff were initially on the tube side and 12 staff on the Metropolitan side. The majority of those present was remote from the site where the fire first broke out and,

apart from the automatic equipment technician and the cleaner, only two members of station staff were in the lower level of the station at the relevant time.

British Transport Police

6. At the time the alarm was first raised there were four British Transport Police officers on patrol in the King's Cross station area. Two police constables, P.C. Bebbington and P.C. Kerbey, were in the temporary station operations room in the tube lines ticket hall, and another two police constables, P.C. Balfe and P.C. Hanson, on the concourse of the British Rail main line station. None of these officers belonged to 'L' Division, the section of the British Transport Police responsible for law enforcement on the London Underground, but to a mobile unit of 'B' Division, which is mainly responsible for policing British Rail Eastern Region.

7. After the emergency call had been made, and before the disaster occurred, these four were joined in the tube side of the station by two more officers, P.C. Kukielka and P.C. Martland, of 'L' Division, and by P.C. Dixon, of the division responsible for British Rail Midland Region.

8. A narrative of the events as they unfolded is given in the following chapter, and the response of the London Underground staff and the police officers considered in Chapters 10 and 11.

Chapter 9

Timetable and Outline of Events on the Night

The evening rush hour passed uneventfully at King's Cross Underground station on Wednesday 18 November 1987 with the usual 100,000 or so passengers passing through between about 16:00 and 18:30.

The precise timings during the fire and the exact order of events cannot always be established with absolute certainty. But I am satisfied that a general pattern of events emerged as I set out hereafter. Where it has been possible to verify a timing by reference to an independent record, that timing is given in bold print. It transpired that several of the clocks, when checked, were found to be inaccurate and I have adjusted times to allow for this.

c19:29   A passenger, Mr Squire, travelling up escalator 4 noticed a small fire underneath a step at the right-hand side of the upper part of the escalator. He reported it at the ticket office to the booking clerk, Mr Newman. Mr Newman telephoned Relief Station Inspector Hayes.

c19:30   Another passenger, Mr Karmoun, seeing smoke two-thirds of the way up the escalator and a glow underneath, pressed the emergency stop diamond at the top of escalator 4 and shouted down to people to get off the escalator. Leading Railman Brickell, the ticket collector at the "way out" barrier, and P.C. Bebbington and P.C. Kerbey, who were in the temporary station operations room in the tube lines ticket hall observing the scene, each went to investigate.

Relief Station Inspector Hayes with Railman Farrell went to investigate the report of a fire, as required by the London Underground rule book. He had been told it was "on the Northern Line escalator".

Leading Railman Brickell went to the bottom of the Piccadilly Line escalators.

P.C. Bebbington descended escalator 4 and saw smoke and a single flame about three to four inches high one-third of the way down the escalators.

19:32   He decided to call his Headquarters information room on his personal radio to summon the London Fire Brigade, but had to go to the surface to make the call as the radios did not work below ground. He waited at the top of the stairs on the Euston Road where he was joined by P.C. Dixon whom he told to await the Fire Brigade. Meanwhile as P.C. Bebbington returned to the Underground, P.C. Kerbey stopped escalators 5 and 6.

c19:32   Further alarm was raised by another passenger, Mr Benstead, with Booking Clerk Newman.

19:33   P.C. Bebbington's call was received at British Transport Police HQ. P.C. Hanson and P.C. Balfe, alerted by P.C. Bebbington's radio call, went from the British Rail main line concourse to the tube lines ticket hall and there joined P.C. Kerbey.

19:33/34   British Transport Police HQ passed the emergency message as a 999 call via the British Telecom emergency call centre to the London Fire Brigade.

c19:35   Relief Station Inspector Hayes arrived in the Piccadilly Line escalator concourse and went into the lower machine room. He saw and smelt nothing.

19:36   Leading Railman Brickell, who had descended escalator 5, saw smoke two-thirds of the way up escalator 4. He and Railman Farrell were told by the police to send passengers up the Victoria Line escalator. Leading Railman Brickell blocked with tape and a builder's skip the foot of the Piccadilly Line escalators. P.C. Bebbington returned to the ticket hall and descended the Piccadilly Line escalator.

19:36   London Fire Brigade despatched four pump appliances and a turntable ladder from Soho, Clerkenwell and Manchester Square fire stations in accordance with the predetermined attendance plan. A forward control unit (FCU) and an area control unit (ACU) were also despatched.

19:37   On hearing the emergency call, P.C. Kukielka and P.C. Martland went to the scene and noticed light smoke at the station entrance.

        While talking to the British Transport Police L Division information room about another matter, the Piccadilly Line controller, Mr R. Hanson was informed of the incident.

c19:38   London Fire Brigade controller Mrs French, told London Underground HQ controller, Mr Tumbridge, of a report of fire at King's Cross.

19:38   Relief Station Inspector Hayes and Railman Farrell went up the Piccadilly Line escalators to the tube lines ticket hall.

        Relief Station Inspector Hayes unlocked and entered the upper machine room: he went down the stairs and then down the steps under escalator 5 from where he saw smoke and flames beneath escalator 4. He returned to the machine room to collect a carbon dioxide extinguisher, but he was unable to get near enough to the fire to use it. Relief Station Inspector Hayes did not attempt to use the water fog equipment. He was preoccupied and forgot about it.

19:39   The police officers in the ticket hall took the decision to evacuate the area.

Piccadilly Line controller Hanson telephoned HQ controller Tumbridge, and told him of the fire.

19:40   Mr Hanson telephoned Piccadilly Line Acting Traffic Manager Weston, who telephoned Metropolitan Line Station Inspector Dhanpersaud. (see 19:41).

Railman Farrell assisted the police in cordoning off the top of escalator 4 and directing passengers entering the ticket hall towards the Victoria Line escalators.

19:40   P.C. Kukielka, by a 999 call from the temporary station operations room, asked for Piccadilly and Victoria Line trains to be ordered not to stop at King's Cross.

19:41   At the request of the police, Railman Farrell went down to the Victoria Line platforms and telephoned the line controller to ask that trains be ordered not to stop at King's Cross.

Booking Clerk Newman was told by P.C. Balfe to stop selling tickets.

Metropolitan Line Station Inspector Dhanpersaud, having been told of the fire by Piccadilly Line Traffic Manager Weston, sent Railmen White and Obcena to investigate.

One of the sets of Bostwick gates at the stairs leading to the perimeter subway from the tube lines ticket hall was closed by an unidentified police officer or officers. Railmen White and Obcena reached the tube lines ticket hall where, having seen the fire, Railman Obcena was told by Railman White to fetch Station Inspector Dhanpersaud.

Piccadilly Line controller Hanson alerted Area Manager Archer at Finsbury Park.

19:42   Station Inspector Dhanpersaud went to the tube lines ticket hall via the Khyber Pass. He opened the Bostwick gates en route and met Relief Station Inspector Hayes who had just come out of the upper machine room.

Station Manager Worrell, who was in the station manager's temporary office on the Metropolitan side of the station as shown in Figure 5, was told of the fire by Piccadilly Line Controller Hanson.

An eastbound Piccadilly Line train stopped, the last to let passengers get out at this platform. A northbound Northern Line train stopped and 50 or so passengers got out.

c19:42   P.C. Hanson ordered the booking office staff to evacuate. Booking clerks Newman, Hythe and Frankland left (19:43/44).

In the confusion no one alerted those in the bureau de change or the nearby public lavatories to the emergency.

19:42   A24 Soho Pump (Station Officer Townsley) arrived.

19:43   Immediately afterwards, C27 Clerkenwell Pump Ladder (temporary Sub-Officer Bell) arrived together with A22 Manchester Square Pump (Station Officer Osborne) followed by A24 Soho Pump (Leading Fireman Kendall) and Turntable (Sub-Officer Trefry) one minute later 19:44.

Relief Station Inspector Hayes and Station Inspector Dhanpersaud entered the upper machine room and operated the circuit breakers.

P.C. Kukielka saw people still coming up the Victoria Line escalators and again telephoned from the temporary station operations room to confirm that trains had been ordered not to stop. An ambulance was requested. P.C. Kukielka and P.C. Martland then went down the Victoria Line escalators and helped P.C. Kerbey to direct passengers from the Victoria Line platforms and concourse area up the Victoria Line escalators.

Station Officer Townsley followed by Temporary Sub-Officer Bell went to assess the situation on the escalators. They saw a fire which Temporary Sub-Officer Bell described as about the size of a large cardboard box but with flames licking up the handrail on the left-hand side seen from below. Station Officer Townsley called upon Station Officer Osborne to send firemen wearing breathing apparatus sets and a jet. Station Officer Townsley and Temporary Sub-Officer Bell went further down to get a better view. As passengers were still coming up the escalator Temporary Sub-Officer Bell went down in order to stop others coming up, whilst Station Officer Townsley returned to the ticket hall.

A westbound Piccadilly Line train stopped, the last to let passengers get out at this platform.

19:44   HQ controller Tumbridge sent the order to the Piccadilly and Victoria Line controllers that trains should not stop. Northern Line trains continued to stop normally until 19:48.

In the ticket hall Station Officer Townsley ordered Temporary Leading Fireman Flanagan to send the message "**Make pumps 4—persons reported**" thereby confirming the seriousness of the fire and the need for ambulances. Temporary Leading Fireman Flanagan went out to do so. Within a very short time the whole ticket hall became engulfed in intense heat and thick black smoke. There was darkness and screaming. Temporary Leading Fireman Flanagan ordered his crew to lead the public out and run for their lives. The flashover had taken place. The time was shown by the digital clock at the head of the Piccadilly Line escalators, which was stopped by the heat of the flashover. It was 19.45.

FLASHOVER

19:45   As Relief Station Inspector Hayes and Station Inspector Dhanpersaud were about to leave the machine room Mr Hayes heard a 'whoosh' and they both heard the crackling sound of fire. Smoke made it impossible for them to make their way out under the Piccadilly Line escalators, so they left via the alternative staircase under the Victoria Line escalators and emerged on the Victoria Line escalator concourse.

Some way down on the Victoria Line escalators P.C. Hanson was shouting to the passengers to hurry up as quickly as possible. He went a short way towards the Piccadilly Line escalators and saw a jet of flames shoot up from the escalator shaft, hit the ceiling of the ticket hall and travel along the ceiling towards him. P.C. Hanson was caught off balance, crawled back to the Victoria Line escalators and shouted to passengers to keep low and get out through the ticket hall by the nearest exit. The heat increased. Flames licked the roof of the ticket hall and swirled towards P.C. Hanson as he made his escape through the tube lines ticket hall to the Euston Road south exit, suffering serious injuries as he did so.

Seeing what had happened Station Officer Osborne called out to the passengers to return to the bottom. He did so himself, assisting Mr Bates, a passenger who had received terrible injuries in the ticket hall a few metres from the top of the Victoria Line escalator. Mr Bates' injuries were so bad that Station Officer Osborne sought to help him by dousing him with water from a fire extinguisher.

P.C. Dixon, who was near the exit on the south side of Euston Road helped P.C. Hanson out into the street. He then sent a "**major incident**" emergency message by radio to the British Transport Police HQ information room. The **19:45:58** message was timed at 19:45:58.

19:46/47   P.C. Martland took Mr Bates to the station inspector's office on the Victoria Line platform concourse.

| 19:46 | Automatic Equipment Technician (AET) Dyer waved down northbound Victoria Line train 227 driven by Mr Barrett, who had received the order not to stop, and so had been driving through on manual control at a walking pace and stopped. Between 150 and 200 passengers were evacuated by this train. This procedure was repeated with two further Victoria Line trains until all passengers were finally clear of the tube lines platforms by 19:55. |

| **19:47** | Station Inspector Dhanpersaud directed passengers from the Piccadilly Line platform (westbound) to the Victoria Line (northbound). |

| **19:47** | London Ambulance Service received initial request for attendance at King's Cross and despatched an ambulance from St. John's Wood at 19:49. |

| 19:49 | Assistant Divisional Officer Shore of the London Fire Brigade arrived. |

| 19:50 | Station Inspector Dhanpersaud went to the Northern Line platform where he was told that trains were still stopping. He rang the line controller. |

| 19:52 | Metropolitan Line platforms cleared of passengers. |

| **19:53** | London Fire Brigade controller Mrs French informed London Underground HQ controller: "**Full fire at King's Cross**". |

| 19:54/55 | Last two passengers on platforms were evacuated by northbound Victoria Line train.

P.C. Martland and P.C. Kukielka took the injured Mr Bates from the station inspector's office to the Midland City subway. They found the London Underground Bostwick gates locked and shouted to AET Dyer for assistance. |

| 19:55 | AET Dyer unlocked the London Underground gates in the Midland City subway. P.C. Martland and P.C. Kukielka took Mr Bates through the subway, found the British Rail Bostwick gates locked, and shouted to attract attention. |

| 19:57 | HQ controller Tumbridge telephoned London Underground Duty Incident Officer, Mr Green, who was at home and informed him of the fire. |

19:59   First ambulance arrived at King's Cross.

c20:00   Attempts by the police to force the British Rail gates and to attract attention by shouting and the use of personal radio failed. AET Dyer and Relief Station Inspector Hayes attempted to contact British Rail by telephone.

20:01   Area Manager Harley arrived by Northern Line train.

            Area Manager Archer arrived by Piccadilly Line train.

            Acting Traffic Manager Nelson and Area Manager Grosvenor arrived by Metropolitan Line train.

            British Transport Police Inspector Wilkinson and P.C. Bardsley arrived by Piccadilly Line train.

20:03   Assistant Divisional Officer Shore ordered:

            "**Make pumps 12**" and "**Make ambulances 4**".

20:05   Woman Police Sergeant O'Neill and eight London Underground staff who had been trapped on the Metropolitan Line platform by smoke were evacuated by train.

20:06   Inspector Wilkinson erroneously told British Transport Police L Division information room that the fire had been extinguished.

20:08   London Ambulance Service put hospitals on standby alert.

20.10   Acting Traffic Manager Weston arrived by Piccadilly Line train.

c20.12   London Fire Brigade Divisional Officer Johnson arrived and took over command.

            Six ambulances were on scene.

20:13   Inspector Wilkinson told British Transport Police L Division information room:

            "**Fire blazing fiercely**".

20:15   London Fire Brigade Deputy Assistant Chief Officer Wilson arrived and took over command.

20:16	London Ambulance Service major accident was declared. Hospitals alerted.
20:17	Midland City subway British Rail gates were unlocked by a British Rail cleaner. Mr Bates was evacuated to hospital by ambulance. Area Manager Harley instructed Station Inspector Dhanpersaud to evacuate all staff via Midland City subway exit.
20:25	Station Inspector Hayes, Railman Farrell and most of the other London Underground staff left the station via the Midland City subway.
20:41	London Fire Brigade Assistant Chief Officer Kennedy arrived and took over command.
20:45	A Northern Line train, whose driver had not received the order to pass through King's Cross without stopping, stopped to let passengers get out. They were ordered to re-board by the police.
c20:53	London Fire Brigade Station Officer Demonte brought the station plans from the London Fire Brigade's plan box in the station to the area control unit.
20:55	P.C. Bardsley reported to British Transport Police L Division information room that trains on Northern Line were still stopping. London Underground HQ Controller Tumbridge was alerted.
c21:00	Assistant Divisional Officer Shore, with breathing apparatus crew, made his way through the tube lines ticket hall and down the Victoria Line escalators and met up with Station Officer Osborne and Temporary Sub-Officer Bell.
21:05	London Underground Duty Incident Officer, Mr Green, arrived by Northern Line train.
21:11	Assistant Chief Officer Kennedy gave the order: "**Make pumps 30**".

c21:15   Station Officer Demonte with breathing apparatus crew was despatched to enter by the Midland City subway. At the end of the subway they met Temporary Sub-Officer Bell, who had been presumed missing. At the bottom of the escalators they met other crews who had entered via the tube lines ticket hall.

21:29   London Fire Brigade liaison officer, Divisional Officer Nesbit, arrived at London Underground HQ control room at 55 Broadway.

21:32   14 ambulances were on scene.

c21:40   Leading Railwoman Ord and Railman Swaby were discovered in the staff mess room off the subway leading to St. Pancras station (shown in Figure 14) and released by firemen.

21:48   Assistant Chief Officer Kennedy sent message:
"Fire surrounded".

21:54   Inspector Wilkinson told British Transport Police L Division information room:
"Fires are being damped down but are not out".

01:46   London Fire Brigade "**stop**" message was sent, indicating that the fire had been contained. Search and salvage operations continued through the night.

Plates 2-31

Plate 2   Looking up Piccadilly Line escalator 5 at King's Cross. Escalator 4 to the left
of the photograph and escalator 6 to the right

Plate 3 Piccadilly Line escalator concourse taken on the day after the fire. Note handrail around access to lower machine room on bottom right

Plate 4   Top of the Piccadilly Line escalators seen from the ticket barriers showing fire damage

Plate 5   Looking up Piccadilly Line escalator 4 showing start of fire damage

Plate 6   General view of fire damage in Piccadilly Line escalator shaft, looking up escalator 4 towards the tube lines ticket hall

Plate 7   Damage to ceiling, facia board and advertisement panel above escalator 4

Plate 8   Remains of the tube lines ticket office looking from the Piccadilly Line escalators

Plate 9   View of Bostwick gates in closed position in passageway approaching King's Cross British Rail station, showing fire damage

Plate 10   Remains of hoarding in tube lines ticket hall showing fire hydrant

Plate 11   View of water fog controls from inside the entrance to the upper machine room

Plate 12   Accumulation of grease and detritus on undamaged part of running track of escalator 4. Taken on 20 November 1987

Plate 13

Grease and detritus on the running track of escalator 5 showing accumulation of fluff. Taken on 1 December 1987

Plate 14   Model of King's Cross Underground station showing layout of tube lines ticket hall

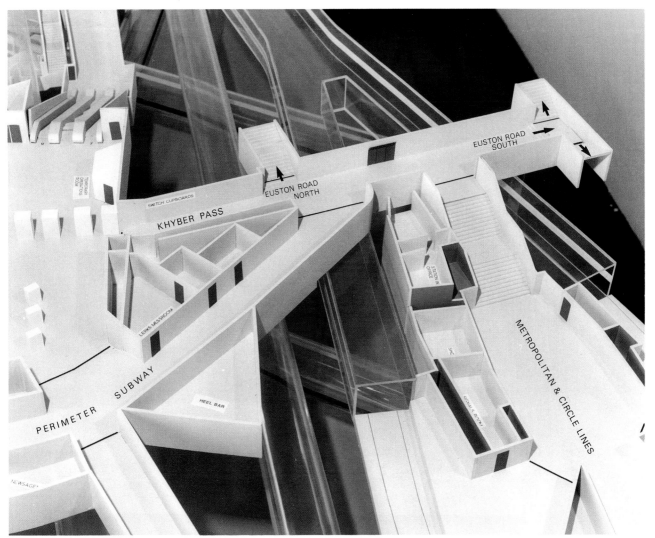

Plate 15   Model of King's Cross Underground station showing the Khyber Pass linking the
tube lines ticket hall on the left with the Metropolitan and Circle Lines on the right

Plate 16 Model of King's Cross Underground station showing the Victoria Line escalators on the left, and the Piccadilly Line escalators on the right, leading to the tube lines ticket hall

Plate 17   London Transport Museum illustrative model of MH escalator

Plate 18   Three step mock-up of MH escalator

Plate 19   Three step mock-up of MH escalator showing treads, risers, skirting board, and balustrade

CHAIN WHEEL

TRAILER WHEEL

Plate 20   Three step mock-up of MH escalator showing running track, chain and wheels

Plate 21   Fire development trials on escalator 4 on 8 January 1988, 7 minutes and 11 seconds after application of lighted match, viewed from beneath

Plate 22   Fire development trials on escalator 4 on 8 January 1988, 7 minutes 54 seconds after application of lighted match. Arrow indicates entry of match

Plate 23   Fire development trials on escalator 4 on 8 January 1988, 8 minutes 41 seconds after application of lighted match. Arrow indicates entry of match

Plate 24   Fire test on six full-scale steps of an escalator at the Health and Safety Executive, Buxton

Plate 25 Fire test on six full-scale steps of an escalator at the Health and Safety Executive, Buxton

Plate 26   Fire test on one-tenth scale model of escalator trough at the Health and Safety Executive, Buxton. Note low lying flames in the trough and jet of flame at the top

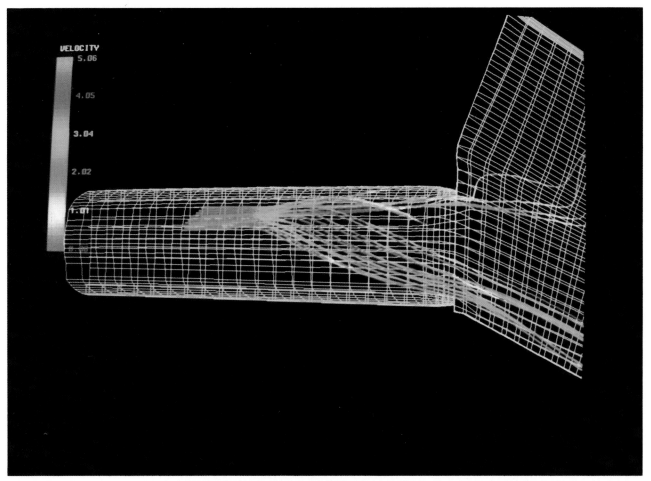

Plate 27　　　　　Computer simulation by Harwell showing flow and direction of hot gases on escalator 4 into the tube lines ticket hall, from a one megawatt fire

Plate 28   View from the bottom of one-third scale model of escalator shaft, at the Health and Safety Executive, Buxton

Plate 29   View from above of fire test on one-third scale model at the Health and Safety Executive, Buxton, showing flames in the escalator trough

Plate 30   View of top of Piccadilly Line escalator shaft in one-third scale model, at the Health and Safety Executive, Buxton, seen from the temporary station operations room in the tube lines ticket hall (see Figure 4)

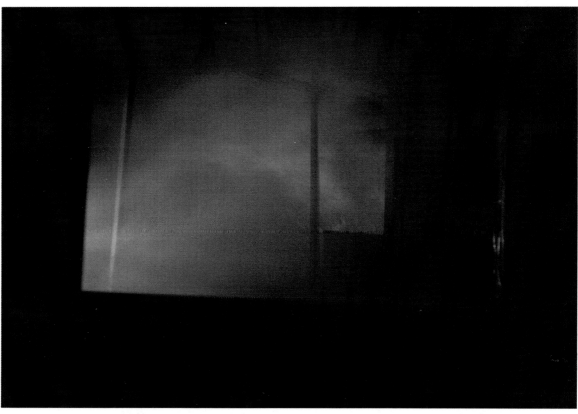

Plate 31   Fire test on one-third scale model from the same position as plate 30, showing flames erupting into the tube lines ticket hall

Chapter 10

The Response of London Underground Operating Staff

1. Details of the operating staff rostered for duty at 19:30 on 18 November 1987 are set out as a matter of conveninece in Figure 13. Their location at the time the alarm was raised is shown in Figure 14.

2. In my view the response of the London Underground operating staff has to be viewed against the background of four critical points:
    (i) they had not been adequately trained;
    (ii) there was no plan for evacuation of the station;
    (iii) communications equipment was poor or not used; and
    (iv) there was no supervision.

3. In these circumstances the operating staff had to do the best they could. It was fortunate that the British Transport Police officers were nearby and were able to take control.

4. There are two other points of general importance which ought to be borne in mind in reviewing the performance of the operating staff. First, the London Underground rule book required staff to deal themselves with any outbreak of fire wherever possible and only to send for the London Fire Brigade when the fire was beyond their control. Secondly, it is apparent that the outbreak of fire was not regarded as something unusual; indeed it was regarded by senior management as inevitable with a system of this age. This attituude was no doubt increased by the insistence of London Underground management that a fire should never be referred to as a fire but by the euphemism 'smouldering'. I am glad to report that London Underground have now agreed to stop using the word smouldering and have agreed that the London Fire Brigade should be summoned immediately there is any suggestion of fire.

The Tube Lines Staff

5. About 15 minutes before the fire on the Piccadilly Line escalator 4 was observed, Leading Railman Brickell at the 'way out' barrier was told by a passenger, Miss Tolmie, of some burning tissue at the bottom of the Victoria Line escalator. He went down and extinguished the tissue by banging it with a magazine before returning to his post. Leading Railman Brickell acted properly and in accordance with the London Underground rule book; it is a matter of speculation what course things would have taken if he had followed the new procedure and called the London Fire Brigade immediately.

6. The fire on escalator 4 was seen by Mr Squire at about 19:29 and reported to Booking Clerk Newman in the ticket office. Mr Newman telephoned Relief Station Inspector Hayes and told him he had received a report of smoke coming from the 'up' escalator on the Northern Line.

It was unfortunate that the place of the fire was described in this way, the accurate description being the Piccadilly Line escalator or escalator 4. Having received the message, without informing either the station manager or the line controller, Relief Station Inspector Hayes set off with Railman Farrell to the Northern Line escalators only to be told by passengers that smoke was coming from the Piccadilly Line escalators.

7. Leading Railman Brickell received a similar report from two passengers and, in spite of being restricted to barrier duties on the grounds of ill-health, went down to the bottom of escalator 5 to investigate. He did not know where the fire hydrant was and was unfamiliar with the water fog equipment. He assisted the police in redirecting passengers from the Piccadilly Line escalators to the Victoria Line escalators.

8. Shortly after he had received the first report, Mr Newman was told by a second passenger that there was a fire underneath escalator 4. He looked out of the ticket office towards the Piccadilly Line escalators:

   "There didn't seem to be any more smoke than when I previously looked out. I didn't think it was very serious, so I didn't leave the booking office."

   Mr Newman had no training in evacuation procedures and saw his duties as limited to what happened in the ticket office.

9. From the concourse at the bottom of the Piccadilly Line escalators, Relief Station Inspector Hayes saw smoke coming from escalator 4, just about half-way up. He went into the lower machine room of the escalators by the trap door, but seeing nothing, he came out and ran up escalator 6 to the upper machine room which he entered via the tube lines ticket hall. It was here that he passed the water fog controls which he failed to operate. He knew about the equipment in general terms, but had never used it or seen it used. He saw smoke and flame, but after returning with a carbon dioxide fire extinguisher was unable to get near enough to use it. In my view his lack of training and unfamiliarity with water fog equipment meant that his pre-occupation with the fire and smoke led him to forget about the system or the merits of its use.

10. Railman Farrell assisted Relief Station Inspector Hayes and went up escalator 6 as well, but when he got to the tube lines ticket hall, the door of the upper machine room slammed in his face and he was unable to follow Relief Station Inspector Hayes. At the request of the police he telephoned the Victoria Line controller at 19:42 from the Victoria Line platforms and asked that an order be put out for trains not to stop at King's Cross. He assisted in sending passengers from the Victoria Line platforms up the Victoria Line escalators to leave the station by way of the tube lines ticket hall. AET Dyer, with police assistance,

halted a northbound Victoria Line train and evacuated a large number of passengers. Railman Farrell left by the Midland City exit shortly after Mr Bates had been taken out at 20:17.

11. Relief Station Inspector Hayes was unprepared by training and experience to take charge of the incident. His failure to notify the station manager or line controller as soon as he received a report of a fire or to operate the water fog equipment were serious omissions which may have contributed to the disaster, although it is possible that the chain of events was too far advanced for any action on his part to have averted the development of the fire, but it might have delayed it.

12. In my judgement, none of those who were concerned with evacuating passengers by way of the Victoria Line escalators up to the tube lines ticket hall are to be blamed for the action they took. In the absence of any evacuation plan they were simply doing the best they could. There was no reason for them to anticipate the flashover.

13. Leading Railman Wood was confined to barrier duties on grounds of ill-health. He gave evidence only briefly, but it was to the effect that as soon as he was told by a passenger about the smell of smoke he went down escalator 5 to investigate. He had some difficulty in controlling passengers, and was personally blamed by some of those he had redirected to the Midland City exit, when they returned after finding it to be locked. I am satisfied that he was trying to assist passengers when he received his injuries.

14. Of the other London Underground staff who should have been on duty on the tube side at the relevant time, Leading Railwoman Eusebe, Leading Railman Swaby and Leading Railwoman Ord were not at their posts and one railman's post was unfilled.

15. Leading Railman Swaby did not give evidence, but it was clear from the evidence of Leading Railwoman Ord that both he and she were taking an extended meal break in a staff mess room at the time of the flashover. The evidence given by Leading Railwoman Ord about meal breaks revealed a disturbing state of affairs, for she told me:

> "On this shift I usually go for my meal relief from 19:00 to 20:30. I know I am only supposed to have a half hour meal break, but it has been an accepted practice since I have been at King's Cross for the ticket collectors to take $1\frac{1}{2}$ hours on late turns only. As far as I know, all the ticket collectors take this amount of time, apart from Mr Wood who only takes an hour. The supervisors leave it to the ticket collectors to work times out for themselves."

16. I could see no reason for Leading Railwoman Ord to make such an admission unless it was true and accordingly I accept her evidence about the position of meal breaks at King's Cross, which can only be described as unsatisfactory. In my judgement the management either knew or ought to have known the position. I repeat the observation I made during the hearing that it would be unfair for those who took advantage of sloppy supervision over a long period of time to be penalised for their actions, although there can be no excuse for what they did.

17. The remaining person who was rostered to be on duty that night was Leading Railwoman Eusebe. She had been given permission to go to hospital and, at the completion of her visit, had telephoned at about 18:30 to be told by Relief Station Inspector Hayes that she need not report for duty.

18. At the material time therefore, there were only two members of London Underground staff on barrier duty in the tube lines ticket hall. In the course of cross-examination, Counsel for London Underground sought to establish that there should have been five members of staff on barrier duty and that this would have been an adequate number to deal with the emergency. Having heard evidence about the training which the staff had received, I reject that submission. It seems to me that the staff were totally unprepared to meet the disaster which happened that night and had to do the best they could in the circumstances.

The Metropolitan and Circle Lines Staff

19. As the station manager at King's Cross that night, Mr Worrell was the most senior member of staff present when the emergency began. But, instead of being at the centre of the station where he could have been in control, Mr Worrell was at the far end of the Metropolitan and Circle Lines platforms where his office had been placed during station building works for the installation of the Underground Ticketing System (UTS) equipment. Mr Worrell had expressed his anxiety to the manager in charge of the station works but he was overruled and so his permanent office became the booking clerks' mess room while the alterations in the tube lines ticket hall were undertaken. The only means of communication in this temporary office was an internal telephone. It is a matter of particular regret that Mr Worrell's representation should have been overruled at a time when the equipment in the temporary station operations room was unsatisfactory. Mr Worrell said that he shared the views of Station Inspector Dhanpersaud on the inadequacy of the equipment in that room.

20. The station manager's office has now been returned to the tube lines ticket hall and the station operations room equipment relocated.

21. Mr Worrell was not told about the fire until 19:42 when the Piccadilly Line controller asked him if he knew of any smouldering in the machine room. Thus, a full twelve minutes had elapsed since the fire was first notified to a member of London Underground staff. Mr Worrell telephoned AET Dyer, who told him that Relief Station Inspector Hayes had gone to investigate. Mr Worrell immediately made his way towards the machine room, saw fire officers and smoke in the station, and shouted to people in the Khyber Pass area to clear the station. He was about to enter the tube lines ticket hall from the perimeter subway when he encountered a blanket of jet black smoke and turned back. Unable to find the entrance to the Metropolitan and Circle Lines ticket hall in the smoke, he continued to the Euston Road south exit and made his way to the surface where he remained assisting with crowd control. Despite his position as senior representative of London Underground, Station Manager Worrell made no attempt to contact the London Fire Brigade to offer advice and assistance. It was over an hour later that he was directed by Acting Traffic Manager Nelson to answer any questions that the London Fire Brigade might have about the station plans.

22. Mr Pilgrim was the relief station manager at King's Cross that night and was present with Station Manager Worrell in his office when the call came at 19:42 informing them of the fire. Station Manager Pilgrim, who was taking a refreshment break, did not regard it as a serious fire and followed Station Manager Worrell after two or three minutes. As he came out into the Metropolitan Line concourse area he saw passengers running down towards the platforms, and dense black smoke at the top of the stairs in the passageway leading from the perimeter subway and Khyber Pass. Thereafter he supervised the Metropolitan Line platforms and arranged for a substantial number of passengers to be evacuated on an eastbound train which arrived at 19:52.

23. Relief Station Manager Pilgrim remained on the Metropolitan Line platforms until all passengers were clear, then gathered all his staff together in the staff mess room away from the platforms and concourse area which were by now full of smoke. An empty train was sent from Moorgate, and with woman Police Sergeant O'Neill, Relief Station Manager Pilgrim supervised the evacuation of eight members of staff on this train at 20:05. He remained behind with Acting Traffic Manager Nelson and Area Manager Grosvenor, taking and making telephone calls until he was led to the surface about an hour later. He met Station Manager Worrell on the surface and reported that all his staff had been evacuated.

24. Station Inspector Dhanpersaud was in the Metropolitan Line inspector's office when at 19:40 he received a call from the Piccadilly Line traffic manager at Earl's Court to the effect that one of the machine rooms appeared to be on fire. As Railman White and Railman Obcena were with him, Station Inspector Dhanpersaud sent them to check the machine room. On Railman Obcena's return Station Inspector Dhanpersaud went with him to the tube side, opening the Khyber Pass Bostwick gates, an action which was to provide an escape route for some people after the flashover. In the tube lines ticket hall, he saw police officers and met Relief Station Inspector Hayes, with whom he went into the upper machine room. There he proceeded to operate the circuit breakers, isolating the electricity supply to all five escalators.

25. Shortly afterwards Station Inspector Dhanpersaud and Relief Station Inspector Hayes made their escape by descending the steps beneath the Victoria Line escalators and emerged into the Victoria Line escalator concourse. There Station Inspector Dhanpersaud saw Mr Bates, who was being ministered to by Station Officer Osborne. Station Inspector Dhanpersaud then assisted in the clearing of the tube lines platforms, ensured that Northern Line trains were passing through without stopping, and isolated the electrical supply to the Northen Line escalators. He then helped firemen and police officers to connect the hose pipe at the bottom of the Piccadilly Line escalators. Within two minutes Northern Line Area Manager Harley arrived and Station Inspector Dhanpersaud went with him to the Victoria Line platforms to evacuate members of staff by means of the Midland City subway. Finally, with other staff gone, he helped AET Dyer to bring trains through on the Victoria Line where a fire-damaged cable had disrupted the automatic operation.

26. Station Inspector Dhanpersaud acted with considerable presence of mind and did a great deal that night to try to achieve the safety of those in the station. He also made a particular impression upon the court in the tone and manner of his evidence.

27. I will consider the role played by the more senior members of operating staff at the end of this chapter.

The Booking Office Staff

28. The booking office staff were, and regarded themselves, as a group apart. They wore no uniform and they belonged in the main to a separate trade union. They had received virtually no training in fire fighting or station evacuation procedures. They regarded their duties as confined to the ticket office.

29. There were six booking office staff on duty at King's Cross that night: there should have been seven. Four men were working on the tube side; two were working on the Metropolitan side. The seventh had left some three and a half hours early with the knowledge of his colleagues. This was a common practice at King's Cross, which must have been known to management.

30. Between 19:15 and 19:20 Mr Anstis, the supervisory booking clerk, left his office on the tube side to visit the station manager's office on the Metropolitan side. Thereafter he went to the Metropolitan Line station inspector's office. Whilst he was there Station Manager Worrell called in from outside that there was some bother on the station. Mr Anstis left after a couple of minutes, and as he walked along the perimeter subway he was confronted by a rush of people screaming and shouting, whereupon he turned round and walked back to the Metropolitan Line. There he assisted in evacuating passengers onto a Metropolitan Line train before going with the other staff by train to Euston Square.

31. Mr Newman was on duty alone in the tube lines ticket office when he received the first report of the fire and telephoned Relief Station Inspector Hayes at once. He received a second report too, but believing the fire not to be serious he did not leave the ticket office. Shortly afterwards he was told to leave by the police. With Mr Hythe, he collected the money and took it to the counting room. He deposited the money in the office and secured it. Mr Hythe had been about to empty and reload the automatic ticket machines at 19:35 when he had smelt burning rubber. As he was completing his task, he heard the cry "Fire—everybody out". He paused to complete his work and then went to leave with Mr Newman.

32. Mr Frankland was on his meal break in the booking clerks' mess room when he was alerted to the fire at 19:43 by Mr Newman and Mr Hythe. They collected him on their way out. Mr Newman and Mr Hythe returned to the ticket office to collect Mr Frankland's coat. Mr Frankland would not have known of the emergency if the others had not gone to get him: the mess room had no communication link.

33. Mr Mistry and Mr Smith were on duty in the Metropolitan and Circle Lines ticket office. After the alarm had been raised they shut the office and assisted on the platforms with the evacuation of passengers and in crowd control.

34. It is apparent from all the evidence which was given at the Investigation that the London Underground staff at King's Cross station that night were woefully ill-equipped to meet the emergency that arose. Those on duty did the best they could using their common

sense in the absence of training and supervision. Had the water fog equipment been used there is reason to think that the progress of the fire would have been delayed and the London Fire Brigade might have been able to deal with it. In fact, not a drop of water was applied to the fire nor any fire extinguishers used by the London Underground staff.

Line Controllers

35. The London Underground HQ controller and individual line controllers have a vital part to play when serious incidents occur on the system. I discuss the shortcomings there were in the communcations equipment in place on the night of the fire in Chapter 16 'Communications Systems'.

36. Mr Tumbridge was the HQ controller on duty at 55 Broadway. He was first informed of a fire in the Piccadilly Line escalator machine room at King's Cross by the Piccadilly Line controller at 19:39. While he was passing this information to the lift and escalator report centre he received a call from the British Transport Police in a direct line to report the fire and the fact that the London Fire Brigade had been called. He did not call the London Fire Brigade to confirm this message. I am satisfied that the London Fire Brigade Wembley control room also informed the HQ controller that fire appliances had been sent to King's Cross although this call was not logged by Mr Tumbridge. I discuss this discrepancy in Chapter 11 'The Response of the Emergency Services: the London Fire Brigade'.

37. Mr Tumbridge then informed the acting traffic manager responsible for King's Cross station, Mr Nelson, of the situation, before having to deal with an unrelated incident at London Bridge station. At 19:43 he received the police request to order Piccadilly and Victoria Line trains not to stop at King's Cross, which he duly passed on to the Piccadilly and Victoria Line controllers. In doing so he assumed that the Victoria Line controller would pass on the request to his Northern Line counterpart (who sits alongside him), although he did not check to see whether this had been done. He requested an ambulance to attend as a precaution at 19:48. The London Fire Brigade called at 19:53 to say a "full fire" was reported at King's Cross station. Mr Tumbridge, although not appreciating the significance of that phrase, alerted the London Underground fire department at Moorgate at 19:55 and then called the Duty Officer, Divisional Operations Manager Green, at home. Mr Green was thus alerted at 19:57, 18 minutes after the fire was first reported to the HQ control room.

38. It is clear that Mr Tumbridge was very busy during the critical half hour after the alarm was raised and did not realise the gravity of the emergency at King's Cross. Had he been informed by a station surpervisor when the fire was first detected, events might have been quite different. At times he was pre-occupied with unrelated incidents at other stations and in making alternative travel arrangements on London Buses following an earlier incident on the Central Line. He was unable to distinguish between the priority of the many incoming calls and did not keep a complete record of all the calls made and received. He was not helped by the fact that the London Fire Brigade liaison officer did not arrive until much later and so vital information which was passing over the London Fire Brigade radio network remained unknown to him. His apparent failure specifically to order Northern Line trains not to stop or to verify whether trains were in fact stopping may have materially contributed to the disaster. The delay in alerting the Duty Incident Officer was unacceptably long, but in the event Mr Green took a further hour to reach the station. When Mr Green did call Mr Tumbridge at 21:05, he was merely told that two people were reported dead, and that HQ control had no further information.

39. The Piccadilly Line controller on duty on the evening of 18 November 1987 was Mr R Hanson. He first learnt of the fire indirectly at 19:38 during a telephone conversation with the British Transport Police about an unrelated incident at Hounslow. He acted promptly in alerting the HQ controller, traffic manager, area manager and station manager within the space of three minutes. He then received a request to order trains on his line not to stop at King's Cross, which was put into effect by 19:45. The only other call he received about King's Cross was from Area Manager Archer at 20:13, who reported that the station was being evacuated. He was unaware until much later that there had been a major incident. Mr Hanson used his colleagues effectively to make calls simultaneously, and it is mainly due to shortcomings in the communications systems—notably the lack of a direct line to the station manager's officer at King's Cross—that they were unable to alert station supervisors any sooner. In the event the station manager learnt of the fire too late (at 19:42) to play any effective part in the local fire-fighting or evacuation.

40. The Victoria Line controller, Mr Vincent, learnt of the fire when at 19:42 he received the police request to order trains not to stop at King's Cross from Railman Farrell. He implemented the order and called the HQ controller, who is likely to have confirmed that he was aware of the situation, and the area manager and traffic manager responsible for the Victoria and Northern Lines at King's Cross. His only other involvement with the incident was to receive a call from AET Dyer at

about 20:05 requesting that British Rail should be asked to open their side of the Midland City exit where passengers were trapped. Mr Vincent passed on this request to the HQ controller who had a wider range of contacts, although Mr Tumbridge had no recollection of receiving the request. It is most likely that the message was passed on but that it proved impossible to contact anyone at British Rail Midland Region. In the event, as we know, the Midland City gates were unlocked at about 20:17 by a British Rail cleaner who heard the cries for help. A more effective response by the line controllers to Mr Dyer's request might have resulted in an earlier release and reduction in the suffering of Mr Bates, although Mr Vincent had no way of knowing that the request he passed on had not been implemented.

41. Mr Vincent, like the other line controllers, did not appreciate the seriousness of the emergency until it was almost over. He carried out the essential task of implementing the order for trains not to stop and informing senior managers expeditiously. He is not to be blamed for failing to inform the Northern Line controller, who might reasonably have been expected to receive directly any order for trains not to stop.

42. The Northern Line controller at the time of the fire was Mr Goldfinch, who was covering the meal relief of the rostered controller. The HQ controller informed him at 19:42 of the reported fire at King's Cross and the possibility that the station might have to close. Mr Goldfinch passed this message to Traffic Manager Hunt and Area Manager Harley. It is most likely that he received an instruction to order trains not to stop at about 19:44, although this and certain other calls received during this period were not recorded in the log. At 19:50 he received a direct instruction to order trains not to stop and implemented it. In the previous eight minutes, three southbound and two northbound Northern Line trains had stopped at the station and passengers had been allowed to get off four of these trains. The Operations Director in his evidence said that the fact that the Northern Line controller did not implement the order until given a further direct instruction at 19:50 may have resulted in passengers being routed towards the fire zone. The controller has now left the service.

43. The Metropolitan Line controller during the first part of the emergency was Mr Gregory, on meal duty relief for the rostered controller Mr Marks, who returned in time to receive and implement the request at 19:56 to order trains not to stop. Mr Gregory had been informed of the fire by the Jubilee Line controller who took a call from the HQ controller. He advised Acting Traffic Manager Nelson and Area Manager Grosvenor. After implementing the order for trains not to stop, Mr Marks received a call at 20:04 from Farringdon station staff requesting an ambulance to carry a badly burned passenger. It was only at this time that Mr Marks realised there was a fire.

44. I make certain recommendations as to the improvement of the HQ controller's equipment which, if implemented, would permit timing and automatic logging of calls, more discriminating treatment of urgent calls, and a faster and more flexible reponse to future incidents. It is essential however that station staff and line controllers should be instructed in the importance of informing the HQ controller of reported fires at the earliest opportunity. HQ controllers for their part must be better trained and practised in the procedure to be followed in the event of fires being reported, for alerting the emergency services, senior managers and others who need to know without delay. The importance of the early attendance of a London Fire Brigade liaison officer at the London Underground HQ control room cannot be over-emphasised.

45. Although many of the delays and omissions in the conduct of line controllers during the emergency can be attributed to inadequancies in the communications equipment in place, it is clear also that there was a general failure to appreciate the severity of the disaster and so to act with the appropriate sense of urgency. None of the controllers thought to check with the London Fire Brigade that it was safe to run trains through the station or indeed to call the station to find out what was happening. In future it is vital that any reported fire is dealt with by line controllers as a matter of the utmost urgency and that the procedure for informing other controllers and senior managers is clarified. The responsibility of the HQ controller for calling the London Fire Brigade, liaising with all the emergency services and keeping line controllers informed of incidents should be clearly set down and a priority prescribed for making calls.

Senior Operating Staff

46. London Underground have a duty officer procedure which provides for a duty officer and duty assistant to be available at all times outside normal office hours to give advice or instruction on dealing with incidents, and to attend in person as incident officer if the incident seems serious enough. The duty incident officer on the evening of 18 November was Mr Green the Divisional Operations Manager for the District and Piccadilly Lines. He was first alerted to the fire at 19:57 by the HQ controller and travelled to King's Cross by car and Northern Line train, arriving shortly after 21:00.

47. Traffic managers and area managers who work on a shift basis are responsible for dealing with any incidents at stations within their areas and, where they attend in person, are required to take charge pending the arrival of anyone in higher authority. At King's Cross, two traffic managers and three area managers arrived by train before the arrival of the duty incident officer, including the traffic manager with primary responsibility for the station, Mr Nelson.

48. On the Metropolitan side, Acting Traffic Manager Nelson and Area Manager Grosvenor arrived together on an eastbound train at 20:01. They assisted in the evacuation of remaining staff by train which was being supervised by Relief Station Manager Pilgrim when they arrived, and contacted the HQ controller and Metropolitan Line controller to keep them informed of the situation. Unable to get through the subway to the tube side or the Euston Road south exit, Area Manager Grosvenor contacted Relief Station Inspector Hayes by telephone and ascertained that passengers had been cleared from the tube side and staff accounted for. Acting Traffic Manager Nelson did not leave by train, but waited until the smoke had cleared enough to use the Euston Road south exit at about 20:49. On the surface he made contact with the London Fire Brigade area control unit and witnessed the arrival of the station plans. He was not asked about the Midland City entrance. He returned to the Metropolitan Line platform and with Area Manager Grosvenor continued to ensure trains were not stopping. After about an hour the London Fire Brigade had damped down the fire in the tube lines ticket hall sufficiently for a room by room search of the area to be made, and Acting Traffic Manager Nelson assisted them in this. He and Area Manager Grosvenor remained on the Metropolitan Line platform until the last train had passed through in contact with the Metropolitan Line controller and HQ controller from time to time.

49. Since responsibility for King's Cross station fell to the division which included the Metropolitan Line, Acting Traffic Manager Nelson was the most senior London Underground officer in the station until the arrival of Incident Officer Green after 21:00. Yet apart from ascertaining by telephone that passengers and staff had been cleared from the lower station, he appears to have considered his duties to rest almost entirely on the Metropolitan side of the station. He did not attempt to leave by train to get to the surface to liaise with the London Fire Brigade at an earlier stage and to offer his detailed knowledge of the layout of the station, or to let those on the surface know that he was available in the station.

50. On the tube lines side, two area managers arrived independently by train very shortly after 20:00. Area Manager Harley (Northern Line) and Area Manager Archer (Piccadilly Line), were joined in the tube side of the station ten minutes later by Acting Traffic Manager Weston who arrived by Piccadilly Line train. After checking that all the platforms were clear of passengers and having seen British Transport Police Inspector Wilkinson and firemen at the bottom of the Piccadilly Line escalators, the managers instructed Station Inspector Dhanpersaud to evacuate all remaining staff and stay in occasional contact with their line controllers or the HQ controller thereafter.

51. Area Manager Harley was occupied for a time with bringing Victoria Line trains through by manual control as the fire above had damaged the circuitry which allowed automatic operation. None of the managers appreciated the scale of the disaster above while they were below, and none attempted to contact the emergency services or London Underground personnel on the surface by telephone. When each of them got to the surface by way of the Midland City exit they saw their main task as liaison with other London Underground personnel. Traffic Manager Weston, who came up shortly after 20:30, assumed that Acting Traffic Manager Nelson was in overall charge. He did not make contact with the London Fire Brigade area control unit once he saw that the Incident Officer Mr Green had arrived.

52. When Divisional Operations Manager Green arrived by Northern Line train shortly after 21:00, he introduced himself to British Transport Police Inspector Wilkinson and Station Officer Osborne, saw that the escalator was still burning and was told that nobody was dead but that one or two passengers had been injured. He then called the HQ controller and was informed that two people had been reported dead. Since the HQ controller could give him no further information, Mr Green made his way to the surface via the Midland City exit.

53. The severity of the accident became clear to Mr Green for the first time on the surface, and he went to the London Fire Brigade area control unit to contact the London Fire Brigade incident officer. He reported to Assistant Chief Officer Kennedy at about 21:20 and was asked to lay a land line to establish communications between the London Fire Brigade and London Underground incident vehicles. No information about what was going on below ground was exchanged. Mr Green assumed that Assistant Chief Officer Kennedy was in full control of the situation and that the firemen below ground were in contact with those above.

54. Mr Green reported the situation to the HQ controller at 21:27 and then asked Acting Traffic Manager Nelson to tell all control grade staff to report to him, accounting for all staff and ensuring that services kept running. He spent the rest of the night liaising with engineering and building services staff about arrangements for re-opening parts of the station for services the following morning.

55. It will be clear from this short account that there was no effective communcation between those present on either side of the station and those outside, and that several opportunities for the exchange of vital information between London Underground and London Fire Brigade personnel were lost. The presence of the two firemen below and the existence of a free access in the Midland City entrance should have been reported. There was uncertainty over which of the London

Underground staff was in charge until the arrival of the duty incident officer and the importance of proper liaison with the emergency services was not understood by the London Underground managers. Their concern with accounting for staff and keeping trains running prevented them from making a proper appraisal of the overall situation and ensuring that relevant information was passed to the emergency services and HQ controller.

56. I deal with the question of staffing and training in Chapter 15 'Station Staffing and Training' and communications equipment in Chapter 16 'Communications Systems'. My other recommendations to arise from this review of the response of London Underground operating staff concern the training of staff in the use of water fog equipment, the location and equipping of station operations rooms, the controller's communications equipment, procedures for determining whether trains should continue to run, planning and instruction on evacuation of stations, fire-fighting equipment, staff uniforms and designated staff assembly and rendezvous points at stations.

Chapter 11

The Response of the Emergency Services

London Fire Brigade

1. The fire at King's Cross presented the London Fire Brigade with four problems:

    (i) they were not called immediately;

    (ii) the crews attending had no detailed knowledge of the geography or station layout;

    (iii) the flashover occurred within two minutes of their first arrival in the tube lines ticket hall; and

    (iv) the officer in charge of the first appliance was killed and the officers in charge of two of the other appliances were cut off below ground. Thereafter communications broke down.

2. In 1963 the London Government Act was passed, paving the way for the estabishment of the London Fire Brigade as it is today. Between 1965 and 1986 the Greater London Council was the controlling authority, but the Local Government Act 1985 replaced the Greater London Council with a new body, the London Fire and Civil Defence Authority, which took control on 1 April 1986.

3. Thus, since 1986 the London Fire Brigade has been a part of, and under the control of, the London Fire and Civil Defence Authority. This authority comprises one councillor from each of the 32 London Boroughs and a representative of the City of London. Its Chief Executive is the Chief Officer of the London Fire Brigade.

4. The London Fire Brigade was summoned to King's Cross Underground station at 19:34 and the first fire appliance arrived at 19:42. It will remain a matter of conjecture what would have happened if the London Fire Brigade had been summoned to deal with the burning tissue at the bottom of the Victoria Line escalator which was extinguished by Leading Railman Brickell at about 19:15. Their presence then would have enabled them to attack the Piccadilly Line escalator fire about 12 minutes earlier and thereby to damp down the fire and possibly avoid the build-up that led to the flashover. Similarly, if the Brigade had been summoned at about 19:30, when the fire on escalator 4 was first reported to a station supervisor, they would have had been there at least four minutes earlier.

5. Because of the risks associated with fire the London Fire Brigade had for some time urged London Underground to call them immediately on any suggestion of fire on the Underground. Their concern was so great that on 23 August 1985 (the day following a fire at Baker Street) the Chief Officer requested Deputy Assistant Chief Officer Kennedy, to

write officially to London Underground about the matter. His letter to Mr Cope, the Operations Director (Railways) was in these terms:

"Dear Mr Cope,

Arrangements for calling Fire Brigade

"I am gravely concerned to find that, contrary to the professional advice of the Brigade, a two-stage procedure has been introduced for notifying the Brigade of fires occurring on the London Underground railway system. Following the recent fire at Oxford Circus underground station, the Brigade made it quite clear that the Brigade should be called immediately to any fire on the underground railway network.

"Experience has shown that a two-stage procedure leads to confusion and, consequently a delay in attendance of the Brigade, as happened at Baker Street last evening.

"We are aware that the incidence of fires on the Underground railway network has fallen considerably since the Brigade's advice to reduce the amount of litter. Nevertheless I cannot urge too strongly that the two-stage procedure be withdrawn and instead clear instructions be given that on any suspicion of fire, the Fire Brigade be called without delay. This could save lives.

"In recognition of the difficulties of operating the railway we have changed the Brigade's procedure to ensure the attendance of a senior officer whenever the Brigade is called to a fire on the underground system."

Nonetheless, London Underground failed to amend Appendix 8 of its rule book which remained in these terms:

D. Outbreak of Fire

D1. There are two types of fire: those that can be extinguished by the use of the equipment available and described in Section C and those that require the attendance of the Fire Brigade. In case of doubt, Fire Brigade assistance must be requested.

6. I report with satisfaction that London Underground have now issued instructions that the Fire Brigade must be summoned immediately to all reported, or suspected, outbreaks of fire or smoke occurring on any part of the London Underground system.

7. Neither Leading Railman Brickell nor Relief Station Inspector Hayes reported the fires which they were investigating and it was not until P.C. Bebbington's call to British Transport Police HQ, logged at 19:33 and transmitted to the London Fire Brigade Wembley control room at

19:34 that the Fire Brigade was alerted. Control Officer French then transmitted the messages which despatched five appliances to King's Cross in accordance with the predetermined attendance (PDA).

8. The PDA plan included a requirement that London Fire Brigade should inform the London Underground HQ controller at 55 Broadway that fire appliances had been sent to King's Cross. Control Officer French told us that she took such a step at about 19:38. The London Underground HQ controller's log did not record the call and the controller, Mr Tumbridge, said he believed he never received it. Having heard all the evidence I am satisfied that Control Officer French did make the call.

9. The PDA for a fire at King's Cross Underground station was for four pump appliances and a turntable ladder, together with a forward control unit equipped with special thermal imaging camera equipment. That requirement had been laid down in 1979 and amended in 1984, following the Oxford Circus station fire. The plan also required the attendance of a senior officer at any fire call on the underground railway system. (See letter of 23 August 1985 from Deputy Assistant Chief Officer Kennedy quoted above). As King's Cross was within the fire ground territory of the Euston fire station any call from King's Cross would normally be dealt with by Euston. But unhappily the Euston appliances were out on another call. So the control officer despatched appliances from Soho and Clerkenwell fire stations together with a pump from Manchester Square. Vehicles are required to notify their arrival to Headquarters by radio. The times recorded at Kings's Cross were:

    19:42 A24 Pump Ladder (Soho) under Station Officer Townsley

    19:43 C27 Pump Ladder (Clerkenwell) under Temporary Sub-Officer Bell, and A22 Pump (Manchester Square) under Station Officer Osborne

    19:44 A24 Turntable Ladder (Soho) under Sub-Officer Trefry, and A24 Pump (Soho) under Leading Fireman Kendall

    19:46 Forward Control Unit (Northern Command HQ) under Station Officer Pryke

    Considering the traffic conditions each of these appliances arrived as quickly as could be expected. Nonetheless, had the appliances from Euston been available they could have been there two or three minutes earlier.

10. On arrival Station Officer Townsley should have been met by a member of the London Underground staff to brief him. Such a guide is highly desirable if the London Fire Brigade is to act effectively and with speed.

Unfortunately, no one from London Underground undertook the task and P.C. Dixon, who had been asked to meet the Fire Brigade, did not succeed because the London Fire Brigade did not go to the place he anticipated. There was no agreed rendezvous point.

11. Station Officer Townsley, as the officer in charge, entered the station via the Pancras Road entrance, accompanied by members of his crew. By this time the evacuation had been started by a member of the British Transport Police.

12. Station Officer Townsley and Temporary Sub-Officer Bell went to make a reconnaissance and, standing between escalators 5 and 6 at the head of the Piccadilly Line escalators, could see a fire burning about half-way down escalator 4. Together with Temporary Sub-Officer Bell, Station Officer Townsley went down escalator 6 a short distance to make a more detailed inspection. He then returned to the tube lines ticket hall where he ordered Station Officer Osborne to arrange for two breathing apparatus wearers and a water jet. He also instructed Temporary Leading Fireman Flanagan to send a message to fire control:

"Make pumps 4—persons reported"

Temporary Sub-Officer Bell continued his descent to prevent passengers coming up the escalators.

13. Situated in the tube lines ticket hall, but hidden behind the contractor's temporary hoarding, was a London Underground fire hydrant with a quantity of canvas hose. In spite of the London Fire Brigade's preference to use their own equipment, this hydrant could have been used to provide a source of water for the fire more quickly than by using the supply from the fire appliances 160 metres away. I recommend later that all hydrants and hoses be changed to London Fire Brigade's specifications and that the London Fire Brigade shall review their use of the occupier's equipment. In certain circumstances this would clearly add speed to their response.

14. At 19:45, within two minutes of the arrival in the tube lines ticket hall of the crew from the first London Fire Brigade appliance, the flashover occurred. As a result the top of the escalators, the tube lines ticket hall and the surrounding passages were engulfed in severe fire with thick black smoke, which forced the fire crews, the police officers, London Underground staff and passengers to retreat rapidly in various directions. Some escaped and some suffered horrific burns, but the fire claimed the lives of 31 people, including Station Officer Townsley. The body of this officer was found at the foot of the steps leading up to the Pancras Road entrance to the station. His uniform and body were virtually unburnt and lying close beside him was the badly burned body of a passenger. In all likelihood this was Miss Byers whom he had

been trying to help to safety. Some witnesses recounted seeing a fireman wearing a white helmet moving across the concourse just before the flashover and someone with a torch exhorting passengers to get out. The evidence I heard points to the fact that this was Station Officer Townsley and that he was trying to help the burned passenger to safety when he was overcome by smoke and fumes. His was a heroic act.

15. The flashover divided the Underground into two worlds, each believing it had lost touch with the other. Those on the surface believed that those beneath were trapped or probably dead: those beneath had no idea what was happening above. Their sense of detachment was complete.

16. When he reached the bottom of the Piccadilly Line escalators, Temporary Sub-Officer Bell set about stopping people ascending and began to clear them away from the concourse. He shouted to the passengers to get back onto a train. Before he began clearing people from the concourse onto the trains Temporary Sub-Officer Bell had observed that the fire on the escalator appeared to be limited. But when he returned, he found that it was a totally different fire and that the flame was going from the steps and sides of the escalator, up round the ceiling and back down onto the escalators. It was curling up the escalator shaft right through to the crest. Temporary Sub-Officer Bell thereafter set about trying to find a branch (nozzle) and hose with which to fight the fire. He was unaware of what was happening in the tube lines ticket hall, or in the Victoria Line escalator concourse. He did not know that his colleagues on the surface believed he was dead.

17. At the time of the flashover Station Officer Osborne was in the tube lines ticket hall at the head of the Victoria Line escalator shaft. He saw a very severe flame shooting from the direction of the Piccadilly Line escalators, which looked like a flame-thrower. By good fortune it did not strike him as it burst up into the ticket hall. He shouted to passengers on the Victoria Line escalator to go back down. Near the top of the Victoria Line escalators he saw a badly burnt man emerging from the smoke. It was Mr Bates. Station Officer Osborne took him to the bottom of the Victoria Line escalators and there used a water extinguisher upon him to put out his burning clothes and relieve his pain. Shortly afterwards P.C. Martland with P.C. Kukielka took control of the situation and evacuated Mr Bates.

18. Meanwhile Temporary Sub-Officer Bell had begun to lay out fire equipment. He himself was poorly equipped because he had failed to bring his axe, his Bardic torch and his personal radio. He had not fought the fire earlier, partly because he beleived it would be attacked by crews with breathing apparatus from the tube lines ticket hall and

partly because he believed to fight the fire from below would endanger those above. To fight the fire, Temporary Sub-Officer Bell climbed the escalator with P.C. Bebbington and directed the jet into the flames. Three times they attacked the fire. He tore panels away from the escalator, the better to attack the fire, but having knocked it out on the surface, Temporary Sub-Officer Bell saw that the fire took hold again and he had to attack once more.

19. On the surface the fire crews found themselves in a difficult position. The officers in charge of three of the appliances, namely Station Officer Townsley, Station Officer Osborne and Temporary Sub-Officer Bell could not initially be found. Badly injured and panic stricken passengers were escaping from the smoke and heat in the ticket hall and entrance tunnels. Meanwhile Firemen Moulton, Button and Flanagan showed initiative and made determined efforts to enter the tube lines ticket hall in breathing apparatus. The heat was so great that at first they were driven back until Fireman Moulton entered again, with Firemen Edgar and Button using their hoses to spray his back and thereby keep the temperature bearable for brief periods. It was about this time that the body of Station Officer Townsley was recovered at the foot of the steps leading up to the Pancras Road entrance.

20. At 19:49, four minutes after the flashover, Assistant Divisional Officer Shore of Euston fire station arrived by car, having been mobilized as part of the predetermined attendance. There was no officer in charge to brief him, and those left on the surface were dealing with the immediate aftermath of the flashover, neither was there any member of the London Underground staff to guide him as to the geography of the station. Assistant Divisional Officer Shore immediately requested additional pumps and four ambulances to attend. Almost at once he was told that three fire officers were missing and had not reported back after going into the Underground. Assistant Divisional Officer Shore then requested further fire pumps making 12 in all knowing that this would command the attendance of more senior fire officers.

21. Assistant Divisional Officer Shore was based at Euston and accordingly King's Cross was a part of his fireground territory. He knew of the Midland City entrance and that a tunnel from Pentonville Road ended up somewhere in King's Cross station. What he did not know was precisely where. It is a matter of regret that Assistant Divisional Officer Shore should not have appreciated the importance of the Midland City entrance particularly given that he remarked upon the absence of smoke there. Furthermore he failed to brief his superior officers about the entrance when he handed over. It is equally to be noted that they did not enquire about the position of any entrances

from the rear of the site which might be relevant for the purposes of rescue. Assistant Divisional Officer Shore nevertheless did well to mobilise further reinforcements during the time that he was in charge.

22. Divisional Officer Johnson arrived at about 20:12 and immediately assumed command, but he remained in charge for no more than three minutes before Deputy Assistant Chief Officer Wilson arrived at 20:15.

23. Deputy Assistant Chief Officer Wilson was in command for 26 minutes, during which time he requested an increase of fire pumps to 20, coordinated the work of various control units and sought plans of the Underground. Station Officer Demonte delivered the station plans, about 20:53. Before that the London Fire Brigade had had to resort to enlisting the help of a British Rail manager who drew for them a plan of the area. Although London Underground failed to provide assistance to the London Fire Brigade about the layout of the Underground, it is equally true that the London Fire Brigade failed to seek assistance as they might have done, for example, through the London Underground HQ controller who could have been reached via the London Fire Brigade Wembley control room.

24. In the absence of help from London Underground, it had proved very difficult to understand the geography of the Underground station. There were two sets of plans held in boxes in the tube lines ticket hall area but one was concealed behind a temporary hoarding and the other was in the perimeter subway too far from the exit to the street to be reached through the dense smoke.

25. In spite of the difficulties under which the London Fire Brigade commanders were working, it is a matter of surprise that no attempt was made to survey the possibilities of entering and approaching the underground station from an alternative rear entrance as laid down in Book 2 Part 3 of the Manual of Firemanship. Deputy Assistant Chief Officer Wilson defended his decision not to adopt this strategic approach by saying that he had insufficient officers to detach to make a reconnaissance through an alternative entrance or an approach by train. Bearing in mind the difficulties which accompanied entry from the front, I believe that Deputy Assistant Chief Officer Wilson should have made a strategic appraisal of the position and attempted an earlier reconnaissance of the possibility of an alternative entrance. If he had insufficient men it would have been a simple matter for him to increase the number of pumps required to attend.

26. At 20:41 Assistant Chief Officer Kennedy arrived and, as he took over command from Deputy Chief Officer Wilson, he realised that the fire-fighters were working under arduous conditions and that some

were suffering from the effects of heat and stress. He therefore requested the attendance of ten more pumps, making a total of thirty altogether. During his period of command search crews led by Assistant Divisional Officer Shore reached the Victoria Line escalator concourse and met Station Officer Osborne by way of the tube lines ticket hall. Other crews reached Temporary Sub-Officer Bell and Station Officer Osborne by way of the Midland City entrance.

27. About 21:40 Leading Railwoman Ord and Railman Swaby were discovered in the staff mess room off the subway leading to St. Pancras station (shown in Figure 14) and released by firemen.

28. At 21:48 Assistant Chief Officer Kennedy was able to send the message:

"Fire surrounded"

indicating that the fire was under control.

29. From about 20:15 the liaison between the fire, police and ambulance, and London Underground staff on the surface had begun to be established. However Assistant Chief Officer Kennedy did not make full use of the opportunities for liaison presented by the arrival of Metropolitan Police Inspector Coleman and London Underground Incident Officer Green. No doubt liaison was not assisted by the late arrival of a number of incident or control vehicles. But I was left with the clear impression that opportunities to pass vital information between the services were missed. Moreover there was complete ignorance upstairs on the surface of what was taking place downstairs at the bottom of the Piccadilly Line escalators or on the platforms.

30. Any evaluation of the performance of the London Fire Brigade has to be seen against the background of the following facts:

   (i) The flashover occurred within two minutes of their first arrival.

   (ii) The officers in charge of two of the appliances—Temporary Sub-Officer Bell and Station Officer Osborne—were isolated and each was out of radio communication with the surface because they had not taken radios with them. These might have given communication on a 'line-of-sight' from escalator concourse to the tube lines ticket hall. Thus the London Fire Brigade had no information as to what was going on down below and did not attempt to obtain it from London Underground. In addition they had no information as to the precise layout of the underground station, and no assistance from London Underground until about 21:15. Their plans of the station were not recovered until an hour after the flashover and even then they proved to be misleading and inadequate.

31. In my view there are a number of lessons to be learned by the London Fire Brigade from the events of that evening:

    (i) Had Temporary Sub-Officer Bell and Station Officer Osborne taken with them their personal radios, communications between them and those at the top of the escalator might have remained opened.

    (ii) Secondly, although the occupier of property should invariably provide a guide to meet the Fire Brigade on arrival, where such a guide is not provided and the Fire Brigade have no detailed knowledge of the geography, it is their duty to obtain details forthwith. We are concerned that on the night of the disaster at King's Cross the London Fire Brigade did not seek out an official of London Underground to obtain details of the complicated layout of the Underground station.

    (iii) Thirdly, the Court was left with the impression that there had been a breakdown of communications at command level between the emergency services. Each diligently pursued its own duty but there was a lack of liaison between them.

32. Later among my recommendations I suggest that there ought to be joint exercises between the emergency services, because I am satisfied that if such joint exercises had taken place, communications would have been better and some of the problems which presented themselves would not have proved as difficult as they did on the night. I am glad to note that these points were accepted by Chief Officer Clarkson. I am equally glad to note that the London Fire Brigade has repeated their wish to continue to work in the closest possible cooperation with London Underground and make available to them its professional expertise and services. I am satisfied on the basis of Dr Ridley's evidence that this has now been accepted by London Underground.

33. My recommendations addressed to the London Fire Brigade include its attendance at pre-start meetings in relation to construction works at stations, reviews of its procedures for handing over command at major incidents, liaison arrangements with London Underground, and its policy and training on the use of alternative means of access, certain improvements in its training and instructions, and improvements to the protective clothing provided for fire-fighters.

34. It is clear that a large number of members of the London Fire Brigade behaved with conspicuous courage and devotion to duty during the disaster in which they lost a very brave officer, Station Officer Townsley.

British Transport Police

35. By coincidence a number of British Transport Police officers were awaiting another duty in the vicinity of King's Cross when they were alerted to the fire. In the event it was the British Transport Police who provided the initial response to the emergency.

36. The British Transport Police is a national, but independent force, responsible for policing duties on British Railways and on the London Underground. It is not answerable to the Home Office, nor is its Chief Constable a member of the Association of Chief Police Officers (ACPO). More worryingly, it was not a member of the London Emergency Services Liaison Panel which had been established in 1973. Happily, that omission has now been rectified.

37. One particular section of the British Transport Police known as L Division, is primarily responsible for law enforcement on the London Underground. Officers of the other divisions of the British Transport Police may be called upon occasionally to help with duties in London Underground, but it is primarily upon L Division that the responsibility falls. The division is 350 officers strong.

38. A constable in the British Transport Police has the full powers of a police constable. It is accepted that their duties as constables override the duties owed to the British Railways Board as employees. The primary duty is that of the office of constable and with it responsibility to preserve the peace, to protect life and also a duty to deal with emergencies.

39. All persons joining the British Transport Police receive the same basic training as any of the Provincial or Metropolitan Police Forces at a Home Office District Training Centre for recruits. There is no training given at Divisional District Training Centres in fire fighting, the use of extinguishers, evacuation procedures, or crowd control, other than in the context of public disorder.

40. British Transport Police officers selected for duty in L Division attend a one-day course at the London Underground's training centre at White City. This is very much a familiarisation course. Until 18 November 1987, British Transport Police officers were made generally aware of evacuation procedures, fire hazards and ordering trains not to stop, but this was usually in the context of the dangers of electric conducter rails and apparatus, and procedures for isolation or removal of current.

Before the Flashover

41. The number of British Transport Police officers in the King's Cross and Euston area on 18 November 1987 was considerably more than usual because they were to carry out special duties at Euston station later in the evening. One unit that was ordered to attend was a mobile unit belonging to B Division, consisting of Sergeant Wilson and five police constables, Kerbey, Balfe, Hanson, Bebbington and Evans. As they were not L Division officers, but principally concerned with work on British Rail Eastern Region, they had no detailed knowledge of the underground or its workings. But since they were not required for duty immediately and had time on their hands, a number of officers were ordered to patrol King's Cross underground and main line stations. Two of these were P.C. Bebbington and P.C. Kerbey.

42. At about 19:30 P.C. Bebbington was keeping observation with P.C. Kerbey in the temporary station operations room in the tube lines ticket hall when he saw a man who had come up escalator 4, press the emergency stop diamond and look back down the escalator. P.C. Bebbington and P.C. Kerbey went to investigate and there saw smoke and flames on the escalator. P.C. Bebbington descended to make an inspection and returned to the tube lines ticket hall to raise the alarm. P.C. Bebbington had with him his personal radio but it did not function well underground. He was not familiar with the London Underground communications system, or the facilities in the temporary station operations room so he decided to run to the surface and alert the Fire Brigade through the British Transport Police HQ information room. His radio message was recorded at 19:33.

43. P.C. Bebbington was joined at the top of the stairs on the north side of Euston Road, by another British Transport Police officer, P.C. Dixon who had heard his call while in St. Pancras station. P.C. Bebbington asked P.C. Dixon to remain where he was and to tell the Fire Brigade the location of the fire on the Piccadilly Line escalators on their arrival. The Fire Brigade vehicles arrived at the Pancras Road entrance and P.C. Dixon, too far away to contact them, ran down into the tube lines ticket hall, where he saw Fireman Ford arriving and pointed towards the escalators.

44. P.C. Bebbington's call was heard by two other British Transport Police officers from the Mobile Unit, P.C. Hanson and P.C. Balfe, who were patrolling the King's Cross main line concourse at the time. Thereupon they went to the tube lines ticket hall.

45. P.C. Bebbington returned to the ticket hall and rejoined P.C. Kerbey who was standing with P.C. Hanson at the top of the Piccadilly Line escalator. In the absence of any London Underground staff in the tube lines ticket hall, P.C. Bebbington decided to prevent the use of the Piccadilly Line escalators and went down escalator 5 to the bottom.

46. With the assistance of Leading Railman Brickell, P.C. Bebbington then diverted passengers from the Piccadilly Line escalator concourse to the Victoria Line escalator, believing that it would be free of fire. At about 19:39 P.C. Kerbey and P.C. Hanson in the tube lines ticket hall indicated to P.C. Bebbington that they had decided to evacuate and to close the station. P.C. Bebbington went to the Northern Line platforms to direct passengers up from the lowest level. He also dialled 999 and asked that Northern Line trains should not stop at the station.

47. Meanwhile, in the tube lines ticket hall P.C. Kerbey and P.C. Hanson, who were in the vicinity of escalators 4 and 5, were attempting to direct people out of the station. P.C. Balfe who was over by the Victoria Line escalator was troubled by the numbers that were coming up the Victoria Line escalators and asked P.C. Kerbey whether there was another exit that could be used. P.C. Kerbey, who knew of the Midland City exit, decided to go and investigate and so, telling P.C. Hanson to remain in the tube lines ticket hall, he descended the Victoria Line escalator with P.C. Balfe. They found that the Midland City exit was blocked by the Bostwick gates which were locked.

48. Two further British Transport Police officers, P.C. Kukielka and P.C. Martland of L Division, having heard P.C. Bebbington's message, arrived by car at 19:37 and immediately went to the tube lines ticket hall where they assisted in directing passengers. But the number coming up by way of the Victoria Line was so great that P.C. Kukielka became worried as to whether the trains had been ordered to stop. He and P.C. Martland decided to go to the Victoria Line concourse where they both tried to speed the evacuation of passengers up into the tube lines ticket hall.

49. At about this time the flashover took place in the tube lines ticket hall, catching P.C. Hanson off balance. He crawled back to the top of the Victoria Line escalator and shouted to passengers to keep low and get out by the nearest exit. The heat intensified and he made his escape by vaulting over a closed barrier and crawled to where he estimated the exit to be. He came across a passenger on the floor, whom he tried to take hold of, but the heat was too intense and his hands would not work because they were seriously burnt. He collided with the glass of the heel bar and cut his hand. Emerging at Euston Road south exit he was helped by P.C. Dixon and then taken to hospital. It is clear that P.C. Hanson acted with great courage in exhorting people to escape the flashover even though badly injured himself.

50. At the bottom of the Piccadilly Line escalator, Temporary Sub-Officer Bell was engaged in trying to fight the fire on the escalator and P.C. Bebbington, with considerable courage, acted in direct support of him on the escalator. P.C. Kerbey and P.C. Bardsley subsequently also helped to fight the fire. P.C. Kerbey and P.C. Balfe took part in the evacuation of passengers by Victoria Line trains and ensured that all the tube line platforms were clear. P.C. Martland and P.C. Kukielka were occupied with the evacuation of the badly burned Mr Bates by way of the Midland City exit.

51. It is apparent that in the absence of any London Underground supervisory staff and an evacuation plan the British Transport Police assumed the initiative. None of the officers initially concerned had any direct experience of the Underground and until the arrival of P.C. Kukielka and P.C. Martland, none were L Division officers. They used their common sense and initiative to devise a plan:

    (i) to divert passengers away from the Piccadilly Line escalator,

    (ii) to evacuate the station, and

    (iii) to prevent incoming trains from stopping.

52. Even though the evacuation from the Piccadilly Line escalator and the diversion by way of the Victoria Line escalator may have led to the death or injury of some of the passengers, no blame should be attached to the officers. In effect they were simply seeking to divert passengers away from the Piccadilly Line escalator which was on fire and to send them to the surface by way of the Victoria Line escalator which they believed would be safe. They could not foresee, nor could anybody foresee, that the flashover would take place involving the tube lines ticket hall and surrounding area.

After the Flashover

53. In addition to the British Transport Police officers in the vicinity who responded to P.C. Bebbington's initial radio call, there were three more officers who were alerted by telephone and went to King's Cross station immediately by train. Woman Police Sergeant O'Neill arrived by Metropolitan Line train at about 19:50, and Inspector Wilkinson with P.C. Bardsley arrived by Piccadilly Line train at 20:01. Further officers were mobilised following P.C. Dixon's "major incident" call. Apart from four police constables who arrived later by train, the other members of the British Transport Police attending the disaster came by road and remained on the surface. At the height of the mobilisation, by about midnight, some 82 British Transport Police officers were present. Assistant Chief Officer McGregor told the Court that nearly every British Transport Police officer on duty within the metropolitan area was sent to the scene.

54. Woman Police Sergeant O'Neill arrived on the Metropolitan Line eastbound platform as London Underground staff were evacuating passengers by train. She called the line controller at 19:56 and requested that Metropolitan Line trains should pass through without stopping. With the members of staff left on that side of the station, including Relief Station Inspector Pilgrim, W.P. Sgt. O'Neill then took refuge from the increasingly dense smoke in the offices at the far end of the concourse between the platforms, and telephoned the L Division information room for assistance. At about 20:05 an empty train sent to evacuate staff arrived, and W.P. Sgt. O'Neill spoke briefly to Acting Traffic Manager Nelson and Area Manager Grosvenor who had just arrived and reported by telephone to the L Division information room, before leaving with the station staff on that train. She returned to King's Cross on foot and was detailed to liaise with the London Fire Brigade area control unit, but was not asked by them to offer specific advice. Later in the evening she escorted people around the tube lines ticket hall, supervised the removal of property, and assisted with crowd control.

55. Inspector Wilkinson was with P.C. Bardsley at Earl's Court station when he received the call to attend King's Cross. They arrived at 20:01, after the evacuation of passengers by train had been completed. Inspector Wilkinson met Temporary Sub-Officer Bell, P.C. Kerbey, P.C. Balfe and P.C. Bebbington in the Piccadilly Line escalator concourse, and established that the remaining London Underground staff were being evacuated. He remained below for two hours, during which time he saw his role as to make himself available to the police officers and fire brigade as a visible presence and to keep the British Transport Police information room informed of events. He played a part in the control and evacuation of passengers from the Northern Line train which stopped by mistake at 20:45.

56. Inspector Wilkinson told the Court that he did not appreciate the seriousness of the fire until much later when he went to the front of the station above ground. Although he made frequent telephone calls to the British Transport Police L Division information room, and quickly corrected his mistaken message that the fire had been extinguished at 20:06, at no time did he seek to establish contact with the London Fire Brigade or his own superior officers on the surface, or to send information which would be of use to them through London Underground staff or his officers who left by the Midland City exit. On two occasions he spoke to London Underground's Incident Officer Mr Green, shortly after the latter's arrival below at 21:05 and again on the surface at 22:20, but on neither occasion did he pass on information about conditions below which might have helped the emergency services.

Recommendations

57. One of the clear lessons of the King's Cross fire for the British Transport Police is the need for training in evacuation, communication, fire-fighting and incident control procedures as they apply to underground stations, and I discuss this issue again in Chapter 15 'Station Staffing and Training'. I consider the improvements in communications equipment required in Chapter 16 'Communications Systems'. I have also included among my recommendations that the British Transport Police should review its arrangements for access to station keys, location information, and liaison arrangements with other emergency services, and should attend pre-start meetings for station works likely to affect passenger flow.

Metropolitan Police

58. The role of the Metropolitan Police at the King's Cross fire was primarily a supporting one, but since there are several lessons to be learned, I propose to review their part shortly.

59. King's Cross station lies within the Kentish Town police division but is close to the divisional boundary with Holborn. At about 19:35 the Duty Inspector at Holborn, Inspector Coleman, was alerted by a call from Woman P.C. Ashley to a fire in the Underground. Inspector Coleman responded quickly and taking Sergeant Martin as his driver, set off in the Holborn duty car. The car was in position as the forward control post at the junction of Euston Road and Pancras Road shortly after 19:45. Inspector Coleman told the Investigation that he had received no special training. Nevertheless with admirable speed and decisiveness he initiated the major incident procedure of the Metropolitan Police. It was no doubt crucial to the success of that procedure that Inspector Coleman was able to use a specially reserved radio channel which was allocated to him and linked his car with Kentish Town and Holborn police stations. That procedure laid down the responsibilities of the first senior Metropolitan Police officer on the scene and the sequence and priorities that he should adopt, bearing in mind the type of incident that had occurred.

60. Meanwhile the central command complex at New Scotland Yard had been alerted by the London Fire Brigade Wembley control room at 19:41. Seven minutes later the British Transport Police indicated that they were dealing with the matter.

61. Following the Metropolitan Police procedure, Inspector Coleman established a rendezvous point for ambulances in Pancras Road and then sent a request for more ambulances to New Scotland Yard. He also asked for traffic units to close all the roads and this message was

relayed at 19:56. Fortunately, a main police traffic garage was situated only two streets away at Drummond Crescent and motor cyclists were quickly deployed at 20:01.

62. Thereafter Inspector Coleman continued to act in the role of the police Incident Officer, requesting reinforcements to deal with the heavy traffic and further ambulances (20:12). He mobilized the despatch of the major incident box from Holborn police station to University College Hospital (20:13) and organised a press rendezvous point together with a request for the area press and publicity officer from the Metropolitan Police to attend. At 20:20 he made his car (a brown Maestro), which had been the police forward control post, the rendezvous point for doctors and nurses attending the disaster.

63. The Metropolitan Police assumed the primary responsibility for organising traffic at the scene. The area was cordoned off with special units to deal with traffic congestion and maintain routes for the emergency services. They also arranged for a helicopter to transfer urgently required medical supplies between hospitals, besides providing support units at University College and St. Bartholomew's Hospitals.

64. Over 100 Metropolitan Police officers were on the scene by 21:00, and at the height of the mobilisation by midnight some 190 officers were present.

65. The organisation of the central casualty bureau at New Scotland Yard was a major task requiring immediate staffing by an inspector, 3 sergeants, 40 constables, together with another 37 police staff for relief purposes. The unit was supported by the divisional casualty bureau and received a total of 14,107 telephone calls during this period. The identification of bodies and the provision of mortuary facilities were further major tasks for police together with numerous other minor jobs.

66. It is apparent that the Metropolitan Police had a properly planned and coordinated major incident procedure which Inspector Coleman was able to initiate with speed after a prompt reconnaissance. In the result an efficient and effective back-up was available to deal with the results of the disaster. I recommend that all emergency services should have and be prepared jointly to implement such a plan. The Metropolitan Police major incident procedure is clearly an ideal base upon which to build.

London Ambulance Service

67. Evidence from the London Ambulance Service to the Investigation was less detailed than that of the other emergency services. The Court

heard only from the deputy chief ambulance officer responsible for operations, and the divisional officer responsible for ambulance control. The London Ambulance Service appears to have discharged its duties properly in response to the disaster at King's Cross. That performance was in spite of a ban on overtime which had reduced from 154 to 124 the number of ambulances available to cover the London Ambulance Service area. Likewise there was a shortfall in the ambulance control staff that evening.

68. The first call was received at ambulance control at 19:47 and within ten minutes an ambulance was on the scene. Another ambulance was there within three minutes and at 20:08 University College Hospital, as the designated hospital, and St. Bartholemew's, as the support hospital, were put on 'yellow' alert, warning of the possibility of a major accident. Eight minutes later, at 20:16 a major accident was declared and University College Hospital and St. Bartholemew's Hospital were put on 'red' alert. Thereafter the number of ambulances on scene rose until a maximum of fourteen were committed by 21:32. Although that number represents the total, each ambulance would and did make as many journeys as necessary.

69. The Investigation revealed three points of concern:
    (i) there was no procedure by which drivers radioed into control on arrival;
    (ii) the emergency control vehicle (Red Major) was not despatched to the scene promptly. It did not arrive until 22:09 almost two hours after a major incident had been declared; and
    (iii) there was difficulty in contacting senior officers and delay in their arrival.

70. I am glad to learn that the first has been dealt with and that ambulances will now report to control on arrival at an incident similarly, to the London Fire Brigade report of 'Status 3'. Equally, fresh instructions have been given to ensure that the emergency control vehicle will be put on standby when a 'yellow' alert is declared and despatched when a major incident is declared. I believe it desirable that the incident officer should decide at that time whether a medical team is necessary or not.

71. If senior officers are to attend the scene I recommend that a more effective way be established of obtaining their speedy arrival. The Assistant Chief Officer of the North West Division did not arrive until 21:10 and the Deputy Chief Ambulance Officer did not arrive until 21:48. Neither the Chief nor Deputy Chief Ambulance Officers could be reached at the first call.

72. My recommendations addressed to the London Ambulance Service include improved procedures for the timing and recording of the whereabouts of ambulances, the removal of casualties and bodies from the scene of a major accident, and the attendance of a senior incident officer.

Chapter 12

The Development of the Fire: eyewitness accounts and scientific investigation

1. There was an extensive history of fires on escalators in London Underground stations, and although some people had suffered from smoke inhalation, nobody had died. Some of these previous fires had been serious and considerable damage had resulted, but in no case had there been a flashover engulfing a ticket hall or landing at the top of an escalator shaft. At King's Cross, only two minutes before the flashover, two experienced firemen, Station Officer Townsley and Temporary Sub-Officer Bell, looked at the fire on escalator 4 from a position between escalators 5 and 6. Temporary Sub-Officer Bell considered it "not a big fire at all", and he likened it to a large cardboard box on fire. Station Officer Townsley may have considered it somewhat more serious, as he said to Temporary Sub-Officer Bell that it would require four fire appliances. The real question to be answered is why two such experienced firemen made that assessment of a fire which within two minutes erupted into the tube lines ticket hall with such ferocity.

2. To explain what happened it is necessary to review the witness evidence in detail. Before the fire dynamics were properly understood, there was much debate between the scientific experts of the parties involved, and extensive computational and experimental work. This revealed a previously unknown phenomenon, which served to explain the eyewitness evidence and the high-speed propagation of flames into the ticket hall and surrounding subways.

3. The reports presented to the Court are listed in Appendix G.

Initiation and development of the fire up to flashover

4. It is probable that the fire started on the running track of escalator 4 at about 19:25. Several possible causes of ignition were examined, of which the chief ones were arson, friction, electrical, and smokers' materials:

    (i) I discuss the arson theory in Appendix K, but in my view the totality of the evidence failed to demonstrate any basis for an allegation of arson.

    (ii) The temperature generated by friction in the escalator wheel bearings was investigated by Mr Swift (Report 11f) and it can be concluded that under the most severe conditions of load the temperature generated is too low to cause ignition.

    (iii) Mr Champion (Report 11j) carried out a detailed inspection of the electrical installations in the vicinity of the Piccadilly Line escalators, and concluded that the cause of the fire was not attributable to an electrical fault. However, he added that the condition of the lighting installation was totally unacceptable in a place of employment subject to the Health and Safety at Work etc Act 1974.

(iv) There was evidence that passengers continued to smoke in the Underground despite the smoking ban introduced after the Oxford Circus station fire. In particular people tended to light up while going up the escalator to leave the station. Examination of the detritus under King's Cross escalator 4 has provided plenty of evidence of the presence of smokers' materials. Dr Wharton (Report 11c) examined various sources of ignition and the probability of a match falling down the gap between the skirting board and the steps causing ignition of the grease and detritus on the running track below. Dr Wharton concluded that it was improbable that ignition was caused by a glowing cigarette alone, but ignition by a flaming match was possible with substantial burning.

5. There is clear evidence from the passenger Mr Squire of a fire underneath escalator 4 at 19:29. P. C. Bebbington who observed the fire on escalator 4 at about 19:32, considered the flame he saw was similar to those seen at 6 minutes 30 seconds after initiation in the controlled fire test on the same escalator carried out on 8 January 1988 and described in a report by Dr Wharton and Mr Moodie (Report 11c). This evidence suggests that the fire on escalator 4 may have been initiated at about 19:25. However, in the test the escalator was stationary whereas escalator 4 was not stopped until about 19:30. There were other differences as indicated in the report which may have influenced the development of the fire.

6. There is considerable witness evidence both before and after the escalator was stopped by Mr Karmoun at about 19:30, which suggests that there was an extensive fire or fires between the centre and the top of the escalator. In particular, P.C. Kerbey observed an orange glow at about 19:33 through the hole in the upper newel post where the handrail returns underneath. This was confirmed by P.C. Balfe who shortly afterwards observed the top of flames as well as an orange glow. Many other witnesses gave evidence of fire underneath the escalator at various positions. Mr Squire was convinced that the fire was going round with the escalator. Although most of the evidence suggests that the fire was concentrated on the right-hand side looking up the escalator, there is evidence, such as that of a passenger Mr Berry, that the fire underneath the escalator stretched from side to side. Both P.C. Kerbey and P.C. Hanson saw smoke coming from the right-hand side looking down the escalator, or the left-hand side looking up. This suggests that the fire had spread beneath the escalator from one side to the other by piloted ignition. The distortion of the angle iron frame beneath the decking and balustrades provided further evidence that there was a seat of fire on the left-hand side looking up and two seats on the right-hand side.

7. The evidence of Relief Station Inspector Hayes, the only witness of the fire from below, conflicted with that of those who saw it from above. It must be noted that the first time he descended the steps beneath escalator 5, Relief Station Inspector Hayes only got as far as the first gap in the supporting wall through which he could see escalator 4. This gap is about one-quarter of the way down the escalator. On his second visit, when the smoke was more intense, he went as far down as the second gap, which is about one-third of the way down, but he was never in sight of one of the main sites of fire which was half-way down the escalator and which was probably where the fire started. As was shown in a report by Cremer and Warner (Report 4e), the field of view of a person on the staircase beneath escalator 5 and looking through the gaps in the supporting walls for escalator 5, is very limited. It can also be seen from Figure 8 that a person standing on the staircase is well underneath the running track of escalator 4. Furthermore, Relief Station Inspector Hayes said in evidence that he had crouched down, which would have made viewing even more difficult, and was uncertain as to the precise location of the fire he observed in relation to the parts of escalator 4.

8. The first observations of flames above the escalator were made about 19:30 by a passenger, Mr Maxwell, who noticed one foot high flames about one-third of the way up, on the right-hand side looking up. Another passenger, Mr Mudge, at about the same time saw flames also on the right-hand side but about one-quarter of the way down from the top. At about 19:32, the same time as P.C. Bebbington made his observation of the fire, P.C. Kerbey noticed smoke and small flames on the right-hand side about one-third of the way down. He observed the fire several times before he eventually went down the Victoria Line escalator, probably just before the firemen arrived in the tube lines ticket hall shortly after 19:43. On the last occasion he observed that the flames were getting fierce and much higher and the smoke was getting worse. P.C. Kukielka and P.C. Martland arrived in the tube lines ticket hall at about 19:38. P.C. Martland took a few steps towards escalator 4 and saw a fire two-thirds of the way down covering an area of one square metre with flames licking over the top of the handrail and concentrated more on the left-hand side looking down. Very shortly afterwards, P.C. Kukielka saw a fire half-way down the same escalator on the right-hand side looking down. Flames were reaching the top of the handrail, and flames were also coming from the steps and panelling and extending half-way across the escalator. He could not see further down the escalator because of smoke. At about 19:40 two passengers, Mr Bate and Mr Eglintine, were perhaps the last people to walk up escalator 6 because Mr Eglintine noted an official stopping people after he had got on. Mr Bate saw the reflection of a fire on escalator 4 in the advertise-ment panels on the adjoining wall at about step 49–50, and a second fire at about step 75. Mr Eglintine did not notice a fire at step 49–50, but he saw a reflection at about step 75 and flame tips above the handrail.

9. The first units of the London Fire Brigade arrived in Pancras Road at 19:42. Temporary Sub-Officer Bell followed Station Officer Townsley down to the tube lines ticket hall where, standing between escalators 5 and 6, he got a restricted view of an apparently small fire on the right-hand side of escalator 4 about one-third of the way down. Flames were licking up to the handrail and the fire extended across two treads. It was at this time that Temporary Sub-Officer Bell said he considered it to be a fire such as might be produced by a large cardboard box. There were no signs of the paintwork on the ceiling blistering or catching alight. He then went down escalator 6, and whilst descending he looked back and saw that the fire had begun to spread. When he got to the bottom the fire had reached the advertisement hoardings on the wall and it was touching the ceiling. Whilst helping to clear passengers from the lower concourse, he was conscious of a rapid build-up of the fire, and when he looked again he noted that it was a very different fire. There were flames going from the seat of the fire and round the ceiling and back down onto the escalators and he noted that the paint blackened and peeled off. He considered that the main source of the flames was the escalator. Probably this observation of the fire was shortly after the flashover, which he did not specifically notice or hear.

10. Firemen Moulton, Edgar and Button were members of Station Officer Townsley's crew who arrived at 19:42, immediately before Temporary Sub-Officer Bell. Fireman Moulton saw a fire six to seven metres down escalator 4, with flames five to six feet high. Fireman Edgar saw a fire on the left-hand side looking down about half-way down escalator 4, with flames about four feet high. The balustrade and also the adjoining treads were alight and burning brightly. Fireman Button saw bright orange flames five feet high about half-way down escalator 4. The fire was right across the steps and above the handrails on both sides of the escalator, but he had no idea how many steps were involved.

11. Several passengers observed the fire from the Piccadilly Line escalator concourse shortly before the flashover. At about 19:43 Mr Saeugling saw flames half-way up escalator 4 over a length of four or five yards, with flames shooting from both sides of the escalator from the bottom into the centre. At about the same time Mr Lee saw flames as high as a person and giving off an orange glow at about two-thirds of the way up. The flames were well on the way to reaching the ceiling on the left-hand side. Miss Parmar saw a blazing fire with orange flames about five to six feet high.

12. The observation of smoke up to flashover was very variable depending on the time, the position of the witness in the tube lines ticket hall, and maybe on their sensitivity or experience of smoke. There is little doubt from the evidence adduced that in the last few minutes before

flashover, conditions were rapidly changing, and it is important to piece together precisely timed observations to produce a coherent whole. In this final period the developing fire had a dominant influence on the air flow patterns in the ticket hall and surrounding passages, so it is probable that people in different places observed different smoke conditions at a particular instant of time. It is also likely that what appeared as heavy smoke conditions to some, may have appeared as insignificant to others, and those subject to smoky conditions for a longer period may then have begun to react to it.

13. The first witnesses to see a fire underneath escalator 4 saw smoke rising from the right-hand side looking up. Mr Squire at 19:29 likened it to the smoke from a single cigarette, and P.C. Bebbington at 19:32 described it as white, whispyish smoke, while others such as Mr Karmoun at 19:30 noted it as black smoke with a rubbery or plastic smell. Yet others, such as Mr Mudge, described it as light grey smoke which smelt rubbery, while a little later at 19:36, P.C. Bebbington noticed great volumes of dark grey smoke. P.C. Hanson and P.C. Balfe (who arrived in the tube lines ticket hall at about 19:34) and P.C. Kukielka and P.C. Martland (who arrived shortly after at 19:38) all noticed some smoke in the ticket hall. At about 19:43 or shortly before, P.C. Hanson considered that the smoke was thickening to the extent of causing breathing difficulties, watering of the eyes and coughing. P.C. Kukielka telephoned the British Transport Police L Division information room at about 19:43 and when asked, confirmed that he needed an ambulance as he was concerned about people suffering from smoke inhalation. At about the same time P.C. Martland did not consider the smoke sufficiently severe to affect breathing or cause coughing. Immediately before the flashover P.C. Hanson observed dense smoke in the tube lines ticket hall, while P.C. Balfe, who was standing at the top of the Victoria Line escalator, noted that the smoke was very thick and passengers were coughing. P.C. Dixon arrived in the tube lines ticket hall at the same time as the fireman at 19:43, and he noted white smoke and immediately started to try to evacuate the ticket hall. Shortly afterwards, the smoke became thick and black and made breathing difficult and visibility poor. Seconds later it became impossible to see or breathe and the heat became intense. P.C. Dixon moved into the Khyber Pass and continued to evacuate people. It then became too hot and breathing was impossible. Unable to see anything, he escaped by the exit on the south side of Euston Road.

14. Booking Clerk Newman was in the ticket office from the first report of a fire by a passenger at 19:30. Early on he noticed white smoke coming up escalator 4 which did not appear to worsen until he evacuated the office, probably around 19:42. Before this Booking Clerk Hythe had been servicing the ticket machines and, although he had not noticed any smoke, he had increasingly smelt burning rubber and begun to feel

intense heat on his face. Booking Clerk Newman told him to close the machine, and they both left the ticket hall having collected Booking Clerk Frankland. As they left the ticket hall there was more smoke which was grey-blue and getting thicker, but they could still see clearly. Smoke was more evident as they walked round the perimeter subway towards the Khyber Pass, and as they reached the exit stairs at the south side of Euston Road, there was a blast of hot air. At the top of the stairs after about 30 seconds they noticed black smoke billowing out.

15. Those firemen in the tube lines ticket hall at about 19:43 appear to have seen a fire burning brightly and giving off no smoke, and only a little smoke in the tube lines ticket hall. However, all of them except for Station Officer Townsley and Temporary Sub-Officer Bell (who went downstairs) went back to street level and they observed smoke and heat, either on the way out or while re-entering from the Pancras Road entrance. Station Officer Osborne arrived slightly later via the entrance on the south side of Euston Road and he noticed smoke at ceiling level in the tube lines ticket hall adjoining the Piccadilly Line escalators. He observed that the policemen guiding passengers out from the Victoria Line escalators were crouching, which he could only attribute to an increase in smoke density even though he considered the atmosphere to be clear. He was about to stop people coming up the Victoria Line escalators before the London Fire Brigade could put water on the fire when the flashover occurred.

16. A group of five British Rail engineers arried at St. Pancras station from Derby at about 19:39. At the entrance to the tube lines ticket hall they found their way barred by a closed set of Bostwick gates. Mr Wilkins put the time of their arrival at the gate at 19:43 but it was probably 19:42. Mr Jones looking through the gate noted a bluey-white smoke which was not particularly dense and smelt like a garden bonfire. Mr Wilkins noted people running from his left to right, up the stairs into the perimeter subway. Mr Hoadley noted two men in dark uniforms, probably policemen, run from the top of the Piccadilly Line escalators. Both Mr Jones and Mr Wilkins noticed a man leave the ticket office having locked it. At about the same time Mr Wilkins noticed two firemen (which suggests a time shortly after 19:43). Immediately after this there was a blast of hot air which, according to Mr Jones, appeared to blow away the white smoke and which was followed by a brown oily smoke, which Mr Jones and Mr Wilkins said smelt like the exhaust of a diesel, and appeared to come from the direction of the Piccadilly Line escalators travelling between the ticket office and the temporary hoarding at ceiling level.

17. Mr Jones and Mr Wilkins decided to get out as quickly as possible, the other three having already gone. As they were departing Mr Jones had

a last look into the ticket hall and noted a fireman in a white helmet, some 20 to 30 feet from the Piccadilly Line escalator and within the ticket barrier, walking towards the Euston Road exit. Mr Jones and Mr Wilkins returned to the surface via the subway to St. Pancras. Whilst crossing the perimeter subway the brown oily smoke caught up with them. When they reached the short downward flight of stairs the visibility improved and it was cooler but, as they reached the steps up to St. Pancras Station, the smoke quickly turned from brown to dense black which smelt to them like a burning plastic cable. They escaped by the stairs to the St. Pancras station concourse.

18. Another passenger, Mr Asquith, met his wife at St. Pancras station at 19:39 and they went down the subway to the Underground station. When they arrived at the perimeter subway they found the entrance to the tube lines ticket hall to their left barred by a closed gate, so they turned to their right to go to the next entrance. Mrs Asquith found it difficult to breathe as although there was no smoke it was hazy and hot, so she stopped at the entrance to the St. Pancras subway. Mr Asquith looked into the tube lines ticket hall through the entrance to the way out barrier and noted it was fairly smoky, but people who were about showed no panic. He heard somebody in the tube lines ticket hall shouting "get out", so he turned to return along the perimeter subway to the passageway to St. Pancras station, and saw black billowing smoke coming towards him at high speed. This was immediately followed by great heat. He managed to get into the St. Pancras subway and catch up with his wife and then escaped to the concourse of St. Pancras station. When questioned he was certain that he had not seen black smoke in the tube lines ticket hall before turning away. Mr Asquith viewed the ticket hall very shortly before the flashover, or maybe even at the instant of flashover.

19. Mr Tigar entered the tube lines ticket hall through the entrance nearest to the temporary hoarding. This must have been shortly before another passenger Mr Holmes, who had arrived at St. Pancras at 19:40, came into the perimeter subway and saw police officers shutting the Bostwick gates at this entrance. It appears probable that Mr Tigar approached escalator 5, which was his usual route, when he saw black boiling smoke rolling up the escalator towards him. He did not see any flames in the smoke but it was very hot and there was a strong smell of burning diesel oil. To escape the smoke he went back through the "way in" barrier to the rear of the ticket hall. He was directed by the police up the steps to the perimeter subway adjoining the Pancras Road subway.

Flashover

20. From 19:43 there was a rapid worsening of the conditions in the tube lines ticket hall. At about 19:45 there was a sudden eruption of black smoke and flames into the ticket hall. The flashover had taken place. The time of 19:45 shown on the stopped digital clock was confirmed by P.C. Dixon who, having escaped via the exit to the south side of Euston Road, and after leading P.C. Hanson to the street, immediately radioed his headquarters for assistance and also informed them of a "major incident" at King's Cross Underground station. This message was recorded at 19:46:03 (i.e. 19:45:58 after being corrected) which, allowing time for P.C. Hanson to escape, suggests the time of flashover at about 19:45. So in a period of about two minutes or less, the fire observed by the firemen on their first arrival had deteriorated from what they perceived as a modest fire into a raging inferno.

21. Very few people who were in the tube lines ticket hall and who witnessed the flashover survived, and most of those who did survive were seriously injured. Others coming up the Victoria Line escalators had a limited view of the flashover looking up the escalator shaft. Temporary Sub-Officer Bell who was at the bottom on the Piccadilly Line escalator shaft probably saw the fire a minute before the flashover and at some time shortly after the flashover.

22. Shortly before the flashover P.C. Hanson was a short distance down escalator 9 on the Victoria Line urging people up the escalator and staircase. He became aware of dense smoke in the ticket hall so he went to investigate. When he got about five feet into the ticket hall he saw:

> "...what I can only describe as a large wall of flame or fire. It was definitely above head high, and immediately following this was like a whoosh...and a large ball of flame, which was about head height, hit the ceiling in the ticket hall itself. This was followed almost instantaneously by dense black smoke...."

P.C. Hanson later amplified this:
> "To be more accurate I would say it was a jet of flame that shot up and then collected into a kind of ball."

and then:
> "I saw it shoot up across the top of number 4 and collect along the roofing..."

In re-examination he was asked:

Q.   "Was this flame limited to the area at the top of escalator 4 as you saw it?"

A.   "Yes."

Q.   *"Can you be sure in your own mind's eye that it did not extend as far over as escalator 6?"*

A.   *"I can be quite sure that what I saw was confined to the escalator nearest to me."*

Q.   *"...was there to the right of the flame that you saw an area of ceiling which you are sure was not involved in flame?"*

A.   *"Yes."*

It is clear from this evidence that P.C. Hanson saw a jet of fire coming from escalator 4 which when it reached the ceiling of the ticket hall formed into what appeared to be a ball of fire. This then spread across the ceiling of the ticket hall and it was followed by dense black smoke. The 'whoosh' either knocked him onto his back or maybe caught him off balance. During his escape there was fire above his head all the time and flames swirling down, which caused his severe burns.

23. Mr Bates had been waiting on the northbound platform of the Victoria Line when he was instructed to leave the platform and directed up escalator 7. When he reached the top he saw orange flames coming from the right-hand side of escalator 4 as viewed from the tube lines ticket hall. It appeared to him that the flames were coming from about two feet from the floor, level with the handrail and that they could have been the tips of longer flames beyond his field of vision. These flames did not appear to present an immediate threat so he continued on into the tube lines ticket hall. He had just taken a couple of paces towards the temporary station operations room when he heard a 'whoosh' and flames shot across from the top of the Piccadilly Line escalators to where he was standing. They hit the wall where the temporary station operations room was situated. The flames were followed instantaneously by thick black smoke. He crouched down and put his hands to his face and then managed to reach escalator 7. He believed that the flames had come from the right-hand side of the Piccadilly Line escalators. It seemed to him that they came from beyond and behind and then across the ceiling of the tube lines ticket hall, and possibly curved and spread downwards to the floor.

24. Numerous other people came up Victoria Line escalator 7 at about the same time as Mr Bates and had similar harrowing experiences. Another passenger, Mr Arari Minta, when he was near the top saw flames shoot from his left and then disappear. A man at the top, probably P.C. Hanson, urged them to get out pointing to the "way out" barrier. Mr Arari Minta then saw a tremendous flash from his left by the temporary station operations room which hit the man who had been directing them out and who then turned and ran towards the exit.

The flames spread across the tube lines ticket hall accompanied by black smoke. Mr Arari Minta dived under the flames which had not reached floor level and escaped via the Khyber Pass to the Metropolitan and Circle Lines platforms. He sustained severe burns. He was evacuated by train to Farringdom station. Mr Kelly had a similar experience except that he saw flames shoot across the ceiling from right to left. He ran to the left but collided with the temporary station operations room. At that stage he was overtaken by flames which he likened to a fire ball. He managed to escape back down the escalator and was evacuated by train. He suffered burns to both hands and his face.

25. Mr Brody saw flames shoot from the Piccadilly Line escalator and circle the tube lines ticket hall ceiling. He rolled on the floor to extinguish the fire on his jacket and managed to escape through the Khyber Pass to the exit on the south side of Euston Road. He suffered 40% burns. Miss Santello had a similar experience to Mr Brody. Flames erupted from her right and went to the left across the ceiling. She tried to escape underneath the flames but the passage was obscured by black smoke. She escaped but suffered very severe burns. Her boy friend, Mr Liberati, was killed.

26. Other passengers at the top of escalator 7, such as Mr Lee and Mrs Korner, saw the flames coming from the right-hand side across the ceiling and rapidly filling the area of the ticket hall visible to them. They managed to escape by returning to the bottom of the escalator.

27. Relief Station Inspector Hayes and Station Inspector Dhanpersaud had gone into the upper machine room at about 19:43. Relief Station Inspector Hayes recalled hearing a 'whoosh' shortly afterwards. Looking up, he could see through the combs at the top of the escalator that it had gone up in fire, and looking up the staircase to the exit into the ticket hall, he could see flames through the gap between the door and frame. Station Inspector Dhanpersaud was also near this exit when he heard the crackling sound and experienced heat from the metal round the staircase to the door into the ticket hall. Since a passenger, Mrs Korner, had already seen the flashover from half-way up escalator 7 at the time that the escalator stopped, this suggests that what Station Inspector Dhanpersaud heard was the crackling of a developing fire after the flashover. Both Relief Station Inspector Hayes and Station Inspector Dhanpersaud escaped down the staircase beneath the Victoria Line escalators into the Victoria Line escalator concourse.

REVIEW OF SCIENTIFIC INVESTIGATIONS

Preliminary Investigations

28. The Health and Safety Executive at Buxton carried out an assessment which provided a factual description of the damage sustained during the fire (Report 11g). The following table gives an estimate of the mass of material burnt during the fire, which amounted to nearly four tonnes. 81% of the total fuel consumed was accounted for by the escalators. Of the fuel burnt in the escalator shaft, 76% was accounted for by the wooden components.

TOTAL MASS OF MATERIAL BURNT AND HEAT RELEASED

	Mass burnt in fire (kg)	Heat Released (MJ)
1. Piccadilly Line Escalator Shaft		
(a) WOODEN COMPONENTS		
skirting board	394	7490
dressguard	104	1872
balustrade	374	6732
decking	187	3366
handrail support	58	1218
facia board	174	3132
risers	253	5313
treads	736	13984
advertisement backboards	152	2432
(b) OTHER COMPONENTS		
escalator wheels	222	5328
ceiling paint	108	1188
grease on running tracks	150	5100
rubber handrail	277	7202
plastic advertisements	6	*
2. Tube Lines Ticket Hall		
(a) WOODEN COMPONENTS		
temporary hoarding (supports and plywood)	282	5358
ticket office (supports and plywood)	223	4237
(b) OTHER COMPONENTS		
melamine	50	*
ceiling paint	200	*
SUB-TOTAL—ESCALATOR SHAFT (ALL FUELS)	3195	64357
SUB-TOTAL—TICKET HALL (ALL FUELS)	755	9595

*calorific values not known

29. Ignition and other tests were carried out by the Health and Safety Executive at Buxton on the characteristics of samples removed from the Piccadilly Line escalators, escalator shaft and tube lines ticket hall (Report 11e). These included ignition tests on the grease and detritus removed from the running track of escalator 4. They showed that ignition was easily achieved by a lighted match, but in none of the tests was ignition achieved by a glowing cigarette. Tests were also carried out which showed that 25% of lighted matches dropped 1.1 metre onto a sample of the same grease caused ignition. Further tests showed that 8% of matches thrown away from the body by a person standing on the right of the escalator, fell down through a 10 mm gap between the steps and the skirting board. This would have been made easier in the absence of the fire cleat on the step (see Figure 9). Many of the fire cleats on the Piccadilly Line escalators were observed to be missing by Mr Milne (Report 4b). These tests provide support for the conclusion in the earlier reports that most of the previous escalator fires had been caused by smokers' material (Appendix J).

30. It was possible for the grease to ignite easily because of the mixture of grease and fibrous materials which formed a wick. Without this wick effect, the grease was not very easy to ignite. Inspection of the unburnt lower portion of the Piccadilly Line escalators showed that there were very considerable deposits of grease and detritus on the running tracks, wheels and chains, as can be clearly seen in Plates 12 and 13. There were also layers of grease and detritus adhering to many of the underneath surfaces of the steps and risers. The lift and escalator maintenance manager told the Investigation that he believed the accumulation of grease on escalator 4 at the time of the fire had probably been there for a number of years.

31. A controlled fire test was carried out on an undamaged section of escalator 4 on 8 January 1988 at the Health and Safety Executive, Buxton (Report 11c). Three attempts were made to ignite the grease and detritus on the running track by dropping a glowing cigarette down the gap between the steps and the skirting board but with no success. The first test using a lighted match caused ignition. The fire growth beneath the escalator, and later above it, was recorded. The fire grew rapidly from the instant of ignition. At 2 minutes and 17 seconds the fire was visible as a glow from above the escalator. At 3 minutes and 45 seconds flames could be seen down the right-hand side of the risers. Beneath the escalator at 6 minutes and 54 seconds the flames were touching the underside of the decking. At about 9 minutes the fire was extinguished before it could consume the balustrade and treads. Plates 21-23 show the fire beneath and above the escalator.

32. For some years it had been the practice of London Underground to apply the Prodorite B2 paint system to existing painted surfaces. In the exacting conditions experienced in the Oxford Circus station fire of 23 November 1984 it had performed entirely satisfactorily. From the beginning of the Investigation there was much debate about the role of the ceiling paint in the development of the King's Cross fire. London Regional Transport and London Underground maintained that the paint on the ceiling of the escalator shaft was a substantial cause of the rapidity of flame spread. Consequently, a number of paint flake samples from the ceiling of the Piccadilly Line escalator shaft were taken by the Chatfield Applied Research Laboratories Ltd and subjected to detailed examination (Report 3). As many as twenty individual paint layers were discovered, of which the topmost six coats corresponded to the components of the Prodorite B2 system.

Opinions put forward and examined in Part One

33. The scientific evidence was first heard at the end of Part One of the Investigation. Four fire experts presented data and expressed opinions on the probable sequence and mechanism of the development of the fire. Since only part of the scientific investigation was complete at that time, and by the nature of the development of scientific understanding, such opinions were necessarily provisional.

34. Mr Moodie based his theory on a fire which began on the running track at about step 48. The spread of fire involving the grease and detritus together with the oil-impregnated skirting board gave an average heat output of 0.15 megawatt beneath the escalator over a 15 minute period. This would preheat a 3-5 metre length of balustrade to a temperature sufficient to ensure a rapid spread of flame. Flames spreading up the skirting board from beneath caused ignition of the balustrade on the right-hand side looking up. With a 3-5 metre length of balustrade alight the heat output woud have been about 2 megawatts. That would have provided sufficient radiative heating spontaneously to ignite a similar length of balustrade and facia board on the left-hand side, increasing the heat output to about 7 megawatts. At this stage there would have been an increased rate of burning, travelling up the escalator and involving the treads. The flames would then have reached up to the ceiling causing ignition of the ceiling paint. Mr Moodie could not envisage the burning of the ceiling paint advancing more rapidly than the burning of the wooden components. The flame length would by now have reached 13-15 metres, sufficient to ignite the right-hand facia board and escalator 6. At this stage the fire would reach the ticket hall. Plates 24 and 25 show fire tests carried out on a full-scale six-step mock-up of an escalator at the Health and Safety Executive, Buxton.

35. Dr Eisner (Report 5a) considered that the mechanism proposed by Mr Moodie did not provide an adequate explanation for the spread of flame into the ticket hall during the last three minutes before flashover. He contended that witness evidence implied a sudden change in the regime of flame propagation, which he concluded could only be provided by the involvement of the ceiling paint. This could be instrumental in rapidly accelerating the spread of flame up and across the shaft as a result of its own involvement and that of the upper shaft portions of escalators 5 and 6. However, he was not aware of any method of calculating flame spread in such a situation and he advised that large scale testing was needed.

36. Mr Tucker (Report 29b) considered that the only plausible mechanism to explain the extremely rapid spread of fire was the involvement of the paint on the escalator shaft ceiling, and this alone could account for the large volume of dense black smoke. He suggested that witness evidence of the fire on escalator 4 two or three minutes before flashover implied that the power output was only 1 megawatt. He envisaged that this fire would have produced flames which reached up the ceiling and ignited it. A rapid spread of flame then occurred causing considerable smoke and producing much of the heat output at this stage. The rapid spread of flame was self-propagating due to the heat transfer by radiation and convection from the long flames produced by the burning paint, which preheated the paint which lay ahead.

37. After the scientific presentations at the end of Part One of the Investigation, it was clear that there was no consensus between the scientific experts, nor even, as Leading Counsel for London Regional Transport and London Underground acknowledged, between the two London Underground scientific experts (Dr Eisner and Mr Tucker). There were several main criticisms of the theory proposed by Mr Moodie. First, Mr Tucker (Report 29d) considered the rate of spread of the fire beneath the escalator to be too high, thus reducing the preheating of the balustrades and hence the speed and spread of flames. Secondly, the large fire postulated before the flame could stretch across the ceiling would have been seen by the firemen at about 19:43, and it would have produced very uncomfortable temperatures in the ticket hall. Mr Tucker's explanation that the spread of fire was accounted for by a very rapid self-propagating spread of flame across the ceiling at a velocity of 2 metres per second was criticised on the grounds that such speeds were unknown in scientific experience. Dr Marshall (Report 17b) demonstrated that the heat transfer from the burning paint to the unburnt paint was insufficient to cause continuing ignition, and that suggested a self-propagating flame spread was barely credible. He also suggested that the observed rates of flame spread in BS 476 Part 7 tests on samples removed from the ceiling did not support the possibility of a self-propagating flame.

Theories proposed and examined in Part Two

38. The second part of the scientific evidence was heard towards the end of Part Two of the Investigation. Five expert witnesses were called to give evidence in relation to the flashover of fire into the tube lines ticket hall.

39. In December 1987 Harwell had been commissioned to carry out numerical simulations of the flow and temperature distribution in the Piccadilly Line escalator shaft and tube lines ticket hall using the HARWELL-FLOW 3D model software package. This was a formidable task and it was necessary to simplify the problem considerably to get results in the time available. It was not until May that the first report (Report 25a) was produced. Several cases of different heat input configurations and different magnitudes of heat input were considered, but the striking and completely unexpected phenomenon uncovered was that the hot gas flow did not rise to the ceiling but appeared to be concentrated in the trench formed by the balustrades and steps. Further up the escalator the flow in the trench appeared to divide, part of it rising out of the trench and spiralling in a clockwise direction over the ceiling viewed from the bottom of the shaft, and the other part continuing up the trench into the tube lines ticket hall. In the ticket hall the flow spiralling over the ceiling of the escalator shaft appeared to travel between the ticket office and the temporary hoarding and then out through the entry from the perimeter subway with some flow sweeping round the back of the tube lines ticket hall. The flow continuing up the trench entered the tube lines ticket hall at ceiling level to the left towards the temporary station operations room. Plate 27 shows a plan view of one of the computed flow configurations. It shows a plan view of a grid of lines representing the outline of part of the escalator shaft and tube lines ticket hall, while the coloured lines show constant velocities in different colours.

40. The Harwell numerical simulation aroused considerable interest. Dr Drysdale (Report 4l) noted that it was well known that fire plumes on inclined surfaces were deflected down onto the surface, as predicted by the Harwell numerical simulation, and this provided an explanation for the high-speed propagation of flames up the escalator trench. The Health and Safety Executive at Buxton carried out some fire tests on one-tenth scale models. Video records of these tests were shown to the Scientific Committee and to the Investigation. These tests clearly demonstrated what has been called the "trench effect", with flames rapidly accelerating up the trench and erupting into the tube lines ticket hall. However, fires do not obey simple modelling rules so the results of these tests, though of interest, could not simply be related to the full scale. Plate 26 shows one of the fire tests on a one-tenth scale model when the flames are just entering the ticket hall.

41. Mr Duggan, a senior scientific assistant employed by London Underground, proposed an alternative theory (Report 15b) in which the ceiling paint played a crucial role. Like Mr Tucker he considered the final phase had been started with a 1 megawatt fire seen by Temporary Sub-Officer Bell. During the development of this fire the hot gas plume would have risen to the ceiling and preheated an area of the ceiling. When the flame reached the preheated ceiling above the fire, which would be prone to delamination, there would have been a rapid spread of flame to the apex, and this would have dramatically increased the rate of fuel emission from the ceiling. Under these conditions of rapid flame spread it was impossible to keep the fire well ventilated, so the hot gas plume would have become fuel rich. This would have generated an ill-defined region of gaseous fuel which was burning only at its surface and which was travelling up the apex of the shaft at the velocity of the hot gas plume. When this entered the ticket hall it provided the fire ball seen by P.C. Hanson.

42. Professor Rasbash (Reports 23a, b) was consulted by Sir Keith Bright and then retained by London Underground. He said his instructions had been ". . . to comment upon the possibility of whether Prodorite could have been a mechanism for producing a fireball, and it is the only area in which really I had studied in any depth". Accordingly he did not consider other possible mechanisms although he would ordinarily have wished to do so. His main thesis was that there was a rapid spread of fire up the advertising hoarding and the adjoining decking due to the corner between them and the flammability of the materials. This rapid spread of fire up the hoarding would have created a band of burning paint following in its wake. Like Mr Duggan he envisaged a fuel-rich situation, which would produce a fuel-rich slug of vapour travelling upwards with a velocity of maybe 2 or 3 metres per second. He considered that 1 kilogram of unburnt fuel vapour would be needed to produce the sudden eruption of flame inside the ticket hall seen by P.C. Hanson.

43. Professor Rasbash also gave details of two tests on samples of the ceiling paint taken from the Piccadilly Line escalator shaft. Regrettably members of the Scientific Committee were not invited to attend these tests. In the first test a sample facing downwards and inclined at 30 degrees was placed above the furnace used in the BS 476 Part 7 test. The ceiling paint delaminated and burnt vigorously; however, burning stopped half-way along the sample, probably due to delamination preventing heating of the paint surface further up. In the second test samples were fitted into a downward facing U-channel, giving a length of 3.2 metres by 0.2 metres. This was placed at an angle of 30 degrees and preheated by a gas burner at the bottom of the trench, which was then raised to play on the beginning of the paint surface. The flames

progressed rapidly over the preheated region, but they were stopped by delaminated material hanging down. At no stage was a self-sustaining flame spread achieved.

44. Mr Moodie (Report 11l) produced an update on his assessment of the fire dynamics. After consideration of the evidence he concluded that the fire development beneath the escalator was more widespread than he had previously assumed, thus providing more extensive preheating of the balustrades and decking. There was also evidence that the fire had spread to the left-hand side looking up, probably by piloted ignition, earlier than he had assumed. More importantly, he considered the implications of the Harwell computer simulation and the one-tenth scale model tests. He concluded that the trench effect provided a possible mechanism for the rapid development of the fire up the trench, and its eruption into the ticket hall. He also noted that the simulation illustrated the development of a corkscrew motion of air within the escalator shaft, and the complex flow patterns and temperature distribution which would occur within the ticket hall. However, he was cautious about accepting this new explanation without further work.

45. The scientific evidence presented in Part Two of the Investigation still demonstrated a considerable divergence of views. The four scientific experts called by London Underground in the two parts of the Investigation (Dr Eisner, Mr Tucker, Mr Duggan and Professor Rasbash) were in agreement that the ceiling paint had a major role in the flashover. On the other hand Dr Marshall and Mr Moodie considered that the paint only had a secondary role in terms of flame spread but probably a major role in terms of smoke production. The London Underground experts could not agree amongst themselves on the mechanism of the involvement of the paint, and none of them provided adequate theoretical or experimental supporting evidence. The Harwell computer simulation and the one-tenth scale model tests provided a possible mechanism for the flashover, but before this could be accepted more work was necessary.

46. I decided to allow further work on the fire dynamics up to 31 July 1988. Subsequently, I extended the deadline to 31 August 1988 to allow the Scientific Committee to hold a further meeting and to attend a fire test at Buxton on a one-third scale model of the King's Cross escalator and shaft, and for the parties to make submissions on this additional work.

Post Part Two Investigations

47. During the Investigation Mr Cockram, London Underground's building services manager, presented a prediction of the air flow in the Piccadilly Line and Victoria Line escalator shafts, based on train movements

during the crucial period 19:30 to 20:00 on 18 November 1987. This is reproduced in the graph at Figure 17. It shows that the air velocity in the Piccadilly Line escalator shaft changed from 1.75 metres per second downwards at about 19:41, to 3.25 metres per second upwards at 19:45. These velocities were computed in the absence of a fire on escalator 4. It will be noted that this change of velocity occurs in the crucial period of build-up to flashover.

48. Harwell extended their computer simulation to model the pressure effects corresponding to the air velocities computed from train movements (Report 25b) with three heat sources including one of 1 megawatt increasing to 2 megawatts. Though these changes brought about changes in the air flow and temperatures predicted, there was still a pronounced trench effect, and separation of flow occurred higher up the trench.

49. Following fire tests on one-tenth scale models of the escalator, the advice of Cambridge Environmental Research Consultants Ltd was sought on scaling criteria. They gave detailed consideration to this problem (Reports 1a, b) and recommended a one-third scale model. They also advised on the scaling-up of fire spread data from such tests to full scale.

50. As a result of the advice, the Health and Safety Executive at Buxton proceeded to build a one-third scale model of the Piccadillly Line escalator 4, the shaft and tube lines ticket hall, which was very fully instrumented. A first test on this model was carried out on 22 July 1988 and the Scientific Committee met at Buxton on 12 August 1988 to view a second test. In the first test the ceiling of the escalator shaft and ticket hall was unpainted. In the second test the metal lining of the escalator shaft and the metal surface of the ticket hall were painted with an arbitrarily selected paint. It was recognised that it was impossible to reproduce the very complex multi-layer paint system on the ceiling of the Piccadilly Line escalator shaft. In these tests the fire was initiated half-way up the escalator. The tests clearly substantiated the trench effect, and also the separation of flow with a stream of hot gas spiralling across the ceiling and involving the paint. It also provided a view of the eruption of fire into the ticket hall in the form of discrete flames and then a more continuous jet from escalator 4 onto the ceiling of the ticket hall and its spread across the ceiling. Plates 28-31 show the one-third scale model before and during a test. (Further details of the one-tenth and the first one-third scale model tests are provided in Report 11n.)

51. Dr Drysdale (Report 4n) reported on further fire tests on one-tenth scale models of the escalator to examine the effect of the geometry of the fire on the development of the trench effect. These demonstrated that if

both balustrades were alight the tips of the flames merged over the centre line of the channel and were deflected up hill. When both sides and the floor were burning these effects were more pronounced. Further tests confirmed the importance of a fire across the floor of the escalator in encouraging the development of the trench effect.

52. Following the meeting of the Scientific Committee on 12 August 1988, final submissions were received from the parties. There was general agreement about the importance of the trench effect and the separation of flow leading to a spiralling flow across the ceiling and a continuing flow up the trench. The views submitted by London Underground were coordinated by their Scientific Adviser, Mr Osborne (Report 15h). There was a general consensus amongst their advisers which Mr Osborne expressed in this first conclusion:

   "The demonstration, by computer simulation and fire modelling, of a 'trench effect' has shown that a mechanism exists for a fire within the escalator trough to develop very rapidly indeed. This is a newly discovered phenomenon, not previously identified in any previous fire situations or tests and not anticipated even in expert circles."

   He noted that there were areas of uncertainty where he thought the trench effect did not provide a complete explanation of the accounts given by witnesses. However, in his final conclusion he stated:

   "The second test left the instinctive impression that it bore a good qualitative relationship to the actual event."

Conclusions

53. I conclude from the witness evidence that the development of the fire until shortly before the flashover was as follows:

   (i) The fire was initiated by smokers' material, probably a carelessly discarded lighted match, which fell through the clearance between the steps and the skirting board on the right-hand side of escalator 4. It fell onto the running track between the chain and trailer wheels, where there was an excessive accumulation of readily ignitable grease and detritus.

   (ii) The fire on the running track probably started in the vicinity of step 48 at about 19:25. Since the escalator was moving, the fire was carried up to at least one other location in the vicinity of step 70 and probably to other sites, and in particular one near the top. The fire was also transmitted to the left-hand side of the escalator somewhere in the vicinity of step 70, probably by flame spread beneath the steps where there was grease and detritus.

(iii) Although the fire beneath the escalator was not as fierce as that above, the heat output was enough to produce significant preheating of the balustrades and decking, which made them more susceptible to ignition and spread of fire.

(iv) The fire on the running track ignited the dry plywood skirting boards, which were impregnated with oil and grease and thus readily ignitable. This provided a path for the fire beneath the escalator to spread to the upper side.

(v) The flames between the steps and skirting board were the source of ignition of the rubber dressguard, the balustrades coated with yacht varnish, and the steps and risers. The fire was at this stage when seen by P. C. Kukielka some few minutes before the flashover.

(vi) Until about 19:43 the main fuel involved in the fire would have been wood, with some grease and the rubber of the dressguard. This would have produced the smoke variously described as white, greyish-white or grey, with a smell mainly of wood fire.

54. The main point of contention amongst the scientists was the explanation for the extremely rapid development of the fire in the last two minutes and its violent eruption into the ticket hall accompanied, or maybe preceded, by very thick black smoke. I have concluded that:

(i) The computational work carried out by Harwell first drew attention to an important and unsuspected phenomenon in the form of the trench effect. In the computer simulation the airflow resulting from the fire in the trench formed by the balustrades and steps, instead of rising more or less vertically to the ceiling and flowing up the apex of the ceiling, flows up the trench. Further up the trench the flow separated into two streams; the top stream rose out of the trench, spiralled in a clockwise direction up the facia board and across the ceiling, as viewed from the bottom of the shaft. The second stream remained in the trench and continued up the escalator shaft into the tube lines ticket hall.

(ii) The experimental work on scale models carried out by Dr Drysdale and the Health and Safety Executive at Buxton served to confirm the existence of a trench effect in which the flames rapidly extend up the trench until they erupt into the ticket hall, as postulated by the Harwell computational work.

55. On the basis of the witness and scientific evidence, I have concluded that the rapid eruption of the fire and black smoke into the ticket hall was caused as follows:

(i) A symmetrical fire developed across the trench formed by the escalator balustrades and steps probably in the vicinity of step 70, with a further fire in the vicinity of step 48. This corresponded with the account of the fire given by Fireman Button.

(ii) At 19:43 or shortly before, the fire had begun to lie down in the trench, a process perhaps accelerated by the switch in direction of the airflow caused by train movements at about this time. The firemen who saw it at this time may not have realised that the flames were stretching up the escalator, but Mr Saeugling from the lower concourse saw flames over a length of four or five metres.

(iii) When the flames lay down, cleaner burning with less smoke and higher temperatures followed, as recalled by witnesses at about this time.

(iv) Higher up the escalator trench, the flow separated into two streams. The upper stream rose out of the trench and swept up over the handrail, decking and facia board, the flames causing them to ignite. This was probably what Temporary Sub-Officer Bell observed when he reached the bottom of the Piccadilly Line escalators. The effect would have been to generate more smoke, which swept across the ceiling and entered the ticket hall on the right-hand side looking up, entering the perimeter subway through the entrance adjoining the temporary hoarding and then sweeping round the subway. Part of the flow would have been round the back wall of the ticket hall behind the ticket office. As the flames spread across the ceiling they would have involved the ceiling paint, causing a rapid increase in the rate of formation of the smoke.

(v) The lower stream, which remained in the trench, continued to accelerate up the trench, followed by an extending flame tip which ultimately erupted into the tube lines ticket hall. At first people in the ticket hall saw a few flickers of flames or detached flames, but this quickly developed into a continuous jet of flame. As these flames were produced by the combustion of the wood components of the escalator, there would have been little smoke in that portion of the flow. These flames followed the airflow from the trench up to the ceiling of the ticket hall, and were deflected by the airflow round the ticket office to the left looking up, crossing the ceiling in front of the Victoria Line escalators. As the flame tips extended less quickly than the airflow, it is probable that some black smoke was already sweeping round the perimeter subway and the back of the ticket hall, when the flames from escalator 4 first erupted into the tube lines ticket hall.

(vi) When the flames from escalator 4 impinged on the ceiling of the ticket hall they ignited the ceiling paint, generating black smoke in addition to that from the ceiling of the escalator shaft. The evidence showed that the massive increase in smoke flow occurred very shortly after the first flames entered the ticket hall.

(vii) The spiralling airflow and the spread of flames across the ceiling would account for the ignition of escalator 5, probably followed by escalator 6. These flames also erupted into the right-hand side of the tube lines ticket hall, causing ignition of the temporary hoarding.

56. Though there have been many previous escalator fires on the London Underground including many severe fires, none of these has produced a flashover. I believe that there are two reasons why a flashover occurred at King's Cross:

   (i) No water or fire extinguishers were used to retard the development of the fire.

   (ii) At 19:43 according to the evidence, the fire was on both balustrades and across the steps of the escalator. Such a fire has been shown to be conducive to the development of the trench effect.

57. There was much discussion of the role of the paint in the development of the fire. The evidence clearly indicated that there were no signs of blistering or ignition of the ceiling paintwork at about 19:43. Within two minutes intense black smoke generated mainly from the burning of the ceiling paint was circulating round the ticket hall and surrounding subway. I conclude that the paint on the ceiling of the escalator shaft was not involved in the fire until shortly before the flashover when flames spiralled across the ceiling and ignited it.

Recommendations

58. Now that the mechanism of the development of fire on wooden escalators is understood, a number of immediate actions are required of London Underground which will break the fire chain and help prevent any repetition of the disaster. My recommendations include the early replacement of all wooden skirting boards, balustrades, decking and advertisement panels by metal ones and then of wooden risers, replacement of missing fire cleats and regular inspections of escalators still at risk, and increased and improved cleaning of all escalators. Other recommendations of particular relevance include the extension of the present prohibition of smoking to all areas of stations below ground (Chapter 13 'The Management of Safety') and the installation of comprehensive fire and smoke detection equipment (Chapter 17 'Fire Certification').

Chapter 13

The Management of Safety

1. I turn now to consider the organisation and approach towards passenger safety adopted by London Underground before and after the fire at King's Cross. The Investigation was concerned with the circumstances of the King's Cross fire disaster and we looked at safety management in detail only insofar as it applied to the risks from fires on escalators. I was not asked to make, nor would I presume to make, an overall judgement on the safety record of London Underground. Dr Ridley accepted, however, that the Court had been given sufficient material on which to base a proper judgement on the monitoring of safety and general arrangements within London Underground to see whether safety standards are maintained.

2. Dr Ridley reminded the Court that, even taking account of the casualties at King's Cross, travel by the Underground remained considerably safer than by almost every other form of transport. Since the end of the Second World War London Underground had safely carried well over 25 billion passengers, and there had been only four years in which fatal accidents had occurred (other than trespassers or suicides). Other witnesses drew particular attention to the internationally renowned quality of engineering on the London Underground.

3. Nonetheless there are lessons to be learned from a complete review of the management of safety within the organisation as a whole. Whether London Underground should be required to undertake such a review must remain for you, but it is of great importance that in addressing the consequences of one particular proven hazard—that of fire on wooden escalators—London Underground should not adopt any less positive and searching an approach to the maintenance and pursuit of improved safety in other areas. In this spirit I offer below some suggestions as to the approach that should be adopted and later make specific recommendations.

Responsibility for passenger safety

4. The corporate aims of London Regional Transport's subsidiary companies are defined in London Regional Transport's standing orders. In the case of London Underground, the first of these is the requirement to:

> ". . . provide consistent with safety, the best value for money rail services, within the resources made available, by the pursuit of service quality, unit cost reduction and effective marketing."

The responsibility for safe operation had in practice been left to the operating company, London Underground. The Engineering Director had responsibility for the maintenance in a safe condition of the infrastructure such as the railway, bridges and tunnels, trains, lifts and escalators, and signalling and communications equipment; the Operations Director had responsibility for the safe operation of the system, the deployment and training of staff, and liaison with the British Transport Police; and the Personnel Director had particular responsibility for the company's obligations and duties under health and safety at work legislation.

5. Many witnesses emphasised that safety was enshrined in the ethos of railway operation, and that staff at all levels were aware of their responsibilities for passenger safety. At the same time, however, they recognised that standards and priorities for different aspects of safety had to be set or assumed. The Engineering Director, Mr Lawrence, recognised that London Underground had a blind spot to the hazard from fire on wooden escalators which was revealed by earlier incidents. Furthermore Dr Ridley recognised that London Underground at its highest levels may not have given as high a priority to passenger safety in stations as it should have done.

6. London Underground appointed specialist safety staff primarily to discharge its responsibilities for occupational safety and not to advise line managers in respect of passenger safety. They did so as a result of their philosophy that passenger safety was inextricably entwined with safe operating practices, and their interpretation of the Health and Safety at Work etc legislation. The safety organisation in place in November 1987 is described in the note to Figure 16. It may be seen that three directors had specialist staff within the lower levels of their command, but no one person had overall charge of safety.

7. In my view London Underground's understanding of its statutory responsibilities for health and safety at work was mistaken. Not surprisingly therefore the staff arrangements put in place to discharge those responsibilities had insufficient regard for the safety of passengers in stations. Section 3 of the Health and Safety at Work etc Act 1974 provides that:

    ". . . it shall be the duty of every employer to conduct his undertaking in such a way as to ensure . . . that persons not in his employment who may be affected thereby are not thereby exposed to risks to their health or safety."

Clearly, passengers passing through an underground station come into this category, contrary to the view of London Underground. Mr C White, the Safety Manager (Operations), told the Court that although the Operations Director bore the responsibility for running the railway in a safe manner, it was impossible to divorce the post of safety manager (commonly seen as concerned solely with occupational safety) from the question of safety of passengers. However, more senior managers including Mr Powell, the Safety Manager (Central Safety Unit), and Mr Straker, the Personnel Director, charged with health and safety responsibilities, categorically said that they did not see passenger safety as being a part of their job. There was also uncertainty about the extent to which safety advisers had specific responsibilities for fire safety matters.

The lessons from earlier fires

8. The approach of London Underground to passenger safety as revealed in the Investigation was not pro-active but re-active. And their reaction to earlier fires and warnings was imperfect, as may be seen from the recurring recommendations made after internal inquiries into fires, summarised in Appendix J. There was no system in place to ensure that the findings and recommendations of such inquiries were properly considered at the appropriate level. With the exception of the Oxford Circus station fire, there was not sufficient interest at the highest level in the inquiries. There was no incentive for those conducting them to pursue their findings or recommendations, or by others to translate them into action.

9. Many of the shortcomings in the physical and human state of affairs at King's Cross on 18 November 1987 had in fact been identified before by the internal inquiries into escalator fires. They were also highlighted in reports by the fire brigade, police, and Railway Fire Prevention and Fire Safety Standards Committee. The many recommendations had not been adequately considered by senior managers and there was no way to ensure they were circulated, considered and acted upon. London Underground's failure to carry through the proposals resulting from earlier fires—such as the provision of automatic sprinklers, the need to ensure all fire equipment was correctly positioned and serviceable, identification of alternative means of escape, and the need to train staff to react properly and positively in emergencies— was a failure which I believe contributed to the disaster at King's Cross.

10. This attitude was underlined during the Investigation when the directors of London Underground were asked in turn whether they would have acted differently if they had had in their possession the information on escalator fires between 1973 and 1987 that was brought together in a single file for the purposes of the Investigation. They were all clear that they would not have taken much different action, in part

because they were confident that passengers could always be evacuated in time. The Engineering Director, Mr Lawrence, told the Court:

> "If I had had the material or the reports of previous inquiries and the recommendations that were part of those inquiries, I do believe that I may have dug deeper . . . I would have read the recommendations about replacing skirtboards, for instance. I would have read the recommendations about special cleaning. I think they could have influenced me to cause other action to be taken . . ."

Dr Ridley was more adamant:

> "I see nothing in the evidence that you have reminded me of, the facts of which you have reminded me, which, going back before King's Cross would have led the Board of London Underground to take a different position. Indeed, although I say I could not have told you immediately before King's Cross how frequently those fires producing smoke took place, that there were such fires producing smoke was known to all senior managers and it was never felt, either by ourselves as individuals or by my predecessors, some of whom I have discussed the subject with, that we should have taken significantly different action from the one that you describe."

11. I referred in Chapter 4 'The Ethos of London Underground' to the received wisdom that fires on the Underground were inevitable. I can summarise the views of the directors of London Underground thus:

    (i) No-one in London Underground, either in recent years or for generations past, had foreseen that a fire starting on a wooden escalator could develop at a speed or with a ferocity which would endanger passengers.

    (ii) Whilst there had been some escalator fires in the past which had caused severe smoke, no passengers had ever been burned, and the true danger of smoke to people had never been foreseen.

    (iii) It was solely considerations of damage to escalators and disruption to services and not of danger to passenger safety which had dictated the action or lack of action by London Underground management.

12. In order to be justified in holding such a view senior management would have had to be certain that there were in place the measures necessary to eliminate the risk of escalator fire developing and spreading. The Operations Director, Mr Clarke, said he was satisfied on the basis of his personal knowledge and experience that there were adequate means of speedy detection of fires in stations, by means

of the noses and eyes of staff and passengers. He believed that water fog equipment and fire extinguishers afforded adequate means to extinguish or control fires once detected. The fire brigade could, if necessary, be called to extinguish the fire, and could be relied upon to arrive speedily. Moreover there were adequate procedures and time to close off escalators and divert or evacuate passengers if that became necessary.

13. However, the evidence of the documents produced by London Underground and the evidence of their witnesses showed that London Underground was not justified in making such unqualified assumptions. Staff training in the use of fire extinguishers and water fog equipment was inadequate and likely to have been very stale. There was no system in place to instil into station staff a sense of urgency and confidence in tackling fire themselves. The value of automatic fire detection equipment was not properly appreciated and it had not been installed. The experience of earlier escalator fires was that the fire brigade was not always promptly summoned or properly met upon arrival. The speedy evacuation of passengers in an emergency could not be compared with the experience with the routine closure of stations, or comfort taken from the rehearsed response of staff in recent emergencies including the Oxford Circus station fire. Exposure to smoke itself was not recognised to be dangerous. Above all proper recognition was not given to the unpredictable nature of fire.

14. The Director General of the Royal Society for the Prevention of Accidents (RoSPA), Mr Warburton, an acknowledged expert in the management of safety, gave evidence after studying the documents available to London Underground directors on which they based their reasoning. He found that there had been a lack of incisive information reaching the directors. Reports of internal investigations of fires did not address themselves to the system in place and offer management positive information to act upon. More generally, the lessons which junior management considered should be learned were not imparted to senior management.

15. Two extracts from the transcript of the evidence of Mr Warburton are given at Appendix M. The first, during his examination by Counsel for the Court, is devoted to the need to minimise the outbreak of fire and of the deficiencies in London Underground's plans for dealing with fires that do break out. The second, taken from his cross-examination by Counsel for London Regional Transport and London Underground, concerns the need for evidence and analysis on which to base a fire prevention policy.

London Underground's actions since the disaster

16. Early on during the Investigation, London Underground decided to identify the action it should take to prevent a recurrence of the disaster. They argued that they and London Regional Transport bore the primary, if not the ultimate, responsibility for identifying such action. Accordingly, they presented the Court with a list of 101 actions they had taken or planned to take, in the words of their Leading Counsel, *"...to ensure as far as it is possible to do that the King's Cross disaster will not be repeated and that the safety of passengers using escalators is ensured."* As the Investigation proceeded, a great many suggestions were made by the Court and other represented parties which were duly considered by London Underground. My recommendations are given in Chapter 20, many of which derive from the modified actions and recommendations from represented parties.

17. I have spoken elsewhere of London Underground's failure to seek out professional advice on safety matters or to heed warnings from within the organisation. It remains a matter of concern that they should apparently consider that the implementation of a definitive list of actions, mainly developed from within, will be capable of preventing the recurrence of a disaster. Such a checklist approach to earlier fires manifestly failed to address the root problems or to elicit the necessary action within London Underground. What is required is an active programme of safety measures, under continuous review in the light of the best available advice.

18. London Underground has argued that although there is still a risk of wooden escalators catching fire, the actions now taken or put in hand will ensure that no fire will ever again endanger passenger safety. I believe a philosophy which takes as its starting point the inevitability of fires is dangerously flawed. A more positive, pro-active approach to safety management is urgently needed to supplement the actions already undertaken.

A managed safety programme

19. Mr Warburton said that he had looked in vain for evidence of someone within the organisation questioning what the worst possible consequences of fire could be. Nobody had asked *"what if. . ."* The available data from sources such as internal inquiry reports and fire hazard surveys should have been properly collected and analysed to permit a true assessment of the risks to be made. This would have allowed a planned safety system to be developed, in which the various hazards could be given appropriate weighting, and targets set for the reduction of the incidence of fires. The aim would be to minimise the number of fires and thus reduce the probability of one of them becoming a major incident. The ultimate objective must be the elimination of all fires.

20. A managed safety programme would help management to make investment choices effectively. Thus the priorities between measures to relieve overcrowding, deter crime or protect against fire could be determined. A continuing programme of safety improvements assessed against actual performance and the reduction of known hazards is so important that management should not be deflected by immediate pressures from pursuing it.

21. In a managed safety programme senior management would be able to judge the progress being made in achieving their goals. Once a reduction in the number of fires can be shown, the safety programme will have achieved results and everyone will be encouraged to continue the programme. At lower management level, a disciplined system should be applied to safety management to carry through the agreed objectives. Designated operating staff would be responsible for regular inspections of their own facility, and the system would be monitored by periodic checks by safety staff or outside bodies.

22. There was some recognition by witnesses from London Underground that a more positive, searching safety programme was needed, though this attitude was by no means universal. The Personnel Director and Engineering Director were each able to accept that the absence of fires causing death or serious injury in the past was not a reliable guide to whether there might be such fires, and that it was necessary to take active steps to reduce the risk of fire. Mr Adams, the Senior Personnel Manager (Operations), had put the matter eloquently in a memorandum to the Operating Management Meeting, written in August 1987 before the King's Cross fire:

    "A safe environment is not one in which there is an absence or a low number of serious injury incidents, but is the result of active participation by management and staff in identifying hazards and then doing something positive about them. In other words, the absence of accidents is a negative measure largely dependent on luck, while the identification then prompt elimination or control of hazards is a positive step and is essential to the discharge of our duties under current legislation."

23. In truth London Underground had no system which permitted management or staff to identify, and then promptly eliminate, hazards. Among my recommendations in Chapter 20 I propose that London Underground should establish a managed safety programme as a matter of priority. I make specific recommendations about cleaning, the state of electrical wiring, the procedure of approval of materials for use underground, consultation before station works are undertaken,

daily checking of fire equipment, and access arrangements at locked exits. I consider London Underground's safety systems and make recommendations about the analysis of reports of fire, consideration given to internal inquiry reports, the rectification of faults found during London Fire Brigade inspections, determination of the safety levels to be met for each station, and organisational changes including the appointment of a Senior Fire Officer, a Chief Safety Inspector and the establishment of a Board safety committee.

24. I also make recommendations concerning the prohibition of smoking in Underground stations, including extending the present ban to shops and staff areas of stations, and measures to reinforce the prohibition.

Chapter 14

The Auditing of Safety

1. I described in Chapter 3 'London Regional Transport and London Underground Limited' that whereas financial matters concerning London Underground, such as productivity and budgeting, were strictly monitored by London Regional Transport, safety was not strictly monitored by London Regional Transport. Sir Keith Bright recognised and accepted this proposition.

2. In my judgement London Regional Transport was under a statutory duty pursuant to section 2(2)(b) of the London Regional Transport Act 1984 to have due regard to the efficiency, the economy and the safety of operation of the public passenger transport services which it provided or secured for Greater London. It is clear on the evidence of Sir Keith that his Board did have proper regard to efficiency and economy: it is equally clear they did not impose the same criteria when it came to safety of operation. In my view Sir Keith was in error in believing that he was entitled to rely on London Underground as the operators to discharge the statutory duty of London Regional Transport. The mere presence of the Chairman of London Underground on the Board of London Regional Transport was not a sufficient safeguard. No doubt this is a matter which will be the subject of consideration by London Regional Transport in due course.

3. In my view it is imperative that a holding company charged with ensuring safety of operation should discharge its duty fully. It is not acceptable that it should try to discharge that duty by delegating it to its subsidiary, coupled with maintaining a loose supervision by having on the Board of the main company a director of the subsidiary company. It is essential that a system should be devised whereby safety of operation can be the subject of audit in the same way as efficiency and economy and I propose that a system should be introduced forthwith. If necessary London Regional Transport should be directed to develop a system of safety reporting which would serve to satisfy their Board that London Underground has in place satisfactory measures to ensure safety of operation. Such reporting should include an independent assessment of hazard from fire, congestion and other aspects that London Regional Transport identifies. Quantifiable objectives should be set wherever possible.

4. I do not believe that the reactions of London Regional Transport to the findings of such a system of safety audit need necessarily interfere with the running of the subsidiary company. The audit can be achieved by system comparable to that which enables London Regional Transport to satisfy itself about the financial state of its subsidiary company. It is clearly in London Regional Transport's interest to take an independent view on the effectiveness and value for money of London Underground's safety programme. If London Regional Transport sets corporate safety objectives, they will be seen to be a part of the overall corporate objectives, and not in conflict with them.

5. London Underground accepted my suggestion that it should have on its Board a non-executive director whose specific responsibility would be safety. The appointment will be subject to the approval of the Board of London Regional Transport. That director should, in my view, be a person with relevant experience who, after independent outside advice, could lay down safety standards and establish performance targets against which the safety standards in the company could be judged. As a non-executive director of London Underground, he will be best placed to report independently to the Board of London Regional Transport on safety matters, and should have direct access to the Chairman of London Regional Transport.

6. If the internal audit has become the yardstick by which financial performance is measured then the safety audit should become the yardstick by which safety is measured. Only with such a management tool can the Board, and hence the general public, be satisfied that all aspects of safety are maintained at the right level.

Chapter 15

Station Staffing and Training

1. The Investigation heard much evidence during Part One about the human state of affairs at King's Cross on 18 November 1987, including specific actions or omissions by the London Underground staff on duty. During Part Two, wider evidence was heard as to the systems of management, supervision, training and recruitment within London Underground. My task has been to inquire into the cause of the accident, the circumstances attending the accident, and the lessons to be learned. I have accordingly concentrated upon an investigation of the system in place which allowed the disaster to occur rather than seeking to make personal judgements upon the people involved. It is only in this way that the lessons for the future can be learned and a repetition of the disaster avoided.

2. I have said unequivocally that we do not see what happened on the night of 18 November 1987 as being the fault of those in humble places. I have also said that the Court had neither heard sufficient evidence nor was qualified to make detailed recommendations on changes required to the system of staffing and staff management in London Underground.

3. Nevertheless, there are a number of general lessons to be drawn from the response of staff at King's Cross on that night and from the other evidence on staffing matters put before the Investigation.

Station Staffing

4. It will be clear from Chapter 9 'Timetable and Outline of Events on the Night' and Chapter 10 'The Response of London Underground Staff' that there was no effective control of King's Cross station by London Underground supervisors or staff at any time before the disaster occurred. While the actions of individuals at the time were understandable , and in several cases involved presence of mind and courage, their overall response may be characterised as uncoordinated, haphazard and untrained. The decision to evacuate passengers and to order trains not to stop was taken by the British Transport Police, who effectively assumed responsibility for station control. The station manager was in an office which had been removed despite his objection to a location remote from the tube side of the station, and he was not informed of the emergency—coincidentally by the Piccadilly Line controller—until twelve minutes after the first report of fire. By that time it was too late for him to play an effective part in evacuation or fire-fighting. More importantly, the training and instruction the supervisory staff had received was wholly inadequate for them to deal with passengers, staff and occupants in an emergency.

5. The single most important need is for better training of staff. The intuitive reaction of station staff in emergencies will depend to a large extent upon the quality of training and practice they have received. This is discussed in the second part of this chapter.

6. London Underground has argued that its current proposals for a new staffing structure at stations will radically alter the status and role of operational staff. The old regime of station inspectors, railmen and booking office staff will be replaced by customer services managers, station services managers, ticket sales assistants and station assistants. Staff will be selected more on merit and qualified to a higher standard; and more staff will be trained for a wider range of duties. There will be a continuous but reduced need for the use of relief supervisors, who will be better instructed.

7. A new management grade provisionally described by London Underground as station 'landlord' is to be established which will have total responsibility for the management of a major station or group of smaller stations. Appointment to these posts will be on the basis of suitability rather than seniority.

8. Although future station staffing will reduce the requirement for relief supervisory staff there is likely to be a continuing long-term need to use them. The future deployment of relief staff must take into account the safety standards of each station. This means that wherever possible relief staff must have knowledge of the station to which they are sent.

9. Several of the station staff present on the night of the disaster were restricted to barrier duties or barred from platform work on grounds of ill-health. Hence they were unfamiliar with parts of the station beyond the ticket hall. The Investigation heard that three of the four leading railmen rostered for duty and present on the tube side of the station were medically restricted. The system which allowed staff to nominate their preferred station had resulted in a substantial proportion of restricted staff congregating at one of the most exacting stations on the Underground. London Underground has accepted that in future safety standards for each station should include appropriate requirements as to the deployment of such staff.

10. Among my recommendations are proposals for the appointment and training of responsible station 'landlords', a review of the deployment of medically restricted staff, improved monitoring and training of relief staff and more promotion on merit.

Management

11. London Underground has accepted that a cultural change is required throughout the organisation. It is important that the proposed changes in staffing arrangements should be seen to be accompanied by improvements in the quality of management at all levels.

12. Dr Ridley has recognised that in the past there was a tendency to 'management by memo', whereby situations were reported without any follow-up. The Court heard from witnesses numerous examples of failures to communciate effectively between management. As a result, information and analysis often did not reach the people who needed to know. When responsibilities were delegated there was no follow-up to monitor performance, and important responsibilities fell between the gaps of different departments. Initiative by middle management was not always rewarded, and safety officers said they felt they were 'voices in the wilderness'. For example, the chief fire inspector, Mr Nursoo, found the same problems of poor housekeeping and electrical wiring in escalator machine rooms year after year. He duly reported this to his superiors but told the Court that he was powerless to require action to be taken. Recommendations from internal inquiries into accidents either did not reach the right people or were not acted on or seen through. Above all, the ordering of priorities and decisions made by the Board were open to doubt because the failure of communciation had led to incomplete information reaching them.

13. The cultural change which London Underground is seeking to bring about throughout the organisation can only succeed if corresponding changes in the method of management are made. In particular, I would expect to see:

    (i) clearer accountability for job performance and systematic monitoring of delegated responsibilities;

    (ii) a more open approach to the exchange of information within the organisation, and a seeking out of relevant information, best practice etc., from outside;

    (iii) an increase in the recruitment of managers with professional expertise other than railway experience, and more use of independent professional advice in training and safety matters; and

    (iv) a structured safety regime, endorsed at the highest level, designed to anticipate and to prevent the unexpected, as discussed in Chapter 13 'The Management of Safety'.

Training

14. The Court heard evidence that the staff who were on duty at King's Cross on the evening of 18 November 1987 were not adequately trained.

London Underground's practice for many years had been to provide initial training for all new recruits, and further formal training when required by staff selected for promotion to prepare them for their new responsibilities. Following the Oxford Circus station fire a programme of two-day refresher courses for station supervisors was run, which included some instruction on fire prevention and evacuation procedures. Other station staff were not similarly trained nor was there any monitoring of the effectiveness of training given.

15. Statements made by the staff on duty at King's Cross on 18 November 1987 indicated that they had little recollection of training in emergency procedures; indeed for most it was so remote that they had forgotten about it. Only 4 out of the 21 staff on duty said that they had had any training in evacuation or fire drills. Staff who failed to show adequate knowledge of their job when examined orally from time to time on rules and regulations could be sent to the railway training centre for further training. However, records showed that in the four years before the fire only 17 staff at King's Cross had been examined in this way.

16. It is accepted by London Underground that, at least until 1987, the quality of staff training at its White City railway training centre had been inadequate. The method of instruction had remained unchanged for many years, consisting largely of laborious note-taking and question and answer sessions. In the words of the training centre manager, Mr Rycroft, it had been all "chalk and talk". The subject matter was often inappropriate or out-of-date. The recording of training received by staff and performance monitoring were unsatisfactory. No central records of additional and refresher training received by staff were kept. Recognising these shortcomings London Underground recruited a training professional in 1987 as Training Manager (Operations), appointed a new training centre manager and charged them with the reorganisation of the centre, retraining of the instructors and introduction of improved training programmes for operational staff.

17. Supervisory staff up to the grade of area manager have now received a one-day refresher course in dealing with the outbreak of fire on stations, including a theoretical evacuation exercise. They have also been instructed in their responsibility for current and future practical and theoretical training of their non-supervisory staff in fire and safety training.

18. Non-supervisory staff and booking clerks are to receive practical and theoretical training on a twice-yearly basis which will include the use of communications equipment and fire and safety training. Every two years operational management and supervisory staff will receive

regular refresher training including the control of station emergencies and the use of fire equipment, public address and other communications equipment.

19. While welcoming London Underground's efforts to make staff instruction more relevant and effective, I have noted with concern that such efforts since the King's Cross fire have depended largely on the ingenuity and dedication of a few individuals with little professional help. The new training centre manager, Mr Rycroft, accepted my impression that he had been 'thrown in at the deep end' with little or no resources, and that he had had to make a valiant attempt to do the best he could. There was no strategic approach to the recruitment and training of instructors. Doubt was cast on the ability of the training centre with its present resources to fulfil the new commitment by London Underground to annual refresher training for all staff. The Operations Director, Mr Clarke, sought to reassure the Court that the new refresher training courses were introduced as short-term measures to meet an immediate gap identified after King's Cross, and that in the longer term the comprehensive training review will result in totally different forms of training being introduced for operating staff. I hope that this is so.

20. The Court was told that safety figured largely in all the various operational training courses, and heard in some detail about a fire safety refresher course provided for all staff in 1988 in response to the King's Cross disaster. But I noted with concern that since November 1987, there had been no input at all to London Underground's training courses from those professionally experienced in fire fighting. The London Fire Brigade had drawn attention in 1985 to the need for greater staff training after the fires at Oxford Circus and Green Park stations. The London Fire Brigade, the National Union of Railwaymen, and the Fire Brigades Union each indicated to the Court that they would be willing to cooperate with London Underground in order to put fire safety training on a more professional basis.

21. Evidence was also heard about London Underground's current staff training in station control. This is mainly concerned with overcrowding, but encompasses the closure and evacuation of stations in emergencies. With the exception of two of the supervisory staff, none of the staff on duty at King's Cross had had, or could recall, training in evacuation procedures.

22. London Underground has now issued station closure instructions for the use of supervisors and has increased the amount of simulated training in station closure, emergency evacuation and crowd control contained in the qualification course for station supervisors. It has also decided in principle that a 'safety procedure' should be prepared for each station in consultation with the emergency services.

23. Instructions to staff about fire and how to behave in emergencies is included in London Underground's staff rule book and appendices. I found that the relevant appendices were excessively detailed and unclear. There were no simple reference manuals for each grade of staff which included relevant extracts from the rule book and its appendices. No use appeared to be made of aide memoire. I understand that consultants are being retained to carry out a detailed review of the appendices to the rule book and to produce them in a simplified format. This should consolidate and simplify the parts relating to fire, remove the detailed instructions with regard to fire appliances, and introduce a requirement for regular training and refresher training into the rule book. The new instructions must be much more simple to read, illustrated where necessary, and supported by practical training.

24. My recommendations on training in Chapter 20 'Recommendations' include closer involvement of the emergency services, with more joint practical exercises, regular refresher training for all management and supervisory staff in controlling station emergencies and the use of fire and commications equipment, and regular fire and staff training for non-supervisory staff and booking clerks, site familiarisation for new station staff, and better training for Incident Officers. I also recommend the preparation of an improved rule book and reference manuals for each station and checklist for the use of supervisors, better training for area managers and group managers on health and safety matters, training to reinforce the smoking prohibition, and better recording and monitoring of training given.

Professional Advice

25. London Underground training procedures have been scrutinised by external bodies on a number of occasions in the past. The Court heard evidence about the findings and recommendations made, and the company's response to them.

26. In 1984/85 at the request of the Railway Inspectorate, the Accident Prevention Advisory Unit (APAU) of the Health & Safety Executive undertook a survey of London Underground's health and safety policies. The report in May 1985 found, amongst other things, that the comprehensiveness and standard of training given to operating and engineering staff was impressive, and recommended that there should be no reduction in the scope of courses. The authors considered that other training needs would be identified from an analysis of the reports on investigated accidents and formal audit reports. They also praised the handling of the recent evacuation during the Oxford Circus station fire when a thousand people had been removed from the area of risk with minimal injury. The Personnel Director, Mr Straker, said that he

had drawn reassurance from this report from an independent body. In its response to the APAU report, London Underground accepted that more could be done to improve the awareness and training of managers and supervisors in the operations directorate, but rejected a recommendation that more resources should be given to the management of occupational safety in that department.

27. Despite having been commended in the APAU report, refresher training for supervisory staff was allowed to slip by the wayside during 1986, until effectively it lapsed in 1987.

28. London Underground has recognised that the King's Cross fire revealed the need for more and better training in fire prevention and evacuation procedures, more on-the-job training at stations, more practical training, and joint training exercises with the emergency services. Because of the new urgency in reviewing training in fire safety and emergency procedures, the Operations Director, Mr Clarke, commissioned an independent report on that issue. The consultants, Health and Safety Technical and Management Ltd (HASTAM) submitted their report in March 1988 (Appendix G, Report 10). They recommended that a strategy for fire safety training and information provision should urgently be drawn up, including a training needs analysis, learning goals and objectives, and that more emphasis should be given to fire prevention and evacuation procedures.

29. London Underground gave its reaction to these recommendations during evidence in Court and in a written review submitted to the Investigation in August 1988 (Appendix G, Report 15e). They found that the conclusions and recommendations were generalised and failed to reflect changes that were already taking place when the consultants carried out their study. They nevertheless have accepted that many of the recommendations are fair and do provide an effective list of priority areas where action is required. The same firm of consultants has been appointed to carry out further work by January 1989. A steering group has been formed under the General Manager (Operations) to carry through action arising from their response to the consultants' report.

30. Since the King's Cross fire, London Underground has had the benefit of a further opinion on its training system from an informed outsider in the evidence of Mr Warburton, the Director General of RoSPA to the Court. He considered that a radical review of the form, content, relevance, and frequency of updating of training was required. Safety training had been ineffective, as was shown by the actions and reactions of staff at King's Cross during the emergency. Training had been largely theoretical, with few staff having 'hands on' experience in the use of fire fighting equipment. There seemed to have been a lack of perception that fire demands a very rapid reaction if it is to be

contained. He considered that the limited knowledge, lack of confidence, confusion and lack of leadership placed all staff on the night in a very difficult position.

31. I welcome the recognition by London Underground of past shortcomings in the quality and effectiveness of staff training and evacuation and fire safety procedures and their willingness to take account of professional advice. Among my recommendations I suggest that priority should be given to the implementation of the improvements to training proposed by the consultants.

Emergency Services

32. Much has been said in this Report about the importance of communications and liaison between London Underground and the emergency services. It is essential that the resolve of the interested parties to work more closely together is carried through into the field of training.

33. Although there has been resistance in the past to practical exercises with the emergency services at complex stations, I believe that the advantages considerably outweigh the disadvantages.

34. To improve the knowledge of the London Fire Brigade personnel of specific features of the London Underground railways, further training is to be provided by London Underground on a number of matters. This will cover escalator and lift equipment, communications, electrical control and ventilation systems. It will allow firemen to get to know station layouts, both in their own and neighbouring firegrounds.

35. The training currently given by London Underground to L Division British Transport Police officers is being extended to other divisions of the British Transport Police serving at police posts close to underground stations.

36. Among my recommendations are proposals for more local familiarisation training and training in technical features of stations for the British Transport Police and the London Fire Brigade personnel, joint exercises at stations with the London Fire Brigade and other emergency services, and greater fire safety and prevention experience for fire brigade officers.

Chapter 16

Communications Systems

1. The Court heard evidence about the various communications systems in use by London Underground staff and the emergency services at King's Cross on the night of 18 November 1987. Proposals for the development and installation of new systems at King's Cross and at other stations were also explained. Most of these proposals had been developed quite independently, but were being reviewed in the light of the lessons learned at King's Cross. The systems have wider application than use during emergencies in stations.

2. I have been given an assurance by London Underground that communications systems are of such importance that they will receive consideration at the highest level. In this highly technical field I do not propose to make detailed recommendations about the types of equipment London Underground should use, but rather to set out the background and some general objectives or principles which I would like to see followed.

London Underground Headquarters Controller and Line Controllers

3. The line controllers, divisional information assistants and signalmen for the Northern Line and Victoria Line are located in a control room at Euston; the Piccadilly Line and District Line controller and assistants at Earl's Court; the Metropolitan Line and Jubilee Line controller and assistants at Baker Street; and the London Underground HQ controller in the control room at 55 Broadway. The British Transport Police L Divsion information room is also located at 55 Broadway.

4. The London Underground control rooms, with the exception of Baker Street, were last modernised in the 1960's. They have signalling equipment and two telephone systems: external lines and an internal automatic telephone system. Three figure numbers reach the line controllers, report centres and offices concerned with maintenance; five figure numbers reach other offices, stations and depots. The system includes normal and emergency (999) lines to the British Transport Police L Division information room. It is possible to dial directly from London Underground into the British Rail internal telephone network.

5. At platform and platform concourse level there are dedicated telephone lines to neighbouring stations and to line controllers. The HQ controller also has direct lines to the London Fire Brigade, the London Ambulance Service, and the British Transport Police L Division information room. The line controllers can also use the public address systems at stations.

6. The British Transport Police L Division information room was modernised during 1986 and 1987 by the installation of an elaborate computer system for command and control purposes known as PLOD (Police Logistical Operational Database). Its facilities included selected direct dialling, message recording, and timed logging.

7. The most important of the calls made during the emergency are described in Chapter 9 'Timetable and Outline of Events on the Night' and Chapter 10 'The Response of London Underground Staff'. It is clear that the station staff, several of whom had a good knowledge of the communications equipment available, failed to make use of it. They did not call the London Fire Brigade upon discovery of the fire, inform the station manager or the line controller promptly, nor use the platform public address system to keep passengers informed during the emergency. There was unacceptable delay in passing on and carrying out the police request that trains should non-stop. In the later stages of the incident no one in the station telephoned London Underground staff and emergency services on the surface either directly or made contact via the HQ controller.

8. The Investigation spent some time establishing the timing of messages sent on the evening of 18 November 1987. The logs of the HQ and line controllers and those of the emergency services had to be reconciled, for clocks proved to have been slow or fast. Calls to and from the emergency services were logged and timed automatically but London Underground staff recorded their calls manually.

9. My recommendations include the provision of a message recording and retrieval system and improved telephone equipment for line controllers, and a computerised information retrieval system for the HQ controller. All telephone points in stations should be prominently signposted, and provided with a list of key telephone numbers.

Public Address Systems

10. The public address system at King's Cross ordinarily reaches each of the eight platforms, concourses and both ticket halls. It can be operated from three points: locally on each platform, the temporary station operations room in the tube lines ticket hall, and the line controllers' offices. There are facilities in the temporary station operations room to override local platform announcements, and the line controllers and information assistants can override them all. Recorded messages from information assistants may be automatically repeated.

11. The public address system does not extend to entrance passages, escalator shafts and some of the other areas of the station used by

passengers, nor to most of the staff areas. In the case of the Victoria Line, the platform public address system cannot be operated from the station operations room or the line controller's office.

12. Announcements from the information assistant located with the HQ controller at 55 Broadway can be broadcast only to ticket offices, station operations rooms and travel information offices, on a separate loudspeaking system known as the Breakdown Broadcast Message System (BBMS). This system is normally used to broadcast travel information to staff.

13. It is remarkable that no use whatever was made of the public address system at King's Cross throughout the fire and evacuation. I include in my recommendations improvements to the existing equipment and its coverage of station areas and more training and practice for staff in the use of the public address system.

Passenger Help Points and Public Telephones

14. At Oxford Circus station London Underground has installed on an experimental basis 38 passenger 'Help Points' allowing passengers to obtain information from the station operations room. The Help Points also have an alarm which is linked to the British Transport Police L Division information room. When the alarm handle is pulled, if the call goes unanswered for ten seconds, it is automatically transferred to the British Transport Police L Division information room. London Underground plans to extend the trial to another twelve stations.

15. An earlier type of passenger communication point was installed on the Victoria Line platforms of King's Cross though it had been out of service for some time. There was no indication to passengers that it was not working nor had the wall panel been removed. During the evacuation of the station Miss Leech and her friend Miss Byers who later died in the fire, attempted to use the inquiry point to report the smoke they had seen. They persevered without success for up to a minute before trying to escape.

16. Public telephones were not provided within the tube lines station at King's Cross, although there were telephones in the perimeter subway. In general there are no public pay telephones beyond ticket barriers at Underground stations. Such telephones could be installed at platform and lower concourse level with obvious advantages for passengers in emergencies and at other times.

17. I have included in my recommendations provision of more passenger communication facilities, including telephones and regular inspection of equipment and its prompt repair or removal where it is not working.

Closed Circuit Television

18. Closed circuit television (CCTV) is provided at King's Cross to monitor the flow of passengers on platforms and parts of the lower concourses and the Metropolitan Line ticket hall. Eight black and white monitors were provided in the temporary station operations room to cover these areas of the station. The operator can change the views on his monitors. Some cameras were also linked to monitors in the British Transport Police L Division information room. The line controllers and information assistants at Euston, Earl's Court and Baker Street can see the platforms on their own lines.

19. The Court heard that on the night of 18 November 1987 some of the monitors in the temporary station operations room were switched off. All five of the cameras covering the Northern Line and some of the Piccadilly Line cameras were out of service, having been removed before the modernisation work in the station. Neither the station manager nor supervisory staff had been consulted about the removal of these cameras. The views provided in the temporary station operations room by the remaining cameras were seriously inadequate and the system was of no material assistance during the emergency. The line controllers did however make some use of the remote monitoring facility to observe smoke in the platform areas and to confirm that the order for trains not to stop was being obeyed. They could see that passengers had been evacuated.

20. I recommend improvements to the standard and coverage of CCTV equipment in stations, and CCTV monitoring in the British Transport Police L Division information room. It is essential that there shall be no alterations which reduce the effectiveness of communications and control facilities in station operations and supervisors' rooms.

Station Operations Rooms

21. Although police officers made some limited use of the facilities in the temporary station operations room during the course of the emergency, it was not manned by a London Underground supervisor. I was disturbed to learn that this had been the position since 1984, when a station inspector's post had been withdrawn and the practice of manning the station operations room had ceased. London Underground has accepted that the station operations room at King's Cross was materially under-equipped especially in CCTV, and that it was not manned by a supervisor in the early stages of the disaster. They conceded that manning of the operations room would have improved communications and control.

22. In my view the station operations room should be the nerve centre for control of the station, and particularly in any emergency. Its location

and manning arrangements are therefore of critical importance. London Underground has now accepted the need to extend the hours of manning of station operations rooms and aims to have continuous manning during traffic hours at the 18 most complex stations by April 1989. It also intends to provide operations rooms at 13 further major stations, and to review the location of existing station operations rooms which are not at ticket hall level. In all cases the operations room must be adequately protected from fire and smoke.

23. I recommend that a properly located and equipped station operations room must be provided at King's Cross, that the improved manning of station operations rooms must be quickly achieved and that the London Fire Brigade and the British Transport Police must be consulted.

Radio in Stations

24. Staff at stations on London Underground have not been provided with radio equipment because current portable radios will only operate below ground if there is a continuous aerial system throughout the station. The only means of communication for staff at King's Cross on 18 November 1987 was the telephone or word of mouth. Members of the British Transport Police and the London Fire Brigade at the scene had their own personal radios, but they did not work between the surface and underground. Officers below ground within the station could not communicate by radio either unless within line of sight.

25. Following a decision made before the fire, new radio equipment is to be installed in 42 underground stations (including King's Cross) for use by British Transport Police officers with connection points for the London Fire Brigade. It is intended that the leaky feeder cable network, around which the system is designed, will include connection points to enable the London Fire Brigade to use their radios within stations. The London Underground system operates on VHF whereas the new personal radios adopted by the London Fire Brigade operate on UHF.

26. Following the King's Cross fire, London Underground decided to accelerate plans for the provision of radio communication for station staff, initially at the same 42 stations. I believe it to be essential that radios used by London Underground and each of the emergency services must be compatible, and that station staff should be issued with radios (or paging equipment) in due course and I include recommendations accordingly.

Train Communications

27. There are three main means of communication with and within trains: train radio, tunnel telephones and public address.

   (i) The train radio network provides two-way communication between the line controllers and the drivers on their respective lines, in tunnels, below and above ground. Line controllers can also contact by this system managers who have portable radios and are close to the running lines. Managers however cannot speak directly to train drivers.

   (ii) The tunnel telephone system lets the drivers speak to the line controllers in emergencies. It is a specialised system of conductors to which can be clipped a portable telephone handset enabling the driver to discharge the traction current.

   (iii) The public address system on trains can only be operated by the crew. It is not fitted on trains of 1959 and 1962 stock. Line controllers cannot normally make public address announcements on trains. In emergencies on Piccadilly Line and Jubilee Line trains the line controller can speak direct to passengers but only after the driver has collapsed and the alarm signal has been activated.

28. I have included a recommendation that all trains must be provided with public address equipment which both driver and guard can use in normal and emergency circumstances.

Training

29. The improved communications facilities which London Underground install will only be effective if staff are properly trained and regularly practised in their use. At present, training for station staff is mainly limited to practical instruction in the use of public address equipment for new entrants or staff on transfer to a new station. More specialised training is given to divisional information assistants. I have already emphasised in Chapter 15 'Station Staffing and Training' the paramount importance of proper training, and I include specific recommendations of regular and up-to-date staff training in the use of the communications equipment.

Chapter 17

Fire Certification

1. The main legislative provisions governing fire safety in occupied buildings are contained in the Fire Precautions Act 1971, as amended by the Health and Safety at Work etc Act 1974. It is clear that the purpose of the legislation was to protect people from the risk of fire in wide classes of premises designated by the Secretary of State. Where premises have been designated they cannot be put to the designated use unless the owner or occupier has applied for or obtained a fire certificate from the local fire authority. The issue of such a certificate is conditional upon the premises meeting certain standards of fire safety.

2. As long ago as 1904 the Board of Trade recognised the especial perils of fire in the environment of the Underground. Following a fire on the Paris Metro in 1903 in which 84 people lost their lives, the Board of Trade drew up a set of requirements for precautions to be taken against the risk of fire in the construction or reconstruction of underground railways in this country. These included prohibiting the use of unsuitable wood, and the provision of emergency lighting and separate entrances and exits on platforms. The Board of Trade also reached agreement with the railway companies that the London Fire Brigade should carry out an annual inspection of stations, although that inspection was initially confined to fire equipment. These inspections have continued on an informal basis and now cover housekeeping arrangements and tunnels.

3. The strict safety measures which flow from the certification of a building above ground were never extended to the Underground where the consequences of a fire could clearly equal if not exceed that of a fire above ground.

4. The relevant legislative regime governing fire precautions and safety at work at King's Cross was the Health and Safety at Work etc. Act 1974, the Fire Precautions Act 1971 as amended, together with the statutory instruments made thereunder and the Offices, Shops and Railway Premises Act 1963.

5. Section 1(1) of the Fire Precautions Act 1971 provides that a fire certificate shall be required "in respect of any premises which are put to a use for the time being designated under this section." Section 1(2) empowers the Secretary of State to designate by statutory instrument particular uses of premises for the purposes of certification and 'railway premises' were so designated under the Fire Precautions Order 1976. Article 2(1) defined railway premises to mean:

    ". . . premises to which the Offices, Shops and Railway Premises Act 1963 applies and premises which are deemed to be such premises for the purposes of that Act."

6. Assuming that King's Cross does not come within the exemption (granted to railway premises employing less than 20 people) which it clearly does not, it follows that a fire certificate is needed provided that the underground station constitutes 'railway premises' within the meaning of section 1(4) of the Offices, Shops and Railway Premises Act 1963, that is to say:

> ". . . a building occupied by railway undertakers for the purposes of the railway undertaking carried on by them and situated in the immediate vicinity of the permanent way."

7. By section 90(1), "except in section 1(4) of this Act, 'building' includes structures." Thus, for the purposes of defining 'railway premises', 'building' and 'structure' are mutually exclusive. Accordingly, the issue to be resolved is whether King's Cross Underground station, or parts of it, constitute a building in this context.

8. I invited Counsel to the Court, Mr Roger Henderson QC and Mr Robert Jay, to set out their submissions on the Law about certification and thereafter I directed that it should be circulated to all the parties. The Opinion is set out in Appendix N. The Opinion recognises that there are two possible interpretations, but submits that the better view is that certification does apply. Although the Railway Inspectorate and London Underground did not support the Opinion, nobody dissented from it.

9. The Railway Inspectorate nonetheless acknowledged that certification could produce possible advantages. The view of London Underground was that the application of fire certification would be an enormous and costly task which would take many years to achieve. They expressed their willingness nonetheless to consider the practicalities in conjunction with the London Fire Brigade, the Railway Inspectorate and the Department of Transport.

10. In my judgment the correct view is indeed that King's Cross Underground station constitutes a building in Law, and I believe that accordingly it should be the subject of certification. But it is clear that the Law is in a state of uncertainty and I recommend that it should be the subject of clarification or amendment.

11. Even if there was doubt as to whether a certificate was needed, I am troubled by the fact that both London Underground and the Department of Transport behaved as though the Fire Precautions Act was irrelevant. The Fire Precautions Act 1971 was based upon and set a standard for fire precautions that represented good practice. If London Underground had a corporate strategy for fire precautions in underground stations—and I heard no evidence to suggest that they

did—the approach and standards embodied in the Fire Precautions Act would have served as a useful benchmark for such a strategy. London Underground's strategy appeared to be to rely on annual inspections carried out by the London Fire Brigade. But these inspections were carried out by invitation and were essentially short visits concerned with housekeeping matters, such as the accumulation of flammable materials and the provision of extinguishers. In the absence of fire certification, the London Fire Brigade was unable to enforce its views concerning structural matters such as the provisions of means of escape.

12. Leaving aside the question of certification, I believe this failure to adopt good practice had a direct bearing on the events of 18 November 1987. This can be illustrated by reference to the provision relating to means of escape (there are of course many other relevant provisions).

13. The required contents of a fire certificate are laid down by section 6 of the Fire Precautions Act 1971. They include in particular "the means of escape in case of fire", and "the means with which the relevant building is provided for securing that the means of escape can be safely and effectively used at all material times."

14. In the view of the London Fire Brigade, expressed in the statement of Deputy Chief Officer Doherty, this provision can be met by ensuring that:

   "There should be no storage of any materials within the escape routes; doors giving access to escape should be fire-resisting and self-closing; doors or gates providing means of escape should be readily available and easily opened; linings should be such that they are not capable of giving rise to firespread and should be regularly cleaned; all lighting to the escape route should be adequate and regularly maintained."

15. None of the means of escape available from the tube lines platforms at King's Cross on 18 November 1987 met those requirements. The Piccadilly Line escalators contained several tonnes of varnished plywood and did not meet the Fire Brigade's requirement. The Victoria Line escalators did not provide a smoke-free route to the surface, because of the absence of any smoke control measures. The Midland City exit was locked and could not readily be opened.

16. London Underground set great store by the use of trains to evacuate passengers from the tube lines platforms in an emergency. However, this procedure depended critically on the availability of staff to communicate with the train drivers, to stop passengers getting off and

to ensure evacuation of passengers already on the platform. In the event there was a crucial absence of adequately trained London Underground staff to cover the six tube lines platforms prior to the flashover.

17. Thus, when the British Transport Police decided in the interests of passenger safety that the tube lines platforms should be evacuated, prior to the flashover, the only option they had was evacuation by way of the tube lines ticket hall.

18. Despite their good safety record, London Underground had experienced serious fires in stations, as appears in the review at Appendix J. Fortunately no one had been killed, but serious smoke-logging had occurred and passengers had had to be evacuated through smoke. The major fire at Oxford Circus station in 1984 had underlined the point that smoke from a fire in a station permeates a major part of the station, interferes with means of escape, and creates a hazard to passengers.

19. On more than one occasion the Court was told by senior London Underground managers that they had inherited the oldest underground railway system in the world and that their ability to improve the fabric of the system was subject to very severe constraint. They contended that fire protection measures that were possible for new systems, such as those in Singapore or Hong Kong, could not be implemented in London. I acknowledged the problem but suggest that a rolling programme of station improvements should take account of fire protection needs as much as any other factors. People who travel on the London Underground are entitled to do so in as much safety as travellers in Hong Kong or Singapore.

20. In any case, the comment about the oldest system in the world does not apply to the Midland City exit. This passage was constructed in 1983/84 and provides an alternative route to the surface, avoiding the tube lines ticket hall. It was not constructed to the standard required by the Fire Precautions Act, since it does not have fire-resisting doors to control the ingress of smoke, flames and hot gases, nor does it have doors that can easily be opened in an emergency.

21. Following the Oxford Circus station fire in 1984, London Underground surveyed all tube stations to identify possible escape routes such as disused lift shafts, which could be used. The cruel irony is that the nearest and possibly the best such escape route at King's Cross was not recognised. If the Midland City exit had been available, before the flashover took place then I regard it as likely that evacuation of the tube lines platforms would have taken place by this route.

22. The subject of certification has wide ramifications and I specifically held during the Investigation that it was outside my terms of reference. But I said I would recommend that the whole matter (particularly with its implications so far as cost is concerned) should be looked at urgently.

23. Whether or not there is to be certification is crucial to my recommendations. If you decide that there shall be a requirement for certification, various consequences will follow and detailed recommendations from me are unnecessary; if you decide there shall not, it is of the utmost importance that the numerous recommendations for safety improvements submitted to the Court during the Investigation and collated by London Underground should be considered separately. The relevant references are given in Chapter 20.

Chapter 18

Role of the Railway Inspectorate

1. The Railway Inspectorate was founded in 1840 and under railway legislation was given powers to carry out inspections of new railways and to recommend to the Board of Trade whether they were or were not fit for public use. That power was extended by later legislation to include:

    (i) inspecting new or altered works (as defined in an agreement drawn up in 1958) on the railways;

    (ii) receiving and analysing accident data; and

    (iii) conducting inquiries into reported railway accidents.

2. The Inspectorate has been concerned for many years with the safety of railway staff and the investigation of accidents to them. With the passage of the Health and Safety at Work etc. Act 1974, an agency agreement was drawn up between the Health and Safety Commission and the Secretary of State for Transport providing for the Inspectorate to enforce the relevant provisions of the Act on the operational parts of the railways, and to carry out preventative inspections. The Inspectorate could thus enforce compliance by issuing improvement and prohibition notices. They were also given the power to prosecute.

3. The scope of the Inspectorate's increased powers and duties and their relationship with those of the fire authority was discussed in passing in the Opinion of Counsel to the Court in Appendix N. The Inspectorate's understanding had always been that, since railway legislation catered for public safety, the Health and Safety Commission and Executive looked to them under the agency agreement to concern themselves only with the safety of staff. Furthermore, the Inspectorate did not believe section 3 of the 1974 Act imposed additional responsibilities on railway operators, who were already subject to a statutory requirement to operate safely and other statutory controls designed to safeguard public safety. Major Rose, formerly the Chief Inspecting Officer of Railways, said that both his Inspectorate and the Health and Safety Executive had believed *". . . that a proper observance by the railways of the statutory duties placed on them by Railway legislation and Transport Acts would equate to a discharge of their duties under section 3."*

4. In my view the Railway Inspectorate was mistaken in its interpretation of the law in believing, if London Underground discharged its duty to have due regard to safety of operation, it had discharged all its statutory duties for the health and safety of passengers. The safety of passengers in Underground stations, and in particular the duty of London Underground as an employer to ensure that they were not exposed to risks from fire, was underlined by the health and safety legislation of 1974. Even making allowances for the Railway Inspectorate's misunderstanding of their responsibilities under the agency agreement, it is my view that the level of resources and degree

of vigour they applied to enforcement activity on London Underground were insufficient. It was in this climate that poor housekeeping and potentially dangerous conditions in underground stations were allowed to persist.

5. The staff complement of the Inspectorate was increased in the mid-1970's to allow work under the health and safety legislation to be carried out. Nonetheless the proportion of time devoted by railway employment inspectors to London Underground varied from as little as three-quarters of one inspector's time in the early 1980's to only one-quarter of one inspector's time in 1987. This reflected in part the problem of staff shortages which had been common in the Inspectorate for several years.

6. Major Rose explained that he did not expect his inspecting officers to look at matters specific to fire protection, such as the existence of wood in escalator shafts, and the accumulation of grease and detritus. He said however that they drew some comfort from the inspections of stations and tunnels customarily made each year by the London Fire Brigade. But the Inspectorate stopped receiving copies of the London Fire Brigade's inspection reports in 1984 after the Inspectorate's accident officer had taken the view that the reports were being satisfactorily made and he need no longer see copies. Major Rose conceded that this was an unfortunate decision. The Inspectorate is now receiving copies of the reports and has received back copies of those it missed. The fact remains that there was no proper liaison between the Railway Inspectorate and the London Fire Brigade regarding their respective interests in safety on the London Underground.

7. In 1973 following two escalator fires which had resulted in the severe smoke pollution of stations, the Chief Inspecting Officer wrote to the then Chief Operating Manager (Railways) at London Transport Executive, saying that such incidents illustrated the problem of dust, fluff and grease on older escalators. He suggested a drive to clear away such accumulations and reduce 'a proven hazard'. There was no record of any later warning that there might be a risk to passengers from fire on an escalator, and Major Rose argued that neither he nor his inspecting officers had ever conceived the possibility of an escalator fire rapidly developing and endangering life. He saw the primary responsibility for detecting fire hazards as lying with the London Fire Brigade in their annual inspection of stations. He did however recall how on one occasion in the course of an occupational safety inspection a railway employment inspector had observed a build-up of grease on the machine cage of an escalator after a cleaning. He had regarded this as a fire risk and reported his finding to London Underground; remedial action was taken as a result.

8.   Major Rose described the approach of the Railway Inspectorate to enforcement activity under health and safety legislation and to formal approvals under railway legislation. They had proceeded when possible by consultation with London Underground, using persuasion and the threat of health and safety legislation enforcement to produce results. The service of prohibition or improvement notices was regarded as a last resort, partly because there was a concern that prosecutions might fail. Furthermore, the Inspectorate did not have the staff resources to undertake time-consuming preparatory work on prosecutions.

9.   London Underground's Engineering Director, Mr Lawrence, confirmed that the route of consultation and persuasion was what he had come to expect of the Inspectorate, and said that he had been extremely surprised in December 1987 to receive a statutory prohibition notice on escalators at four stations—the first such notice he had known. Figures submitted in evidence showed that there had been two prohibition notices and one improvement notice served on London Underground since 1980 and no prosecutions. In the same period four prohibition notices had been served on contractors working for London Underground.

10. The question was raised in Court as to whether this informal approach led to a relationship which was too cosy between the London Underground and the Inspectorate. Major Rose denied this, arguing that the amount of information on safety measures which a railway is legally required to give to the Inspectorate is extremely limited, and that it is mainly by a system of liaison and relatively informal exchanges with the operators that the Inspectorate is able to exert a positive influence on the development of railway safety.

11   The Court heard of an example from 1987. After an adverse inspection of escalator machine rooms by the Railway Inspectorate, senior London Underground officials gave undertakings and there was an agreed programme of action for several months and a general 'blitz' on safety conditions in machine rooms. Nevertheless, the adverse conditions were not remedied until the service of a delayed prohibition notice in December.

12. In my view the powers of enforcement under the existing health and safety legislation are adequate to allow the Railway Inspectorate in its present form to fulfil its responsibilities for the safety of passengers. There needs, however, to be an increase in the number of staff coupled with an increased willingness to use its powers where necessary notwithstanding the uncertainties in the outcome of any prosecution. The experience in 1987 of the inspection of escalator machine rooms illustrates how long known unsatisfactory conditions can be allowed to persist if prompt enforcing action is not taken.

13. For the future, the Railway Inspectorate has proposed that:

(i) vigorous efforts will be made to overcome recruitment difficulties and to provide the equivalent of one full-time Inspector for London Underground;

(ii) in addition more effort will be put into monitoring London Underground's safety management arrangements, concentrating on their systems and the implementation of the list of actions;

(iii) there will be improved liaison with the Fire Brigade;

(iv) a review of the requirements for reporting of accidents will be undertaken, and London Underground will be encouraged to carry out better analysis of accidents and report such analysis to the Inspectorate;

(v) the Inspectorate will work with London Underground and the emergency services on emergency and evacuation exercises, ensuring that a wider range of staff are involved;

(vi) the Inspectorate would welcome regular liaison meetings with a Board-level safety committee at London Underground, matched by increased communication at lower managerial level.

14. In my view the Railway Inspectorate in recent years has not made full use of its powers or devoted sufficient resources to London Underground to create the tension necessary to ensure safety. Their misunderstanding of the duties imposed by section 3 of the Health and Safety at Work etc Act 1974 led them to take a more relaxed approach with London Underground than they would otherwise have done. I believe their general relationship with London Underground lacked the creative tension necessary to instil discipline and produce prompt results within the organisation. A more vigorous use of enforcement powers would probably have alerted London Underground senior management to the unsatisfactory state of affairs in stations sooner, and produced general improvements in housekeeping standards. The degree of liaison and cooperation with the London Fire Brigade was insufficient, and the decision to stop receiving copies of fire inspection reports was wrong.

Recommendations

15. I include among my recommendations that the Railway Inspectorate must be brought up to establishment, must adopt a more vigorous enforcement policy, and do more to keep the management systems of London Underground under review. There should be a review of the requirements for the construction and operation of underground railways, changes in the procedures for accident reporting, and regular liaison meetings between the Railway Inspectorate and London Underground at senior levels. I discuss the wider question of whether there should be a single passenger safety inspectorate in the next chapter.

Chapter 19

Matters for further consideration

1. A number of issues were raised during the Investigation which, in my view, went beyond the circumstances attending the accident and I ruled that evidence on them should be heard briefly or not at all. As a result of my consideration of the evidence as a whole, I make here a number of observations and recommendations for your consideration.

Financing of London Regional Transport

2. The question was raised as to whether the steady reduction in subsidy to London Regional Transport imposed by the Government's 1984 financial objectives for the corporation had had an adverse effect upon safety standards in London Underground. The budgeted shortfall between London Underground's income and expenditure at the start of the year was reduced as follows:

> 1984/85: £144 million
> 1987/88: £108 million

The corresponding actual end-year shortfalls were:

> 1984/85: £120 million
> (£136 million at 1987/88 prices)
> 1987/88: £104 million

that is to say, a reduction in real terms over three years of about 24%. Over the same period investment expenditure increased by about 48% in real terms.

3. In my judgement there is no evidence that the overall level of subsidy available to London Regional Transport was inadequate to finance necessary safety-related spending and maintain safety standards. I accept the evidence of the most senior management in London Regional Transport and London Underground that if funds were needed, funds were available. There does, however, remain the question of how the available resources were allocated and used by London Underground. I have drawn three conclusions:

   (i) There was a feeling among London Underground managers that the financial climate would rule out proposals to increase spending in certain areas. The lift and escalator manager, Mr Styles, for example, said that between 1985 and 1987 he did not press for investment to relocate the water fog controls or replace the wooden parts of escalators with metal ones. He did not do so despite their recommendation by internal inquiries into escalator fires and his support for such investment because he felt that they would have stood only a thin chance of being authorised. There was also evidence that when the budget for escalator cleaning was reduced, the effects were not fully considered at an appropriate level.

(ii) The current criteria for evaluating investment proposals adopted by London Underground may have discriminated against investment in stations. Dr Ridley suggested that the measure of cost per train mile used to judge the efficiency of spending proposals might be less appropriate than the cost per passenger mile, which would better reflect the increase in numbers of passengers passing through stations. He said that he would be making a proposal in due course to the Department of Transport.

(iii) There has been a tendency in London Underground in the past for capital expenditure to be less than the budgeted figure. This may have served to reduce necessary investment in safety measures. The principal civil engineer for London Underground, Mr Mead, presented expenditure figures for the lift and escalator department which showed that actual capital expenditure had been below budget provision in all but two of the seven years up to 1987/88, and that there had been an underspend of £1.4 million in 1987/88. He accepted that had the money been fully spent in every year safety in stations would have been better. Dr Ridley, however, denied that capital under-spending was an endemic problem in London Underground, although it had been so in the past. He produced the following summary of London Underground's financial results for the past five years:

London Underground Budget

£ million	LRT Budget Plan	Approved Budget	Actual Result	Actual Result (87/88 prices)
1983				
Income	288	271	301	365
Expenditure				
Cost of operations	293	296	291	353
Investment	105	99	106	129
	398	395	397	482
Shortfall	110	124	96	117
1984/85				
Income	258	290	313	357
Expenditure				
Cost of operations	313	317	316	360
Investment	120	117	117	133
	433	434	433	493
Shortfall	175	144	120	136
1985/86				
Income	333	331	358	385
Expenditure				
Cost of operations	323	315	316	340
Investment	132	128	135	145
	455	443	451	485
Shortfall	122	112	93	100
1986/87				
Income	376	386	390	406
Expenditure				
Cost of operations	334	324	320	332
Investment	174	174	171	178
	508	498	491	510
Shortfall	132	112	101	104
1987/88				
Income	404	408	428	428
Expenditure				
Cost of operations	328	317	335	335
Investment	198	199	197	197
	526	516	532	532
Shortfall	122	108	104	104

Dr Ridley argued that London Underground's overall capital shortfalls against the original budget provision of £3 million in 1986/87 and £2 million in 1987/88 were the result not of poor management, but rather deliberate responses to requests from London Regional Transport to alter the provision in the year to conserve funds within the corporation as a whole.

4.   Accordingly, I have included among my recommendations that the criteria for investment appraisal should be reviewed, that funds allocated to London Underground should be fully used, and attention paid to safety in decisions on the allocation of resources.

Staffing Levels

5.   A related question was whether the reduction in recent years in numbers of London Underground staff, especially station staff, had had an adverse effect on passenger safety. I made clear during the Investigation that London Underground's system and management of matters such as evacuation, training and staffing insofar as they were intended to achieve safety were of direct relevance. Accordingly, evidence was heard in Part Two about matters including the decline in the staff/passenger ratio at King's Cross station, the reduction in the establishment of cleaning staff, the ending of permanent manning of the station operations room, the adequacy or otherwise of the number of rostered staff to effect an emergency station evacuation, and proposals for further reductions in station staff at King's Cross. Representations were made to the effect that any proposals for reducing staff numbers should be dropped until a reappraisal of the safety implications has been carried out.

6.   I found no evidence that the reduction in the number of operating or maintenance staff contributed directly to the disaster at King's Cross. I did, however, note with concern that in one matter we examined in detail, that of smoke detection, no explicit consideration had been given by London Underground to the increased value of automated smoke detection systems in the context of station de-staffing proposals, despite the fact that noses and eyes had been recognised as the first line of defence against fire. In my view, the issue is not purely the number of staff in stations but rather the need to establish a proper level of safety at each station which can then be met by the provision of either automated aids or the proper disposition of staff. Accordingly I have included a recommendation that the safety standards being determined by London Underground for each station should address the relationship between staff numbers and automated aids.

Underground Ticketing System

7. Three aspects of the Underground Ticketing System (UTS) being installed at King's Cross and other central stations were raised during the Investigation. First, the station works necessary to permit the installation and the degree to which they may have contributed to the disaster. I discussed this in Chapter 11 'The Response of the Emergency Services: The London Fire Brigade', Chapter 13 'The Management of Safety' and Chapter 16 'Communications Systems'. Secondly, the question of the design of the UTS gates and their effect upon emergency evacuation from the station. Thirdly, the effect of the reduction and re-disposition of station staff with the introduction of automated ticket checking.

8. I am pleased to note that London Underground has now undertaken discussions with the Railway Inspectorate and with the London Fire Brigade about the effect of the UTS equipment. As a result action has been taken to retain exits which would otherwise have been closed at King's Cross and another station and to improve emergency egress at other stations by the fitting of alarm panic bars to exit doors. I have recommended that the safety issues arising from the introduction of automated ticketing at stations should be properly considered in discussion between London Underground and the London Fire Brigade and carefully monitored thereafter.

Congestion

9. We heard evidence about the greatly increased use of the Underground system in recent years and the effects of congestion on passenger safety at King's Cross station and more generally.

10. The station supervisors at King's Cross described how, in the months preceding the fire, congestion in the station, particularly in the Khyber Pass, had reached intolerable levels. At peak times it was not unusual for the inward and outward flow of passengers in the Khyber Pass to come to a complete standstill. The presence of a relief station manager to assist with crowd control served to ease the situation somewhat, but congestion would still reach levels which required Metropolitan Line trains to be held in the platforms until the passageways had cleared, or even on occasions for trains to be required to pass through without stopping. Such habitual overcrowding in the very area of the station which bore the brunt of the fire is clearly a cause for concern, and the spectre of a far greater toll of death and injury had the fire occurred during the peak period cannot be ignored.

11. Plans for the construction of a direct subway link between the tube line lower level and the subway leading to the Metropolitan Line to relieve

congestion have been developed by London Underground in the past and I understand that new proposals are being considered now. I recommend that measures to relieve the severe congestion at King's Cross should be taken without delay.

12. More generally, Dr Ridley gave evidence that the number of journeys on London Underground made by passengers had increased by 62% since 1982 while service levels had increased by 11% over the same period. Since 1985/86 the numbers of passengers had been at an all-time record. He said that it had been his ambition on joining London Underground to see the historic decline in ridership level out, but that it all got rather out of hand, and that the point where the extra passengers were filling up empty spaces on trains was soon surpassed and congestion became a problem. In Dr Ridley's words "...the most powerful pressure on us, on the management, on the system, and on the organisation was from congestion..."

13. Dr Ridley subsequently made the following statement to the Court:

    "I see three principal dangers to passenger safety at stations; one, from congestion; two, from crime; and three, from fire. They are all crucially important. It is crucially important that they be taken very seriously. I have tried to stress that nothing is more important than the problems arising from the very high congestion that currently exists on the system and I can tell the Court that all the information that I have seen suggests that the public is more concerned about crime than about fire but I am sure they are concerned about fire. ... With the benefit of hindsight I believe we have given higher priority to safety problems arising from congestion and crime than to fire, and this was based on our experience of risk".

14. Other witnesses gave evidence that there had been no exercise to determine the volume of passengers that can safely use exits or to determine the effects of narrowing or blocking passageways during station modernisation.

15. In Chapter 13 'The Management of Safety', I suggested that the monitoring of congestion should be an integral part of the managed safety programme. In my view it is essential for senior management in London Underground to have detailed and up-to-date information on the incidence of congestion and the associated risks to passenger safety in order not only to determine priorities for investment in congestion relief schemes, but also the need for immediate remedial measures to reduce the risk of accidents. Accordingly, I have recommended that satisfactory monitoring arrangements be put in place, research undertaken and expert advice sought as to the safe passenger flows and capacity of exits and passageways etc.

Crime

16. Reference was made during the Investigation to London Underground's actions in association with the British Transport Police to combat crime on the Underground. Dr Ridley's view of the importance of the crime problem in the minds of London Underground management and passengers alike is given above. It became apparent that several of the areas of concern in this Investigation, such as improvements to communication equipment, staff training and better deployment of staff, had been covered by the Department of Transport's Report of a study into the scale and nature of crime on the Underground which was produced in 1986 by a working group chaired by London Underground. Any work on the implementation of the recommendations of the 'Crime on The London Underground' Report should in my view be undertaken with the safety measures arising from the King's Cross disaster and the recommendations in this Report. The benefits of improved communications systems, closer liaison with the police, a brighter station environment, and more effective deployment of staff clearly have an impact upon fire safety as well as the protection of passengers and staff from crime.

Smoking and Littering Byelaws

17. I have included recommendations for discouraging smoking and dropping litter in stations arising from Chapter 13 'The Management of Safety'. The Investigation also heard some evidence of the inadequacy of byelaws and enforcement activity in this area. Accordingly, I have also recommended that the Government should give its support to any proposals by London Underground to introduce a byelaw against the dropping of litter in Underground stations.

18. The current byelaw in force on London Underground states that:

    "No person shall smoke or carry a lighted pipe, cigar or cigarette in any lift or vehicle or elsewhere upon the railway where smoking is expressly prohibited by the Executive by a notice exhibited in a conspicuous position in such lift or vehicle or upon or near such other part of the railway..."

    The areas around and on the escalators at King's Cross had been included in the ban since February 1985 when the Board of London Regional Transport extended the prohibition to cover all station areas lying within the ticket barrier at the 119 sub-surface and deep level stations on the Underground. However, the Investigation heard that there were probably no 'no smoking' signs in place on the advertisement panels of the Piccadilly Line escalator shaft on 18

November 1987, nor in a conspicuous position nearby and so in point of law to smoke while on the escalator would not have been unlawful. Similarly the lighting and discarding of a match would not contravene the current byelaw.

19. London Underground had indicated that it will consider tightening up the present byelaw prohibiting smoking in sub-surface stations. I recommend that the Government should lend its support to any proposals to make a more effective ban and to increase the penalties for persons convicted or contravening it.

A Passenger Safety Inspectorate

20. I believe that the time may now have come for a review of the role of the Railway Inspectorate, together with other inspectorates, to see whether it should become part of a passenger safety inspectorate concerned with monitoring and supervising standards in passenger transport on a much wider basis. The safety of people in stations and terminals is just as important as their safety while in transit. A more coordinated approach, bringing the several Inspectorates together, could produce great benefit.

Public Safety Information

21. It became clear during the Investigation that it had not been the practice of London Underground or the London Fire Brigade to disclose publicly the results of annual fire inspections of Underground stations undertaken by the London Fire Brigade. The London Fire and Civil Defence Authority had expressed some concern that the release of advice given by the London Fire Brigade as a result of any inspection made by request of an occupier (more particularly if it had been made under section 1(1)(f) of the Fire Services Act 1947) could have the effect of discouraging other people from seeking such advice. I view with dismay the suggestion that information gained by a statutory authority which has a bearing on the safety of the public using a system for mass transportation should not be made publicly available. The travelling public have a right to know about the safety arrangements made by transport operators and the safety of places in which they habitually gather.

22. Accordingly, I was pleased to note that immediately after the King's Cross fire and in response to a Parliamentary Question, the Minister of State arranged for the most recent reports of the inspections undertaken by the London Fire Brigade and by London Underground's Chief Fire Inspector to be disclosed. London Underground also indicated during the course of the Investigation that it is willing for the

content of future inspection reports, including any comments it has on the reports, to be published. I attach considerable importance to this and would hope to see the principle followed more widely in areas where the safety of the travelling public may be at stake.

23. Quite apart from the formal position on the publication of safety inspection reports, I suggest that you and London Underground may like to consider the wider benefits to be gained from improved communication with the public about safety improvements put in hand in the wake of the King's Cross disaster. The Director General of RoSPA drew attention in his evidence to the importance to staff morale, customer confidence and public image of a public campaign by companies in America who had very serious problems with their products and openly declared the problems and reported over time on how they had overcome them.

24. My preference would be to have London Regional Transport publish an annual report, perhaps addressed to the London Regional Passengers' Committee, in which progress, achievements and proposals of the safety programme are set out. Relevant information should also be included in London Regional Transport's Annual Report and Accounts and London Underground should consider what further occasional publicity would be beneficial in restoring confidence. This reporting should be in addition to the independent monitoring of progress conducted by the Department of Transport. London Underground should discuss with the London Fire Brigade their proposals for communicating safety information to the passenger.

Staff Consultation and Trade Unions

25. I hope that London Underground's response to the tragedy of King's Cross will be marked by closer cooperation between management and staff. I welcomed many of the constructive suggestions put forward by the National Union of Railwaymen and other trade unions during the course of the Investigation and noted with satisfaction London Underground's proposed action to invite trade union representation at future internal inquiries into incidents.

26. At the same time several of the parties expressed their disappointment at the re-emergence during the proceedings of old grievances over terms and conditions of staff employment, at the apparent lack of employee involvement in the development of London Underground's list of actions, and the continuing lack of a comprehensive system of safety committees and safety representatives throughout the organisation. I am not in a position to offer specific recommendations in this field, but

I express the hope that the signs of improved cooperation between management and staff will continue in the cause of passenger safety. Both management and unions should have but one overriding aim—to serve the public safely.

27. A particular cause for concern was the continued lack of a comprehensive system of safety representatives and safety committees in the operating department of London Underground as provided for in the health and safety legislation. Joint safety committees have been established in London Underground at departmental and, in some cases, divisional level as part of the machinery for consultation and negotiation with the trade unions. The committees usually met twice yearly, and concerned themselves with occupational health and safety issues, and not directly with passenger safety or fire safety matters. The committee concerned with station operations was the Railway Operations Department Joint Safety Committee. Although there were 100 safety representatives at station level, it had not proved possible over the years to reach agreement on the establishment of local safety committees to the extent that had been achieved in the engineering departments. Until the end of 1987 there had been no health and safety representative at King's Cross station for two and a half years.

28. The Operations Director, Mr Clarke, told the Court that there had not been satisfactory arrangements for safety committees in place in 1987, notwithstanding criticism of the arrangements in the Health and Safety Executive Accident Prevention Advisory Unit (APAU) 1985 report, and that discussion with the trade unions on the formation of such committees had been continuing for a long time. The General Secretary of the National Union of Railwaymen, Mr Knapp, for his part, said there had not been the organisation for proper consultation at all levels on safety matters. Although the trade unions had the power to nominate representatives with whom consultation must take place, he argued that there was only one committee on which they could sit and that it did not meet on a very regular basis. The NUR nevertheless offered its support for the implementation of a proper system of safety representation.

29. In the light of the proper interpretation of the Health and Safety at Work etc Act 1974 as encompassing visitors and passengers who pass through stations, I regard it as most important that the stalemate over the appointment of safety representatives and safety committees in London Underground should be broken. Accordingly I have recommended that the trade unions should appoint safety representatives as necessary to allow a comprehensive system of safety committees covering all stations.

30.   I have also recommended that the trade unions and London Underground, with contribution from the safety representatives and safety committees, should increase and improve the degree of employee participation in the preparation and execution of the safety programme.

Emergency Planning

31.   Section 30 of the Fire Service Act 1947 contains the powers of entry etc for members of the police and fire brigade engaged in extinguishing a fire and, protecting premises from fire or in rescue operations. It also provides that the senior fire brigade officer present at a fire shall have sole charge and control of all operations for the extinction of the fire. The London Fire Brigade and the British Transport Police have argued that in practice there is no difficulty in determining who takes control of fire-fighting and evacuation operations at fires, but that for the avoidance of doubt the roles and statutory responsibilities of the relevant services should be clearly defined. Accordingly, I have recommended that a review of section 30 of the 1947 Act should be undertaken to seek to clarify the responsibilities of the police and fire brigade.

32.   I raised the question during the hearings of whether there should be a national disaster plan. On reflection, it seems to me that an office or desk in a Government department which would coordinate the valuable information that exists relating to disasters and their consequences could serve as a focal point for sharing experience and knowledge. It is unsatisfactory that those coping with the consequences of major disasters should very often have to start from scratch, and that the lessons to be learned from earlier accidents involving deaths and injuries should not be as widely disseminated as possible.

33.   In this context I noted with concern that the British Transport Police had set out to draft a major incident manual without any direct help from other police forces, emergency services or operators such as London Underground. They knew of no forum where police forces, fire brigade, ambulance service and operators could come together. In fact, as discussed in Chapter 11 'The Response of the Emergency Services', the Metropolitan Police had a well-developed and workable major incident procedure which could have formed the basis of discussion. The existence of a well-publicised disaster planning desk could have facilitated a more effective use of the resources of the British Transport Police.

34.   Similarly, there is a vast amount of valuable information about the medical treatment and counselling of victims of disasters which all too often is dissipated. It could be shared with the local agencies involved in the next disaster. The Department of Psychiatry of University College and Middlesex School of Medicine have made a number of suggestions following their involvement with the aftermath of the King's Cross disaster which would merit consideration by Government. These include the establishment within 48 hours of a disaster of a steering group of social services, health services, emergency services, relevant academic departments and voluntary agencies, together with an adviser from central government, which would provide contacts for those responding to disasters, a 'knowledge base' on matters such as providing psychological support, the compilation of a register of people 'at risk' a coordinated agency approach to survivors, and so forth.

Identification of Bodies

35.   It is usual at the scene of multiple fatal accidents for the police to take charge of the identification, recording and removal of bodies. In the exceptional circumstances of the fire at King's Cross, it was not safe for police officers to enter the ticket hall and surrounding areas at the time that fire-fighters were discovering casualties. Therefore the fire brigade took a decision to remove some bodies to a place where they could be examined for signs of life. In fact no live casualties were recovered in this way and the uncertainty as to the position in which individual bodies had been found put a number of obstacles in the way of the subsequent forensic investigation. The fact that a single numbering system for bodies was not used from the outset may also have resulted in a misattribution of blood samples, and made the task of assigning levels of toxic materials to particular bodies more difficult.

36.   It is a matter of regret that the circumstances in which each person died could not be determined and communicated to their relatives. The London Fire Brigade has recognised the need for improved procedures for the identification and handling of bodies, and since the fire has proposed a system of body-tagging by fire officers in situations where casualties have to be moved before police officers have recorded their position. I asked during the Investigation that the London Fire Brigade should consult the relevant police forces and the ambulance service to ensure that the proposed identification system was acceptable to everyone concerned. I have included a recommendation that an agreed system for the identification and recording of the position of casualties is put in place by the London Fire Brigade as a matter of priority.

37.   Since this is an issue, however, which potentially affects the emergency services throughout the country, the Government may consider it worthwhile to review standing arrangements for the handling and receiving of casualties to see whether a standardised system needs to be developed and adopted by all fire services.

Coroner's Inquests

38.   I was appointed by you to inquire into the causes and the circumstances attending the accident—a remit which covered the cause of death of the 31 people who died. I was however, aware, that the St. Pancras coroner would hold the usual statutory inquest in due course. After hearing expert evidence about the role of toxic gases in the fire and the findings of pathologists on post mortem tests, I determined that the matter of the cause of death in individual cases could not be pursued any further in this Investigation. On the evidence available to me no reliable assessment could be made of the relative importance of various materials present in the station to the production of toxic fire fumes or to the source of toxic materials found in the bodies. In the event, the coroner decided the matter should not be taken any further.

39.   Insofar as there is a question for London Underground as to the continued presence in stations of materials known to produce toxic fumes under certain conditions, I have recommended that the assessment of risks and priorities for removing materials should be reviewed as a matter of priority. In my view the overlap between an Investigation under the Regulation of Railways Act 1871 and the coroner's inquest raises a point which you might like to consider.

40.   It does not seem to me to be in the public interest, or in the interest of the bereaved, to have two separate public inquiries in cases of this sort. In Scotland the Lord Advocate enjoys the discretionary power to suspend the normal requirement for an inquiry into a sudden death if he is satisfied that the cause of death has been ascertained elsewhere. There is no such discretion in England. Accordingly, I have recommended that the Government should review the requirement in England to hold a separate coroner's inquest into the cause of death where a public Formal Investigation into the accident has been appointed. In this way unnecessary distress to the relatives and witnesses, with the inevitable additional expense to the public purse can be avoided.

Implementation of Recommendations

41.   In the following chapter is a summary of the recommendations made in this Report with an indication of the priority I would attach to their implementation should they be accepted.

42.   Dr Ridley gave me his personal assurance that any recommendations pertaining to London Underground and accepted by the Board of London Underground will be implemented vigorously. Sir Keith Bright also told the Court that London Regional Transport has supported and will continue to support Dr Ridley in taking steps to overcome the shortcomings identified. I welcome these assurances and earnestly hope that a programme of action can be agreed with London Underground and effectively implemented without delay.

43.   You will also, no doubt wish to consider the adequacy of the arrangements put in place to monitor the implementation of the actions. I have made suggestions elsewhere for an independent safety audit of London Underground (Chapter 14), a more active enforcement role for the Railway Inspectorate (Chapter 18), and for public reporting of progress with safety improvements (Chapter 19 above). The agreed programme of actions arising from this Report should provide a starting point for all those activities. I would suggest in addition that London Underground and London Regional Transport should be required to make regular reports to you, in such form as may be specified, on their progress with the implementation of agreed actions, their response to any outstanding matters requiring consideration, and on any new or revised actions they propose to take to improve safety on the Underground.

Chapter 20

Recommendations

1. During the Investigation, London Underground provided a list of actions they would take in order to prevent a recurrence of the King's Cross disaster. Some had already been completed, some were of a continuing nature, and others involved action in the medium and long term. The Court asked for some explanations and additions, and the list finally presented to the Court included 104 actions. This is referred to in Appendix G as Report 15f.

2. During Part Two of the Investigation, I invited the parties to submit their recommendations to London Underground and invited London Underground to give their response. These were collated by London Underground in the document 'Response to the Recommendations From Other Parties' in July 1988. This is referred to in Appendix G as Report 15g.

3. After considering this document and all the evidence put before the Investigation, I make the recommendations summarised below. For fuller details and the source, reference should be made to the 'List of Actions by London Underground Limited' and the 'Response to the Recommendations From Other Parties'. A table at the back of this chapter gives a reference to the corresponding London Underground action or represented parties' recommendation number.

4. London Underground agreed with the suggestion that some indication should be given about the level of priority to be attached to each of the recommendations. I have given an indication of the urgency and priority I judge to be appropriate by using the following terms:

    Most important: ****
    Important: ***
    Necessary: **
    Suggested: *

    The most important recommendations should be implemented without delay, although it would be encouraging to see work begin on the other categories concurrently, and in all cases as soon as may be.

Chapter 7: Escalators on the Underground

Most Important ****

(1) All escalator trusses shall be fitted with linear heat detectors and machine rooms with smoke detectors. Priority should be given to escalators with wooden components and consideration given to moving the water fog valves to a protected location outside the machine room. The eventual aim should be for the detection equipment to activate an alarm system, automatic sprinklers or water fog equipment where suitable.

(2) A replacement programme of six or more escalator renewals per year shall be established. Escalator design shall be reviewed to allow easier and more effective cleaning.

Necessary **

(3) Effective barriers must be provided to prevent access to escalators. They must be robust, secure and prominent.

(4) The water supply to sprinkler equipment shall be fitted with a pressure gauge and by-pass valve. London Fire Brigade should be invited to attend London Underground water fog tests.

Suggested *

(5) Trap doors must be made secure.

(6) A non-inflammable escalator lubricant must be sought and used. Methods of lubrication must be improved.

(7) The remote monitoring equipment being fitted to escalators and lifts shall be modified so as to record any activation of smoke or heat detectors. This work should be completed by the end of 1989.

Chapter 10: The response of London Underground Staff

Most Important ****

(8) All messages received or made by HQ and line controllers must be timed and recorded with an effective retrieval system. A telephone system incorporating the most up-to-date facilities shall also be provided, as should data and video transmission equipment.

(9) Station instructions for emergencies and closure must be agreed with the London Fire Brigade and used in training station staff.

(10) Fire hydrants and cabinets must be marked with outrigger signs.

(11) A rendezvous point for the emergency services and a staff assembly point at each station must be agreed and marked.

(12) Station evacuation plans should include evacuation by train.

Important ***

(13) Water fog equipment must be regularly tested and staff trained in its use.

(14) Principles for the location and equipping of station operations rooms must be agreed by all those concerned and followed by London Underground in their future planning.

(15) London Underground fire equipment shall be modified to London Fire Brigade standards and the amount and type of fire equipment in stations agreed.

(16) London Underground shall undertake further research into the effect of trains on air movement in the Underground. London Underground should provide criteria by which line controllers, who have received a report of fire, can judge whether it is safe to continue to run trains.

Necessary **

(17) The computerised action checklist system for the HQ controller (Gazetteer) shall be provided.

(18) Station staff, including booking office staff, shall have distinctive uniforms which give a clear indication of rank.

Suggested *

(19) Water gas fire extinguishers shall be made safe to use in the vicinity of electrical equipment.

Chapter 11: The response of the Emergency Services

Important ***

(20) In agreement with the London Fire Brigade, London Underground shall produce and maintain up-to-date station plans, and place them in boxes it has provided, at locations agreed or specified by the London Fire Brigade.

(21) The London Fire Brigade shall attend all pre-start meetings and important later meetings in relation to construction works on the Underground. Details of the works shall be included on the Fire Brigade's central risks register. Fire equipment and London Fire Brigade plan boxes affected must be relocated before work starts.

(22) The British Transport Police shall also attend those pre-start meetings for works likely to affect passenger flow and movements in stations.

Necessary **

(23) The emergency services shall review the exchange of information between themselves and London Underground during an incident, both at their controls and at the site. The London Fire Brigade should send an officer to attend at London Underground HQ as soon as a major incident seems likely to develop. At the site of incidents, the London Fire Brigade must nominate an officer to liaise with London Underground and each of the emergency services.

(24) The London Underground HQ controller and the British Transport Police L Division information room must maintain a list of the position of all station plans and key holders. British Transport Police officers shall hold or have access to keys for all station entrances and exits.

(25) The British Railways Board as employers of the British Transport Police shall discuss with the Home Office closer links between the British Transport Police and other police forces.

(26) The London Fire Brigade shall review its procedures and criteria for handing over and assuming command during major incidents.

(27) The London Fire Brigade shall review its policy and training on the use of alternative means of access to an underground fire.

(28) Links between the London emergency services and the British Transport Police shall be strengthened.

(29) The London Fire Brigade shall ensure that its officers are made familiar with the geography and layout of underground stations on their own and adacent fireground territories.

(30) The London Fire Brigade shall review its instructions and training arrangements for command and control.

(31) The London Fire Brigade shall review the provision of protective clothing for its personnel, and in particular gloves, in the light of the injuries sustained by fire-fighters at King's Cross.

(32) The London Ambulance Service shall improve its procedures for timing and recording the whereabouts of its ambulances.

(33) The London Ambulance Service shall review its procedures for the removal of casualties and bodies from the scene of a major accident.

(34) The London Ambulance Service shall improve its arrangements for the attendance of a senior incident officer when a major incident may develop and shall review the procedure for the attendance of its command and control vehicle at major accidents.

Chapter 12: The Development of the Fire

Most Important ****

(35) The wooden skirting boards and balustrade, decking and advertisement panels of all escalators must be replaced with metal by July 1989.

Important ***

(36) Replacement of the wooden risers must be urgently sought in view of the discovery of the 'trench effect' and the conclusions of the report referred to in Appendix G as Report 4n.

(37) The initial programme for manual cleaning of tracks and step chains together with the spaces behind balustrade and decking panels must be completed.

(38)   The frequency of escalator cleaning must be determined from surveys of the rate at which grease and fluff builds up at different sites.

(39)   Escalators shall be manually cleaned at least every six months until the rewiring of machine rooms is completed. Thereafter they shall be mechanically cleaned in accordance with the programme determined under Recommendation 38. Escalator steps must be removed as necessary, and the means of access and protective clothing improved for those doing the work.

(40)   Station supervisors must personally inspect escalators, and both upper and lower machine rooms, every two hours until wooden parts have been removed.

(41)   The treatment of timber risers and step boards with oil and spirit must cease. Missing fire cleats must be replaced.

*Suggested **

(42)   Further research shall be undertaken into the dynamics of fires in escalator shafts by London Underground using the available scale models and computer simulation.

Chapter 13: The Management of Safety

*Most Important ****

(43)   The recommendations of internal inquiries into accidents must be considered at director level.

(44)   Trade union participation in internal inquiries shall be encouraged.

(45)   London Underground shall regularly examine fire equipment and ensure that defects are reported and remedied at once or alternative arrangements made.

(46)   The annual inspection by the London Fire Brigade of underground stations and tunnels shall continue, and unsatisfactory features must be remedied and reported on within six weeks. Copies of the reports shall be sent to the Chief Safety Inspector and Railway Inspectorate and arrangements shall be made by London Underground to publish the reports in consultation with the London Fire Brigade and the London Regional Passengers' Committee.

(47)   Keys must always be readily available for unmanned locked gates at station exits. There shall be communication equipment or remote monitoring equipment at these gates.

(48)   Locked emergency gates shall be fitted with alarmed panic bars.

(49) Station ventilation systems must be checked to ensure that contaminated air cannot be introduced into the rooms they serve. Instructions must be issued on any action to be taken in the event of a fire.

(50) London Underground shall maintain a formal system for health and safety monitoring at all levels of management.

Important ***

(51) Electrical wiring in escalator machine rooms and shafts shall be inspected and defects rectified.

(52) A survey must be carried out of all remaining VIR cable installations and a renewal programme established. The electrical wiring, lighting, decoration, and general state of machine rooms and shafts must be improved. The waterproofing of electrical equipment to permit mechanical cleaning must then be undertaken.

(53) All machine rooms and shafts must be specially cleaned by the end of 1988 and regularly cleaned thereafter. Essential cleaning materials shall be kept only in small quantities and in correctly marked containers in fire-proof bins.

(54) Reports of fires and smoke shall be produced promptly and an analysis made available for management and Board meetings, the Railway Inspectorate, the London Fire Brigade, and the London Regional Passengers' Committee.

(55) The Senior Fire Officer of London Underground, under the direction of the new Chief Safety Inspector, shall review the scope, effectiveness and organisation of the fire section and station fire equipment in consultation with the London Fire Brigade.

(56) The Chief Safety Inspector shall review existing safety arrangements, identify hazards, recommend policies, objectives and systems to meet those hazards, and thereafter audit the effectiveness of the system. He should have direct access to the Chief Executive of London Underground and the power to call for any reports, logs and correspondence relating to safety.

(57) In consultation with the emergency services the Chief Safety Inspector shall carry out a survey of each station in order to recommend the means of achieving satisfactory safety levels. The survey must particularly address the most effective combination of equipment and staff.

(58) The scientific adviser of London Underground shall be provided with separate funds for research and development.

(59) London Underground must establish a managed safety programme under the control of the Director and Company Secretary initially to implement the recommendations in this Report. In time it should be extended to cover other activities.

(60) London Underground shall continue the cleaning programme it has started in all areas of stations. Consideration must be given to limiting the sale on its premises of merchandise which produces significant quantities of litter.

(61) The Board of London Underground shall establish a safety committee and lay down its terms of reference.

(62) London Underground shall undertake an investigation of the problems of passenger flow and congestion in stations and take remedial action. They shall obtain advice from the London Fire Brigade and those with technical expertise. Reports of the most serious incidents of congestion must be made to the Board of London Underground and to the Railway Inspectorate.

(63) The present prohibition on smoking shall be extended to all areas of stations wholly or partly below ground, including staff accommodation and shops.

(64) By audible and visual warnings London Underground must encourage passengers not to smoke. Stubbing bins shall be provided at station entrances.

Necessary **

(65) The sale of smokers' materials at Underground stations shall be banned.

(66) Rubbish must be removed at least daily from machine rooms. Bin rooms must be located at ground level or protected against fire and frequently cleared.

(67) London Underground shall review the administration of the Code of Practice for the use of materials. All materials used in new works, modernisation, or maintenance must comply with the Code of Practice unless a specific waiver is obtained.

(68) The restriction on the use of materials shall be extended to other engineering departments and must be applied to the work of contractors.

(69) London Underground shall survey materials present on the system, evaluate the risks involved from those materials and devise a programme to remove those which constitute a hazard.

(70)   London Underground shall not permit alterations to any station operations room or supervisor's office which would reduce the effectiveness of communications and control.

(71)   Proper job specification and inspection arrangements shall be put in place for all maintenance and cleaning activities.

(72)   London Underground must institute and maintain a set of standards for cleaning and maintenance.

(73)   The lift and escalator engineer shall maintain and repair the lighting systems in lift and escalator shafts.

(74)   Combustible items such as paper and card shall not be stored at stations unless properly protected from the risk of fire. This recommendation and the Code of Practice shall apply to all occupiers of premises on the Underground.

(75)   London Underground shall agree with the relevant local authority, who is responsible for cleaning areas around stations such as access passages and toilets.

Suggested*

(76)   Escalator dust trays must be emptied daily and the design examined to see if the contents can be kept damp.

(77)   London Underground shall inform the London Regional Passengers' Committee, as the statutory body which represents the interests of passengers, of the conclusions and recommendations of internal inquiries into accidents which might affect passengers.

Chapter 14: The Auditing of Safety

Most Important ****

(78)   A non-executive director with special responsibility for safety shall be appointed to the Board of London Underground. He shall have direct access to the Chairman of London Regional Transport.

(79)   London Regional Transport shall establish a system whereby the safety of operation of London Underground can be the subject of audit. The Board of London Regional Transport shall receive reports on such audit.

Chapter 15: Station Staffing and Training

Most Important ****

(80)   Station operations rooms shall always be adequately staffed by suitably trained personnel.

(81) London Underground shall establish a programme of continuing instruction at work by supervisors for station staff in fire and safety with the assistance of the London Fire Brigade and British Transport Police. At stations equipped with water fog equipment supervisors must be given practical training during the regular testing of the equipment.

(82) Every two years all management and supervisory staff shall receive refresher training in controlling station emergencies, and the use of fire and communications equipment.

(83) Every six months fire and safety training must be provided for non-supervisory staff and booking clerks. Staff must be given site familiarisation training before they are permitted to take part in the running of the station. Specific provision shall be made for the instruction of staff in shops and other premises in Underground stations.

(84) Instructions to staff as to the calling of the fire brigade shall be re-drafted in plain English. They must contain only relevant matter.

(85) Fire safety training for cleaning and engineering staff working on stations shall be provided. London Underground must obtain expert advice.

Important ***

(86) Fire and safety training for station staff shall be reviewed in the light of the advice from consultants.

(87) Detailed records of all training given to individual staff shall be available locally to station supervisors.

(88) There shall be a joint exercise with the emergency services at least twice each year. London Underground must involve as many different fire stations, staff and members of the public as possible.

(89) All staff shall be trained in the emergency use of public address and other communications systems.

(90) Potential London Underground incident officers must be trained and practised in their duties.

(91) A station 'landlord' shall be appointed and trained to have total management responsibility at each major station or group of smaller stations.

(92) Relief supervisory staff shall only be appointed to a station for which they are qualified.

(93)   London Underground shall engage consultants:

  (i)   to rewrite the rule book and its appendices in plain English;

  (ii) to produce check lists for station supervisory staff and duty cards for members of staff;

  (iii) to produce relevant extracts from the rule book and appendices appropriate to each grade of staff; and

  (iv) to prepare station information books for each station.

Illustrations and diagrams must be used whenever possible.

(94)   London Underground shall consult the Railway Inspectorate and the London Fire Brigade before issuing these documents and any future revisions.

(95)   London Underground shall train London Fire Brigade Personnel on technical features of stations, such as escalator and lift equipment, electrical controls and the means of isolating the electrical supply.

Necessary **

(96)   London Underground shall only allocate staff to a role for which they are physically suitable. In the cause of safety, a proper balance must be ensured at each station.

(97)   Potential station supervisors must be trained in the evacuation and closure of stations.

(98)   Area and group managers must be trained to discharge their responsibility under health and safety legislation.

(99)   The British Transport Police shall review the training given by London Underground to its officers to ensure that it is appropriate to their responsibilities.

(100) London Underground shall provide familiarisation training for members of all the emergency services.

(101) London Underground and the British Transport Police must decide the most effective way to enforce the smoking prohibition and then train staff and officers accordingly. The criteria for prosecutions should be reviewed.

(102) London Underground shall review its policy on the promotion of staff and promote more on merit.

(103) London Underground shall reconsider and take advice on the Health and Safety at Work etc Act 1974, and institute a series of training courses for middle and senior management.

(104) London Underground shall review the standards of its electricians and provide appropriate training where necessary.

(105) London Underground shall make sure that all its written communications are in plain English and properly presented. They must check that instructions are being followed.

*Suggested **

(106) London Underground shall encourage staff to undergo further training by offering financial incentives and appropriate marks of distinction on uniforms.

(107) London Underground should consider the display of posters in stations explaining action to be taken in the event of fire.

(108) The British Transport Police should review the performance of its officers in the King's Cross emergency and give additional fire training.

(109) The London Fire Brigade shall improve the training of its operational staff in fire prevention and safety and provide experience.

Chapter 16: Communications systems

*Most Important ****

(110) The quality and scope of public address equipment must be improved. It shall cover a wider area of stations.

(111) The radio equipment in underground stations for the British Transport Police must be made compatible with that used by the London Fire Brigade.

(112) London Underground shall regularly inspect communications equipment. Where it is out of order it must be clearly labelled. Defective equipment must be immediately reported for repair.

*Important ***

(113) A new station operations room must be provided at King's Cross suitably located and properly equipped.

(114) Closed circuit television equipment shall be improved to allow coverage in colour of wider areas of stations. Monitoring facilities shall be provided in the British Transport Police L Division information room and line controllers' rooms.

(115) Platform and kiosk telephones, together with controls for public address equipment, must be clearly marked. At all telephone points there should be a list of key telephone numbers. An aide memoire of

important telephone numbers should be issued to London Underground staff and the emergency services. Public pay telephones shall be provided more widely inside stations.

Necessary **

(116) Station staff shall be issued with radios. Station radio equipment shall be made compatible with that used in the running tunnels.

(117) Paging equipment for junior station staff may be considered as an alternative to personal radios.

(118) There shall be public address equipment on all trains for use by the crew and the line controller.

(119) The London Fire Brigade must improve the means of radio communications between fire-fighters below ground.

Chapter 17: Fire certification

Most Important ****

(120) The law on fire certification as it relates to underground stations is in a state of uncertainty. Steps should be taken to resolve the position.

Important ***

(121) Comprehensive fire and smoke detection equipment, providing for remote monitoring and automatic operation of extinguishing devices, shall be fitted in underground stations as appropriate.

(122) London Underground shall initiate a programme of research into the fire qualities of paint. The surface to which it is applied and the method of application must be considered. The result of this research must be incorporated in the Code of Practice.

(123) London Undergound shall consult the London Fire Brigade and Railway Inspectorate about the means of escape and fire precaution measures in all future station refurbishment schemes.

(124) London Underground shall undertake a survey to identify secondary means of escape from stations and the costs of conversion.

Necessary **

(125) London Underground must study the best way in which smoke and ventilation can be controlled.

(126) London Underground shall mark passages, lifts, staircases and escalators in stations for easy identification.

Suggested*

(127) London Underground shall re-examine its Code of Practice as it relates to the fire-loadings in escalator shafts and other regions of stations.

(128) The regular meetings at three levels of senior management between London Underground and the London Fire Brigade, and those between the Railway Inspectorate and the London Fire Brigade shall continue.

Chapter 18: Role of the Railway Inspectorate

Most Important****

(129) The Railway Inspectorate must be brought up to establishment to carry out its responsibilities under section 3 of the Health and Safety at Work etc. Act 1974.

(130) The Railway Inspectorate must be more vigorous in the discharge of its duties on London Underground.

Important***

(131) The Railway Inspectorate shall keep the management of safety by London Underground under review. It must enlist outside advice.

(132) An observer from the Central Transport Consultative Committee, as the statutory body which represents the interests of the travelling public nationally, should be invited to attend meetings of the Railway Industry Advisory Committee.

(133) Fires which occur outside traffic hours on London Underground must be reported. The Department of Transport should secure such reports until the 'Railways (Notice of Accidents) Order 1986' [SI 1986 No 2187] has been amended.

(134) Separate accident statistics for London Underground shall be shown in the Railway Inspectorate annual reports.

(135) The 'Department of Transport Railway Construction and Operation Requirements' in respect of underground railways and stations shall be reviewed, together with the letter dated 10 November 1958 to the railway undertakings entitled 'Submission of new works for approval by the Minister under S.41(1) of the Road and Rail Traffic Act 1933', in the light of:

    (i) the circumstances of the King's Cross fire;

    (ii) building regulations;

    (iii) legislation on fire prevention and precautions; and

    (iv) experience with other underground railway systems.

(136) The designs for new stations or significant alterations to stations shall be scrutinised by the fire authority and the Railway Inspectorate with special regard to passenger safety and fire precautions.

(137) There shall be twice-yearly meetings to discuss safety matters between the Chief Inspecting Officer of Railways, those of his staff responsible for enforcement on London Underground and the Engineering and Operations Directors and the Chief Safety Inspector of London Underground.

(138) Each year the Board safety committee of London Underground shall meet the Chief Inspecting Officer of Railways.

*Necessary***

(139) 'The Offices Shops and Railway Premises (Hoists and Lifts) Regulations 1968' [SI 1968 No 849] must be amended to require escalators and travolators in Underground stations to be inspected every six months by a competent person.

(140) The Railway Inspectorate shall review its role in enforcing fire precautions under health and safety legislation in the light of this Investigation.

Chapter 19: Matters for further consideration

*Most Important*****

(141) London Underground shall review its proposals for the working of the Underground Ticketing System (UTS) at stations and take advice from the Railway Inspectorate and the London Fire Brigade.

*Important****

(142) London Underground shall build a direct subway link between the tube lines and the Metropolitan and Circle Lines at King's Cross or provide alternative satisfactory means of relieving the serious congestion.

(143) The trade unions shall appoint safety representatives as necessary under 'The Safety Representatives and Safety Committees Regulations 1977' [SI 1977 No 500] to provide a comprehensive system of safety committees covering all stations.

(144) There must be more employee participation in the preparation and execution of London Underground's safety programmes in accordance with section 2(6) of the Health and Safety at Work etc. Act 1974.

(145) Explicit consideration by the Boards of London Regional Transport and London Underground shall always be given to safety when decisions on resource allocation and investment are being made.

(146) The numbers of passengers using the system must be duly reflected in the criteria for investment appraisal in London Underground.

(147) Funds allocated to London Underground must be fully used, and particular attention paid to the safety implications of any changes to the budget.

Other Recommendations for which priorities should be determined:

(148) London Underground shall regularly inform the travelling public about safety on the Underground and any proposed changes.

(149) Legislation against the dropping of litter on London Underground shall be introduced and a review undertaken of the byelaw prohibiting smoking and the penalties for the offence.

(150) Consideration should be given to the establishment of a single passenger safety inspectorate charged with monitoring and supervising standards in all passenger transport.

(151) The duplication involved in holding both a public inquiry and a coroner's inquest should be avoided.

(152) Consideration should be given to a national disaster planning desk where the experience gained from disasters and their investigation and civil emergencies can be retained. Advice on the coordination of individual emergency plans should also be available at a national level.

(153) A uniform documentation procedure for handling and receiving fatalities should be considered. In London all the services must meanwhile agree a common system for identification of casualties and recording the position in which they are found.

(154) The recommendations in the report of the study 'Crime on the London Underground' [HMSO 1986 ISBN 0 11 5508058] must continue to be implemented.

(155) A review shall be undertaken of section 30 of the Fire Services Act 1947 to clarify the responsibilities of the police and the fire brigade.

Implementation of Recommendations

Most Important ****

(156) London Underground and London Regional Transport shall make regular reports to the Secretary of State for Transport upon their progress with the implementation of those recommendations directed at them.

(157) Reports on the progress made by London Underground shall also be included in the annual reports of London Regional Transport, the London Regional Passengers' Committee and the Railway Inspectorate.

Report Recommendation	Priority	Report Chapter	London Underground Action	Represented Parties Recommendation
1	****	7	25	19, 20, 35, 37–39
2	****	7	—	1, 2
3	**	7	6, 7	23, 24
4	**	7	—	21, 22
5	*	7	21	16
6	*	7	22	17
7	*	7	27	—
8	****	10	40, 41	231, 258, 261, 267–269
9	****	10	55	127, 129, 132, 133, 135, 302, 305, 409
10	****	10	61	58
11	****	10	85(ii)	128
12	****	10	—	132
13	***	10	11, 23, 24	18, 294
14	***	10	32(iii), 33	211, 214–216, 218–221, 223–226
15	***	10	60	55, 59, 60, 62, 63, 65, 66, 407
16	***	10	—	130
17	**	10	42	—
18	**	10	79	313, 314, 332
19	*	10	59	12, 57, 61
20	***	11	91, 92	143–149, 344(i) & (vii)
21	***	11	86(i) & (ii), 87, 88	137–142
22	***	11	86(iii)	414
23	**	11	—	338, 339, 342, 343
24	**	11	—	413, 415, 435
25	**	11	—	434
26	**	11	—	418
27	**	11	—	419
28	**	11	—	420
29	**	11	—	402, 403, 405, 421(iii)
30	**	11	—	422, 423
31	**	11	—	432
32	**	11	—	438
33	**	11	—	—
34	**	11	—	437
35	****	12	1, 2	—
36	***	12	—	—
37	***	12	8, 9, 14	—
38	***	12	13(i)	5, 7

Report Recommendation	Priority	Report Chapter	London Underground Action	Represented Parties Recommendation
39	***	12	10, 12, 13(ii)	3–6, 13
40	***	12	5	—
41	***	12	3, 4(i)	—
42	*	12	—	—
43	****	13	28(i)	—
44	****	13	28(ii)	337
45	****	13	62–65	54, 56, 63, 64, 66, 142, 146
46	****	13	89	209
47	****	13	98	413
48	****	13	99	98, 100
49	****	13	—	44, 45
50	****	13	—	380–381
51	***	13	20(ii)	—
52	***	13	20(i) & (iii)	8a, 12, 13, 14
53	***	13	15, 16, 17	8b, 9, 10, 86
54	***	13	26	29, 30, 380
55	***	13	66, 67, 68	55, 59–63
56	***	13	70, 71(i)	160, 161, 350, 354, 365, 369, 370, 374, 378–383
57	***	13	102	127, 132–135, 330, 360, 378, 379, 385–391, 397, 400
58	***	13	103	273
59	***	13	104	351, 352, 379
60	***	13	—	88
61	***	13	71(iii)	354, 381
62	***	13	—	—
63	***	13	94	71–74
64	***	13	96,97	77, 78
65	**	13	—	75, 76
66	**	13	19	89, 90
67	**	13	44, 45	53
68	**	13	48(ii)	150–153
69	**	13	48(i)	49–52, 372
70	**	13	35, 84	136, 137
71	**	13	—	8c, 25, 27
72	**	13	—	158, 159
73	**	13	—	15
74	**	13	—	84, 85
75	**	13	—	168
76	*	13	18	11
77	*	13	—	367

Report Recommendation	Priority	Report Chapter	London Underground Action	Represented Parties Recommendation
78	****	14	71(ii)	348, 349, 354, 359, 365, 381, 382
79	****	14	—	—
80	****	15	32(i) & (ii)	212, 213
81	****	15	50, 51	286, 294, 302, 305
82	****	15	53	42, 113, 280, 285
83	****	15	52	290–294, 297, 301, 302 305, 344(ii), 389–391
84	****	15	85(i)	—
85	****	15	—	298
86	***	15	49	281–284, 303
87	***	15	54	288, 297, 305
88	***	15	57	129, 286–289, 344, 401
89	***	15	—	285
90	***	15	69	340, 341
91	***	15	74	8c, 26, 27, 49, 82, 83, 161, 217, 241, 242, 315–327, 356, 372, 397
92	***	15	75–77	292, 295, 309–311, 329
93(i)	***	15	82(i)(a), 82(ii)	127, 299, 383 385–394, 397
93(ii)	***	15	82(i)(d), 82(ii)	
93(iii)	***	15	82(i)(c), 82(ii)	
93(iv)	***	15	82(i)(b), 82(ii)	
94	***	15	82(iii)	182, 306
95	***	15	90	266, 404–406, 408, 421(iii)
96	**	15	78	312, 328, 329
97	**	15	56	134
98	**	15	82(iv)	161
99	**	15	93(i)	288, 345, 409–411
100	**	15	93(ii)	410, 412, 416
101	**	15	95	80, 204
102	**	15	—	320
103	**	15	—	279
104	**	15	—	308
105	**	15	—	395, 396
106	*	15	—	296
107	*	15	—	307
108	*	15	—	345, 409
109	*	15	—	421(i) & (ii)

Report Recommendation	Priority	Report Chapter	London Underground Action	Represented Parties Recommendation
110	****	16	36	230, 231, 236, 238, 239, 241, 242, 344(iv)
111	****	16	37	255, 257, 264, 265, 344(v), 417
112	****	16	—	231
113	***	16	34	230
114	***	16	36	223, 230, 248, 250, 251
115	***	16	—	232–235
116	**	16	38, 39	230, 231, 254, 256, 257
117	**	16	—	256
118	**	16	—	244–247, 259
119	**	16	—	344(iv), 417
120	****	17	—	—
121	***	17	30	32–34, 36–39
122	***	17	43, 46	—
123	***	17	—	—
124	***	17	—	92
125	**	17	29, 31	43, 44, 46, 47, 48, 220
126	**	17	—	—
127	*	17	47	428
128	*	17	—	375, 398
129	****	18	—	169, 170
130	****	18	—	171, 172
131	***	18	—	173
132	***	18	—	178
133	***	18	—	28
134	***	18	—	31
135	***	18	—	177
136	***	18	—	199
137	***	18	—	181
138	***	18	—	183
139	**	18	—	205
140	**	18	—	179
141	****	19	101	112
142	***	19	100	276–278
143	***	19	—	67
144	***	19	—	346, 355, 368
145	***	19	—	271, 353
146	***	19	—	270
147	***	19	—	—

Report Recommendation	Priority	Report Chapter	London Underground Action	Represented Parties Recommendation
148	—	19	—	357, 358, 361, 373, 384
149	—	19	—	79, 87, 204
150	—	19	—	—
151	—	19	—	—
152	—	19	—	—
153	—	19	—	—
154	—	19	—	240
155	—	19	—	344(iii)
156	****	19	—	352, 440
157	****	19	—	440

Note:

In Chapter 17 I indicated that certain recommendations had not been included in Chapter 20 but must be considered separately if it should be decided not to apply fire certification to underground stations. The relevant numbers of recommendations by represented parties are as follows:

41, 91–111, 114, 119–127, 131, 175, 184–200, 202, 203, 206–208, 222, 249, 360

Chapter 21

Conclusion

1. For over a century London Underground has run an exceedingly safe railway system. It has a very good record and travel by the Underground remains considerably safer than by almost every other form of transport. But London Underground, and its holding company London Regional Transport, had a blind spot—a belief that fires were inevitable, coupled with a belief that any fire on a wooden escalator, and there had been many, would never develop in a way which would endanger passengers. In my view that approach was seriously flawed for it failed to recognise the unpredictability of fire, that most unpredictable of all hazards. Moreover it ignored the danger from smoke, which is almost certainly more deadly than fire.

2. During the Investigation I indicated that I would consider the question of commendations of individuals at the end of the hearings. Later I said that I would like further time to reflect on the matter. Having done so, I do not consider that it is appropriate to make commendations in this Report, for such a course would be thought to be the definitive list of all those who had acted with courage and dedication. In truth there were many from whom I did not hear, who acted with courage and dedication, such as the doctors and nurses. Indeed there were also many civilians and members of the emergency services who did not give evidence because they could not help me with my immediate task of establishing the cause of the accident.

3. There are two individuals whom I would like to mention. Station Officer Townsley died a hero's death, giving his life in an attempt to save another. Police Constable Hanson's presence of mind and courage must have enabled many people to escape with their lives. The Court salutes not only those two but all the members of the public, the emergency services and London Underground staff who helped others in any way.

4. I turn now to deal with costs. The Investigation has no power under the Regulation of Railways Act 1871 to make an award of costs, but you indicated that you would listen sympathetically to any recommendations that I made.

5. In my view it is proper that those who died or were injured should have the benefit of full representation at an Investigation such as this and access to technical experts. I granted leave to those who applied and said that I would expect them to join together for the purposes of the Investigation. They gladly accepted my invitation and so a consortium of solicitors was formed to represent the majority of those who died and those who were injured. I recommend accordingly that you should order the payment out of public funds of their standard scale costs to be agreed with the Treasury Solicitor, or failing such an agreement to be taxed.

6. In my view it is not appropriate that the Association of London Authorities, the London Fire and Civil Defence Authority and the British Transport Police should receive an order for costs out of public funds. They are public authorities, funded by ratepayers' or taxpayers' money, and although I acknowledge the substantial contribution which was made to the proceedings by the London Fire and Civil Defence Authority the suggestions they made were ultimately for the general good of the ratepayers of London.

7. I recommend that those trade unions who appeared should receive a contribution towards their costs. Although their members were all represented by their respective employers, the Court was assisted at times by the submissions made on behalf of the trade unions. I recommend that the National Union of Railwaymen, the Fire Brigades Union and the Associated Society of Locomotive Engineers and Firemen should receive one-third of their standard scale costs out of public funds to be agreed with the Treasury Solicitor, or failing such an agreement to be taxed. I recommend that the Transport Salaried Staff Association, who played only a minor part in the proceedings, should receive the sum of £500 towards their costs.

8. Prodorite Limited, the manufacturers of the paint system used on the escalator shaft, applied for leave to appear after the first two scientific experts retained by London Regional Transport and London Underground alleged that the paint had been a substantial cause of the flashover. Quite clearly such an allegation was extremely damaging in commercial terms, for the finger of suspicion had been pointed at Prodorite. It is clear from the evidence which I heard that there was no substance in the allegation. It would be quite wrong having defeated such an allegation if Prodorite were left to pay their costs. There is no power under the Act to make an order for one party to pay the costs of another party and accordingly I recommend that you should consider the payment of Prodorite's standard scale costs out of public funds to be agreed, with the Treasury Solicitor, or failing such an agreement to be taxed.

9. This has been a long and searching Investigation into a terrible disaster in which 31 people lost their lives and many more were injured. Having set out as an Investigation into the events of one night, its scope was necessarily enlarged into the examination of a system—the human and physical state of affairs which was in place at King's Cross on that night. I am conscious that during the Investigation a number of people felt bruised by the searching questions which they were invited to answer; but with a tragedy of this dimension the Court had to know why this state of affairs had come about. Such was the purpose of this Investigation with its inquisitorial process. If their answers and this Report serve the ends of safety and remind people that above all they must place safety first, the Investigation will have achieved its goal.

Appendix A

Text of Letter of Appointment

Regulation of Railways Act 1871

In the matter of a fire at King's Cross Underground Station on 18 November 1987

Whereas

(1) a fire occurred at King's Cross Underground Station on 18 November 1987 (hereinafter called "the accident") which was an accident of which notice is for the time being required by or in pursuance of the Regulation of Railways Act 1871 to be sent to the Secretary of State for Transport (hereinafter referred to as "the Secretary of State"), and

(2) it appears to the Secretary of State that a formal investigation of the accident is expedient

Now therefore the Secretary of State, in exercise of the powers conferred by section 7 of the Regulation of Railways Act 1871 and now vested in him, hereby makes the following Order –

The Secretary of State directs that a formal investigation of the accident and of the causes thereof and of the circumstances attending the same be held, and he hereby appoints **John Desmond Augustine Fennell OBE QC** to hold the same with the assistance of **Major Anthony Gwyn Burton King**, an inspecting officer of railways, **Dr Alan Frederick Roberts, Sir Peter Howard Darby CBE**, and **Professor Bernard Crossland CBE** as assessors.

Signed by authority of the Secretary of State
25 November 1987.

A J GOLDMAN
An Under Secretary in the
Department of Transport

Appendix B

Procedural History

1. On 24 November 1987, the day following my appointment, I visited the scene of the disaster and the incident room set up at King's Cross by the British Transport Police.

2. The Court held a preliminary public hearing on 2 December 1987 at Church House, Westminster, at which I outlined the terms of reference of the Investigation, discussed the procedure to be followed, and heard applications for legal representation.

3. I granted representation to various parties on the ground that they had a direct interest in the Investigation. They were:
   i) the deceased and injured;
   ii) London Regional Transport and London Underground Limited;
   iii) the London Fire and Civil Defence Authority;
   iv) various trade unions whose members had been involved;
   v) the Association of London Authorities representing 15 London boroughs and in particular Camden where the accident happened;
   vi) the London Regional Passengers' Committee, a statutory body set up under the London Regional Transport Act 1984 to represent the interests of passengers; and
   vii) Otis Elevators plc.

4. I granted leave to the trade unions whose members had been involved, notwithstanding that both London Regional Transport and London Underground Limited and the London Fire Brigade made express statements indicating that they appeared to represent the interests not only of management but of every single member of their respective organisations.

5. Where I felt unable to grant representation I encouraged those making the application to provide their evidence to the Treasury Solicitor so that it could be considered by Counsel to the Investigation whose role was one of complete independence. I am glad to say this was done.

6. The Court encouraged the victims of the disaster and their families to consider shared representation and a consortium of solicitors led by Russell, Jones and Walker was formed to represent their interests. I indicated to the consortium that I would arrange for them to have access to the technical experts engaged by the Treasury Solicitor so that they would have whatever help they needed fully to represent

their clients' interests. In each case where it appeared that a deceased or injured person was not represented I wrote a personal letter to that person or their next of kin inviting them to apply for leave to appear and offering to help with professional representation. Thus, I am glad to report that all those who died were represented apart from one whose family wished not to take part in the Investigation for compassionate reasons.

7. I indicated that where a person's conduct might be called into question either at the outset or during the Investigation, I would sympathetically consider an application for that person to be represented.

8. A second preliminary hearing was held on 25 January 1988 at Church House, Westminster. Although that hearing was primarily to discuss technical matters, I granted leave to appear to three further parties:

    i)   the Associated Society of Locomotive Engineers and Firemen;
    ii)   Prodorite Limited; and
    iii) the British Railways Board and the British Transport Police.

    I granted leave to Prodorite Limited, the manufacturers of the paint system used on the ceiling of the Piccadilly Line escalator shaft at King's Cross station, in view of the suggestion that their product substantially contributed to the flashover.

9. I also ruled that as far as any allegation or criticism of the conduct of another person or party was concerned, notice of such matter must be given by letter to the Treasury Solicitor who would then, having consulted Counsel to the Investigation, write a letter setting out the basis of such criticism to the party concerned thus enabling that criticism to be met. In adopting this course I was following the recommendation made by the Royal Commission on Tribunals of Inquiry (the Salmon Commission), which I indicated would form the basis of the procedure at this Investigation.

10. The formal hearings began on 1 February 1988 at the Methodist Central Hall, Westminster. Eyewitness evidence both oral and written was given first, followed by expert evidence as to the mechanics of the flashover. In Part Two of the Investigation the Court heard extensive further evidence, principally from London Regional Transport and London Underground Limited, about the human and physical state of affairs which was in place at King's Cross on the night of the disaster. There was also further scientific evidence. During Part Two the Court received from London Underground a list of 101 actions which it proposed to implement by way of changes to the present system. That

list was later enlarged to incorporate suggestions from the Court and the parties. Finally, the Court considered the lessons to be learned from the accident.

11.   At the outset of Part Two, I was invited to make rulings on the scope of the evidence to be received during the remainder of the Investigation. The Association of London Authorities submitted that the Court should consider the funding of London Underground. I ruled that such a question was *ultra vires* the Investigation, which was concerned with what happened in the accident at King's Cross on the night of 18 November 1987, and why it happened. But I went on to make it clear that I would allow proper questions directed to the underlying philosophy of the management towards safety and how decisions were made, together with the basis upon which they were made insofar as they related to what happened in the disaster.

12.   At a later stage, the Association of London Authorities made an application as to the payment of their costs by the Secretary of State, but in the absence of any assurance that I would recommend these should be paid, they withdrew from the Investigation on 3 May 1988. I invited the Association of London Authorities to submit any evidence they would have presented and they duly made such evidence available to the Investigation. It was taken fully into account.

13.   The Court heard 114 witnesses in Part One which lasted 40 days and 36 witnesses in Part Two which lasted 51 days. Some of the witnesses called for Part Two had already given evidence in Part One. Over 80,000 documents, over 100 reports and 15 videos were submitted in evidence.

14.   The formal hearings moved to Church House on 3 May 1988 and were completed on 24 June 1988. In all the Court sat for 91 days.

15.   Apart from the public hearings, the Court met on several occasions to discuss the progress of the Investigation. The Court made a visit to the British Transport Police L Division information room and London Underground Headquarters Controller's Room at 55 Broadway. We also visited Oxford Circus Underground Station and saw the new Underground Ticketing System (UTS) and communications equipment in operation.

16. At the outset of the Investigation a Scientific Committee was set up under the chairmanship of Professor Crossland. The first meeting was held on 25 January 1988, and five meetings were held thereafter. They were attended by Cremer and Warner as consultants to the Court and by experts retained by the represented parties. The object of the Scientific Committee was to try and establish common ground and, where this was not immediately established, to agree upon a technical programme to evaluate the merits of the various theories. In this way it was possible for many of the technical problems to be clarified and programmes of experimental work to be executed. The scientific work continued until 31 August 1988, by which time it had achieved significant results.

Appendix C

List of Parties and their Representation

1. **Mr John Hendy QC** and Mr Terry Gallivan of Counsel, instructed by Mr Grahame Kean, representative of the *Association of London Authorities*, appeared on behalf of that Association.

2. **Mr Charles Pugh** and Mr Matthew Scott of Counsel, instructed by Messrs. Russell, Jones and Walker acting for a consortium of solicitors, appeared on behalf of the *bereaved and injured*.

3. **Mr. Christopher Kemp**, solicitor, appeared on behalf of the *British Railways Board*.

4. **Mr Anthony Seys Llewellyn** of Counsel, instructed by Mr Simon Osborne, Solicitor for British Railways Board, appeared on behalf of the *British Transport Police*.

5. **Mr Roger Henderson QC,** Mr Robert Jay and Mr Ian Burnett of Counsel, instructed by the Treasury Solicitor, appeared on behalf of the *Court*.

6. **Mr Benet Hytner QC** and Mr Allan Gore of Counsel, instructed by Messrs. Robin Thompson and Partners, appeared on behalf of the *Fire Brigades Union* and the *Associated Society of Locomotive Engineers and Firemen*.

7. **Sir John Drinkwater QC,** Mr Charles George and Mr Charles Gibson of Counsel, instructed by Mr David Atkinson of the Legal Services of the *London Fire and Civil Defence Authority*, appeared on behalf of that Authority.

8. **Mr Rufus Barnes** and Mr John Cartledge, appeared on behalf of the *London Regional Passengers' Committee*.

9. **Mr Lionel Read QC**, Mr Christopher Carling and Mr Nigel Cooksley of Counsel, instructed by Mr Ian King, solicitor to *London Regional Transport and London Underground Limited*, appeared on behalf of that statutory Corporation and that Company.

10. **Mr Geoffrey Barber** appeared on behalf of the *National Association of Fire Officers*.

11. **Mr Alan Cooper** and Miss Michelle Brown of Counsel, instructed by Messrs. Pattinson and Brewer, appeared on behalf of the *National Union of Railwaymen*.

12. **Mr Raymond Kidwell QC** and Miss Anna Guggenheim of Counsel, instructed by Messrs. Jarvis and Bannister, appeared on behalf of *Otis Elevators plc.*

13. **Mr Simon Tuckey QC** and Mr Victor Lyon of Counsel, instructed by Messrs. Linklaters and Paines, appeared on behalf of *Prodorite Limited.*

14. **Mr Christopher Symons** of Counsel instructed by the Treasury Solicitor, appeared on behalf of the *Railway Inspectorate of the Department of Transport.*

15. **Mr Michael Tomlinson** appeared on behalf of the *Transport Salaried Staffs Association.*

Appendix D

List of Those Who Died

1. AGYAPONG, Miss Betty
   Student

2. BEST, Terence Alonzo
   Council employee

3. BRYANT, Mark David
   Cold store supervisor

4. BURDETT, Andrew
   Office worker

5. BYERS, Miss Elizabeth Norma
   Schoolteacher

6. CHAPPELL, Miss Treena
   Bank employee

7. COTTLE, Dean
   Schoolboy, aged 7

8. COTTLE, Mrs Susheila Nirmala
   Housewife

9. DEARDEN, Miss Sarah
   Financial journalist

10. EVE, Neville Harold
    Office worker

11. FAIREY, Miss Jane Alison
    Stockbroker

12. FALCO, Mrs Natalie Angela
    Widow

13. GEORGE, Jonathan Redvers
    Engineer

14. GOVINDARAJAN, Kuttalam
    Manager, Bureau de Change

15. HALL, Graham David
    Company director

16. HOLDEN, Michael
    Council employee

17. HUMBERSTONE, Ralph
    Casual employment

18. KEARNEY, Miss Bernadette Frances
    Auxiliary nurse

19. KEEGAN, Michael Anthony
    Materials controller

20. KHAN, Shoabib
    Student

21. LIBERATI, Marco
    Student

22. MARKS, Philip Geoffrey
    Architect

23. MORAN, Laurence Vincent
    Musician

24. NEWCOMBE, Lawrence Sonny
    Staff nurse

25. PARSONS, Stephen Alan
    Installations manager

26. ROOME, Christopher
    Stockbroker

27. ST. PRIX, John Fitzgerald
    Self-employed painter and decorator

28. SINGH, Rai Mohabib
    Assistant manager

29. TARASSENKO, Ivan
    Musician

30. TOWNSLEY, Colin James
    Station officer, London Fire Brigade

31. *UNIDENTIFIED MAN

*Despite the widest publicity and extensive enquiries by the police and other authorities, the identity of this man remained unknown when the Report went to press.

Appendix E

List of Witnesses for Part One

1. ANSTIS, Brian
   Senior Booking Clerk, London Underground Ltd

2. ASQUITH, Jeremy
   Designer

3. ATKINSON, Peter Maurice
   Chief Inspector, British Transport Police

4. BAKER, Stephen Andrew
   Project Controller

5. BALFE, Patrick Michael
   Police Constable 2439, British Transport Police

6. BARDSLEY, Richard Philip
   Police Constable 2625, British Transport Police

7. BARKER, Mrs Eileen Margaret
   Housewife

8. BARRETT, Arthur Stanley
   Automatic Train Operator, London Underground Ltd

9. BATE, David Christopher
   Data Processing Manager

10. BATES, Richard John
    Journalist

11. BEBBINGTON, Terry Alan
    Police Constable 2476, British Transport Police

12. BECK, Colin
    Architect

13. BEDFORD, Mrs Susan Alice
    Physical Education Teacher

14. BELL, Roger William
    Temporary Sub-Officer, London Fire Brigade

15. BONNER, Miss Lesley
    Journalist

16. BRICKELL, Philip Howard
    Leading Railman, London Underground Ltd

17. BROOKES, Miss June
    General Manager

18. BUTTON, Stuart
    Fireman, London Fire Brigade

19. CLARKE, Timothy
    Area Operations Assistant, British Railways Board

20. CLARKSON, Gerald Dawson
    Chief Officer of the London Fire Brigade and Chief Executive of the London Fire and Civil Defence Authority

21. CLIFT, Anthony John
    Detective Superintendent, British Transport Police

22. COLEMAN, Alan
    Inspector, Metropolitan Police

23. COUPER, Allan William
    Inspector, British Transport Police

24. CROSBY, Thomas Patrick
    Deputy Chief Ambulance Officer, London Ambulance Service

25. CURRAN, Neil Charles
    Computer Manager

26. CURTIS, Hugh Robert
    Lift and Escalator Service Fitter, London Underground Ltd

27. DEMONTE, Roger
    Temporary Station Officer, London Fire Brigade

28. DHANPERSAUD, David
    Station Inspector, London Underground Ltd

29. DINGLEY, Miss Judith Ann
    Journalist

30. DIXON, Julian Mark
    Police Constable 2639, British Transport Police

31. DOHERTY, Michael John
    Deputy Chief Officer, London Fire Brigade

32. DWYER, Noel Thomas
    Fitter's Mate, London Underground Ltd

33. DYER, Malcolm
    Automatic Equipment Technician, London Underground Ltd

34. EDGAR, John
   Fireman, London Fire Brigade

35. EGLINTINE, Peter
   Computer Programmer

36. EISNER, Dr Herbert Sigmund
   Consulting Scientist

37. EMANUEL, Anthony Lenus
   Leading Railman, London Underground Ltd

38. FARRELL, Matthew James
   Railman, London Underground Ltd

39. FLANAGAN, David Charles
   Leading Fireman, London Fire Brigade

40. FORD, William
   Fireman, London Fire Brigade

41. FRANKLAND, Robert David
   Booking Clerk, London Underground Ltd

42. FRENCH, Mrs Patricia Ann
   Control Officer, London Fire Brigade

43. FROST, Brian Lesley
   Divisional Officer, London Fire Brigade

44. GREEN, Ronald John
   Divisional Operational Manager (District and Piccadilly Lines), London Underground Ltd

45. GRIFFITH, Elliott Carlisle
   Rest Day Cover Leading Railman, London Underground Ltd

46. HALL, Miss Sarah Jane
   Solicitor

47. HALLIDAY, David John Xavier
   Fire Investigator, Metropolitan Police Forensic Science Laboratory

48. HALSTEAD, Mrs Jennifer Ann
   Housewife

49. HANSON, Roy Christopher
   Line Controller (Piccadilly Line), London Underground Ltd

50. HANSON, Stephen Terrence
   Police Constable 2550, British Transport Police

51. HARLEY, Ivor Russell
   Area Manager (Northern Line), London Underground Ltd

52. HAYES, Christopher
   Relief Station Inspector, London Underground Ltd

53. HILLS, Dennis
   Part-time cleaner, Cleaning Services Organisation, London Underground Ltd

54. HOADLEY, Jonathan Wilfred
   Senior Technical Officer

55. HOLMES, Kenneth
   Engineer

56. HUMPHREY, Charles Barry
   Station Officer, London Fire Brigade

57. HYTHE, Peter William
   Leave Cover Booking Clerk, London Underground Ltd

58. IZIENICKI, Gabriel Leonard
   Maintenance Manager (Lifts and Escalators), London Underground Ltd

59. JOHNSON, Colin Thomas
   Divisional Officer, London Fire Brigade

60. JONES, Philip Andrew
   Assistant Design Engineer

61. KARMOUN, Abdeslam Ahmed
   Computer Programmer

62. KENNEDY, Albert Richard
   Assistant Chief Officer, London Fire Brigade

63. KERBEY, Kenneth John Leonard
   Police Constable 1102, British Transport Police

64. KORNER, Mrs Shirley
   Psychiatric Social Worker

65. KUKIELKA, Richard
   Police Constable 2248, British Transport Police

66. LANE, Paul Joseph Steven
    Bank Clerk

67. LEE, Andrew William
    Merchant Banker

68. LEECH, Miss Rosalind Mary
    Secretary

69. LEVER, Miss Jean
    Publican

70. MARSHALL, Dr John Geoffrey
    Consulting Scientist

71. MARTLAND, Grahame Phillip
    Police Constable 2612, British Transport Police

72. MEHMET, Ilfray
    Tailor

73. MENDELLE, Paul Michael
    Barrister

74. MOODIE, Keith
    Principal Scientific Officer, Research and Laboratory Services Division, Health and Safety Executive

75. MORGAN, Miss Lesley
    Travel Executive

76. MOULTON, Robert Edward
    Fireman, London Fire Brigade

77. MURPHY, Miss Barbara Elizabeth
    Furniture Restorer

78. NELSON, Leonard
    Acting Traffic Manager (Metropolitan and Jubilee Lines), London Underground Ltd

79. NEWMAN, Derek Michael
    Booking Clerk, London Underground Ltd

80. NOLAN, Terence Patrick
    Contract Engineer

81. O'NEILL, Mrs Sharon Margaret
    Woman Police Sergeant 256, British Transport Police

82. OBCENA, Patricio
    Railman, London Underground Ltd

83. ORD, Miss Kathleen Isobel
    Leading Railwoman, London Underground Ltd

84. OSBORNE, Peter Kenneth
    Station Officer, London Fire Brigade

85. PAGE, Colin Phillip
    Electronics Engineer

86. PAGE, Peter John
    Assistant Station Manager at King's Cross, British Railways Board

87. PARMAR, Mahendra
    Railman, London Underground Ltd

88. PILGRIM, Carl Winston
    Relief Station Manager, London Underground Ltd

89. POWELL, Martin Ivor
    Fireman, London Fire Brigade

90. PREECE, Miss Patricia Ann Frances
    Divisional Ambulance Officer, London Ambulance Service

91. PRYKE, Alan James
    Station Officer, London Fire Brigade

92. RANASINGHE, Indunil Noel
    Leave Cover Relief Booking Clerk, London Underground Ltd

93. SHORE, Clifford John
    Assistant Divisional Officer, London Fire Brigade

94. SINGH, Manjit
    Fireman, London Fire Brigade

95. SMITH, David Robert
    Relief Booking Clerk, London Underground Ltd

96. SQUIRE, Phillip Jeffrey
    Dustman

97. TIGAR, Jeremy John
    Salesman

98. TOMBE, David
   Police Constable 184 AL, Metropolitan Police

99. TOSELAND, Dr Patrick Arthur
   Consultant in the Department of Clinical Chemistry at Guy's Hospital and Senior Lecturer in the Department of Forensic Medicine in the Medical School

100. TRAYNOR, John William
    Fireman, London Underground Ltd

101. TREFRY, Vernon Ronald
    Sub-Officer, London Fire Brigade

102. TUCKER, David Mansfield
    Consultant Scientist

103. TUMBRIDGE, Malcolm Leonard
    Relief Line Controller, London Underground Ltd

104. TURNER, Raymond
    Detective Sergeant 2846, British Transport Police

105. WESTON, Christopher Donald
    Acting Traffic Manager (District and Piccadilly Lines), London Underground Ltd

106. WHITE, Bertram Arthur
    Railman, London Underground Ltd

107. WILKINS, Stephen John
    Railway Signals Engineer

108. WILKINSON, Ian Michael
    Inspector, British Transport Police

109. WILLIAMS, Timothy
    Senior Administrative Officer

110. WILSON, John William
    Deputy Assistant Chief Officer, London Fire Brigade

111. WINGROVE, David John
    Editor

112. WISE, Richard James
    Chartered Accountant

113. WOOD, John
    Leading Railman, London Underground Ltd

114. WORRELL, Joseph Michael
    Station Manager at King's Cross, London Underground Ltd

Appendix F

List of Witnesses for Part Two

1. ADAMS, Ronald Charles
   Senior Personnel Manager (Operations), London Underground Ltd

2. BRIGHT, Sir Keith
   Chairman and Chief Executive of London Regional Transport

3. BUTCHER, Clive Gordon
   General Manager (Operational Development) London Underground Ltd

4. CLARKE, William Robert
   Operations Director, London Underground Ltd

5. CLARKSON, Gerald Dawson
   Chief Officer of the London Fire Brigade and Chief Executive of the London Fire and Civil Defence Authority

6. COCKRAM, Ian James
   Building Services Engineer, London Underground Ltd

7. COLLINS, David Howard
   Area Manager (Metropolitan and Jubilee Division), London Underground Ltd

8. DISMORE, Andrew Hartley
   Solicitor, Robin Thompson and Partners

9. DUFFIE, Michael Leslie
   Principal Architect (Architectural Services Group), London Regional Transport

10. DUGGAN, Gary James
    Senior Scientific Assistant (Development), London Underground Ltd

11. FITZHUGH, Dr Henry Antonie
    Marketing and Development Director, London Underground Ltd

12. IZIENICKI, Gabriel
    Maintenance Manager (Lifts and Escalators), London Underground Ltd

13. JONES, Dr Ian
    Computer Science and Systems Division, Harwell

14. KNAPP, James
    General Secretary, National Union of Railwaymen

15. LAWRENCE, Leslie Stanley
    Engineering Director, London Underground Ltd

16. MARSHALL, Dr John Geoffrey
    Consulting Scientist

17. MATTHEWS, David Glynn
    National Health and Safety Officer, Fire Brigades Union

18. McGREGOR, William Ian
    Assistant Chief Constable (Operations), British Transport Police

19. MEAD, David Richard
    Principal Civil Engineer, London Underground Ltd

20. MILLS, David Brynley
    Train Radio Manager, London Underground Ltd

21. MOODIE, Keith
    Principal Scientific Officer, Research and Laboratory Services Division, Health and Safety Executive

22. NURSOO, François Marc
    Chief Fire Inspector, London Underground Ltd

23. PERRY, Dennis Reginald
    Traffic Superintendent (Operations), London Underground Ltd

24. POWELL, Richard Geoffrey
    Safety Manager, London Underground Ltd

25. RASBASH, Professor David Jacob
    Emeritus Professor of Fire Safety Engineering, Edinburgh University

26. RICHARDS, David
    Project Officer, London Underground Ltd

27. RIDLEY, Dr Tony Melville
    Chairman and Managing Director of London Underground Ltd

28. Rose, Major Charles Frederick
    Lately, Chief Inspecting Officer of Railways, Department of Transport

29. Rycroft, Trevor James
    Training Centre Manager (Operations), London Underground Ltd

30. Stollery, Michael Arthur
    Principal Executive Assistant (Architectural Services Group), London Regional Transport

31. Straker, Roger Norton
    Personnel Director, London Underground Ltd

32. Sutton, Roger
    London Regional Treasurer, Fire Brigades Union

33. Styles, Jeffery
    Officer (Special Duties), London Underground Ltd

34. Wallace, Mrs Maudlin
    Chargehand Escalator Cleaner (Lifts and Escalators), London Underground Ltd

35. Warburton, Richard
    Director General, Royal Society for the Prevention of Accidents

36. White, Cecil Edwin
    Safety Manager (Operations), London Underground Ltd

Appendix G

Reports Presented to the Court

1. **Cambridge Environmental Research Consultants Ltd**

    (a) *"Fluid mechanics and physical modelling of King's Cross Fire flow in the booking hall."*
    28 July 1988

    (b) *"Fluid mechanics and physical modelling of King's Cross Fire."*
    29 July 1988

    (c) *"Notes following a meeting at H.S.E. Buxton, on August 12, 1988."*
    23 August 1988

2. **Professor D. Canter PhD FBPsS FAPA FBIM** Head of Department and Professor of Psychology, University of Surrey (with the assistance of I. Donald BA MSc PhD and P. Wood BSc PhD)

    "Behavioural and Psychological Aspects of the Fire at King's Cross Station."
    3 May 1988

3. **The Chatfield Applied Research Laboratories Ltd**

    "Examination of paint coatings – King's Cross Underground Station."
    8 March 1988

4. **Cremer and Warner Reports**

    (a) **The Cremer and Warner team**

    "Investigation into the King's Cross Underground Fire. Report on the technical investigation of the Fire on the 18th November 1987 based on analyses of evidence from the fireground and associated information."
    20 January 1988

    (b) **D. D . Milne B Eng MSc**

    "Edge Cleats No.4 Escalator."
    22 February 1988

    (c) **J. L. Britton BSc Tech**

    "Inspection of MH-Type Escalators lower machine chambers."
    23 February 1988

    (d) **B. N. Pain CBE QPM**
    Specialist Consultant

    "King's Cross Underground Fire, Wednesday 18 November 1987. Police Actions: 19.30 to 20.00 hours."
    24 February 1988

(e) **D. E. Shillito CEng FIChemE FInstE FRMetS**

"*The viewing of the No.4 Escalator right-hand running track from the stairway beneath No.5 Escalator.*"
3 March 1988

(f) **The Cremer and Warner team**

"*Preliminary comments on the significance of errors and omissions in the drawings of King's Cross Underground Station supplied by LUL to LFB. An Aunt Sally for discussion.*"
14 April 1988

(g) **D. J. Willmot QFSM MIFireE**

"*King's Cross Fire Investigation. Proof of Evidence. Information required for fire fighting purposes.*"
10 May 1988

(h) **B. N. Pain CBE QPM**
Specialist Consultant

"*Investigation into the King's Cross Underground Fire. Proof of Evidence. Police and Ambulance Service Actions Part 2.*"
11 May 1988

(i) **T. C. Marrs MD MSc FRCPath Dip RC Path and J. E. Bright MIBiol CBiol**
Chemical Defence Establishment, Porton Down

"*Final Investigation into the King's Cross Underground Fire. Report on Blood cyanide analytical techniques and significance of levels obtained.*"
June 1988

(j) **Cremer and Warner Team**

"*Summary – Escalator Fires (1973 – November 1987).*"
Report no: 88057 undated

(k) **Cremer and Warner Team**

"*Case of Waterfog fitted and operated (1958 – 70) excluding motor incidents, behind advert panels etc. In other words cases where it was felt waterfog would not have been useful.*"
1 June 1988

(l) **D. D. Drysdale BSc PhD FIFireE**
Unit of Fire Safety Engineering,
University of Edinburgh

"*Fire at King's Cross Underground Station, 18 November 1987. Some observations on the mechanisms of fire growth.*"
5 June 1988

(m) **Cremer and Warner Team**

"Examination of "Cellactite" Panels at King's Cross Underground Station, Piccadilly Line Escalator Shaft on the 20th June 1988."
21 June 1988

(n) **D. D. Drysdale BSc PhD FIFireE**
Unit of Fire Safety Engineering,
University of Edinburgh

"An experimental study of the behaviour of flames in an inclined rectangular channel."
July 1988

(o) **D. D. Drysdale BSc PhD FIFireE and D. E. Shillito CEng FIChemE FInstE FRMetS**

"King's Cross Fire Investigation, Fire Dynamics. Joint opinion on the one-third scale tests, Buxton, July and August 1988."
25 August 1988

5. **H. S. Eisner BSc MSc PhD and FIME**
Consultant on fires and explosions in mines

(a) *"King's Cross London Underground Fire, 18th November 1987: Report of Investigation."*
19 January 1988

(b) *"King's Cross London Underground Fire, 18th November 1987: Final Report of Investigation."*
23 March 1988

6. **B.C.R. Ewan BSc PhD Chementech Limited**

(a) *"The King's Cross Underground Fire. A consideration of the contribution of the ceiling paint system to the rapid acceleration of fire."*
12 March 1988

(b) *"The King's Cross Underground Fire. A consideration of the contribution of the ceiling paint system to the rapid acceleration of fire: First Updated Report."*
May 1988

7. **Fire Research Station, Cardington**

"Ceiling lining material with PRODORITE paint coating. Paint coats on plaster base with metal re-inforcement."
25 May 1988

8. **C. D. Foster BSc PhD CChem MRSC FIFireE MInst Pet**
   J. H. Burgoyne, Consulting Scientists and Engineers
   > *"Preliminary Report on an Investigation into the cause and spread of the Fire at King's Cross Underground Station on 18 November 1987."*
   > 20 January 1988

9. **D. J. X. Halliday BA**
   Metropolitan Police Forensic Science Laboratory
   > *"Fire Investigation Report King's Cross Underground Station."*
   > Undated

10. **Health and Safety Technology and Management Ltd (HASTAM)**
   Aston Science Park
   > *"Review of Fire Safety Training and Information in London Underground Ltd."*
   > 28 March 1988

11. **Health and Safety Executive Reports**
   (a) **K. Moodie BSc MSc and R. K. Wharton BSc PhD**
   Research and Laboratory Services Division
   > *"Fire at King's Cross Underground Station, 18 November 1987. Part 1: Damage Assessment."*
   > 8 December 1987

   (b) **K. Moodie BSc MSc**
   Research and Laboratory Services Division
   > *"Fire at King's Cross Underground Station, 18 November 1987. Part 2: Interim proposals for assessment of fire."*
   > 8 December 1987

   (c) **R. K. Wharton BSc PhD and K. Moodie BSc MSc**
   Research and Laboratory Services Division
   > *"Fire at King's Cross Underground Station, 18 November 1987. Part 3: In situ fire test."*
   > 19 January 1988

   (d) **K. Moodie BSc MSc**
   Research and Laboratory Services Division
   > *"Fire at King's Cross Underground Station, 18 November 1987. Part 4: Investigation Progress Report."*
   > 19 January 1988

   (e) **R. K. Wharton BSc PhD**
   Research and Laboratory Services Division
   > *"Fire at King's Cross Underground Station, 18 November 1987. Part 5: Ignition Tests and characteristics of samples."*
   > 9 March 1988

(f) **P. K. Swift TEng (CEI) MIMEMME**
Research and Laboratory Services Division

*"Fire at King's Cross Underground Station, 18 November 1987.
Part 6: Temperature measurements during laboratory tests on
escalator wheels."*
23 February 1988

(g) **K. Moodie BSc MSc**
Research and Laboratory Services Division

*"Fire at King's Cross Underground Station, 18 November 1987.
Part 7: Assessment of Fire Dynamics."*
7 March 1988

(h) **K. Moodie BSc MSc S. F. Jagger BSc PhD H. Beckett HNC(Mech
Eng) and R. J. Bettis PhD**
Research and Laboratory Services Division

*"Fire at King's Cross Underground Station, 18 November 1987.
Part 8: Laboratory Fire growth tests."*
22 March 1988

(i) **S. F. Jagger BSc PhD and K. Moodie BSc MSc**
Research and Laboratory Services Division

*"Fire at King's Cross Underground Station, 18 November 1987.
Part 9: Fire Growth Calculations."*
21 March 1988

(j) **M. J. Champion CEng MIEE**
Technology Division

*"Report of an Inspection of Electrical Installations in the vicinity
of Nos. 4, 5 and 6 escalators at King's Cross Underground Station,
London, N1."*
11 March 1988

(k) **R. J. Bettis PhD**
Research and Laboratory Services Division

*"Fire at King's Cross Underground Station, 18 November 1987.
Part 10: Burner Trials in an inclined inverted channel."*
6 June 1988

(l) **K. Moodie BSc MSc**
Research and Laboratory Services Division

"Assessment of Fire Dynamics – an update."
8 June 1988

(m) **S. F. Jagger BSc PhD**
Research and Laboratory Services Division

"Fire at King's Cross Underground Station, 18 November 1987.
Part 9: Fire Growth Calculations (Revised Version)."
9 June 1988

(n) **K. Moodie BSc MSc S. F. Jagger BSc PhD R. J. Bettis PhD**
Research and Laboratory Services Division

"Fire at King's Cross Underground Station, 18 November 1987.
Part 11: Scale model fire growth tests."
29 July 1988

(o) **K. Moodie BSc MSc**
Research and Laboratory Services Division

"Fire at King's Cross Underground Station, 18 November 1987.
Part 12: Assessment of Fire Dynamics (updated version)."
18 August 1988

(p) Record of meeting of Scientific Committee held at HSE, Buxton
on 12 August 1988.
18 August 1988

(q) **S. F. Jagger BSc PhD**
Research and Laboratory Services Division

"Fire at King's Cross Underground Station, 18 November 1987.
Part 13: A preliminary assessment of the second fire growth test
on the Buxton one third scale model escalator."
25 August 1988

12. **London Borough of Camden**

(a) *"London Borough of Camden – Chief Engineer."*
22 December 1988

(b) *"Submission to the 'Committee of Investigation into the King's*
Cross Underground Fire'. Report by the Director of Works."
5 January 1987

13. **London Fire and Civil Defence Authority**
London Fire Brigade

(a) *"Fire Investigation Report. Fire at King's Cross Underground*
Station at 19:36 hours on 18 November 1987."
12 January 1988

(b) *"A study and review of Fire Safety in underground railway*
systems within major cities in Europe and Asia."
February 1988

14. **London Regional Passengers' Committee**

   (a) **LRPC 1:**
   Bundle of 47 pages comprising:

   Letter dated 23/12/87 from LRPC to Mr Desmond Fennell OBE QC.

   List of Questions tabled for consideration by the King's Cross Fire Inquiry.

   "Passenger Safety and Protection from Fire on London's Tube Railways", a London Passenger Transport Research Group Report (Appendix A).

   "Passenger Safety and Protection from Fire on London's Tube Railways", minute of discussion at LRPC Facilities Sub-Committee meeting of 12/3/85 (Appendix B).

   "Statement by London Underground Ltd on the circumstances surrounding, and the actions following, the Oxford Circus station fire on Friday 23/11/84" (Appendix C).

   "Oxford Circus Fire", minute of discussion at LRPC Information and Facilities Sub-Committee meeting of 21/11/85 (Appendix D).

   "LUL Detrainment Exercise", report submitted to LRPC Information and Facilities Sub-Committee meeting of 30/11/87 (Appendix E).

   "LUL Detrainment Exercise", minute of discussion at LRPC Information and Facilities Sub-Committee meeting of 30/11/87 (Appendix F).

   (b) **LRPC 2:**
   Bundle of 44 pages, comprising correspondence between LTE/LUL, LTPC/LRPC, and members of the public, between 1969 and 1984, regarding passenger flow arrangements in the "Khyber Pass" and the operation of the ticket barriers in the King's Cross tube lines ticket hall.

   (c) **LRPC 3:**
   Bundle of 64 pages, comprising a letter to LRPC dated 8/2/88 from the Public Transportation Safety Board of the New York State Department of Transportation (with attachments), regarding passenger safety precautions and procedures, with special reference to protection from fire.

   (d) **LRPC 4:**
   Bundle of 54 pages, comprising correspondence regarding the locking of emergency exit barriers and the transcript of a presentation on fire safety precautions at Underground stations made to LTPC by LT and LFB on 23/2/72.

(e) **LRPC 5:**
Bundle of 138 pages, comprising excerpts from the System Safety Plan of the New York City Transit Authority, relating to:

The concept of a System Safety Plan;

The designated responsibilities of specific Departments vis-a-vis fire precautions in stations;

The role of the System Safety Department;

Hazard identification and risk assessment procedures;

Examples of current (1987) System Safety goals;

The broad characteristics of the New York subway system (for purposes of comparison);

Standing instructions for responding to emergencies (edited to exclude non-relevant contingencies) including the role of the civil emergency services;

Maintenance procedures for fire extinguishing apparatus;

Standing instructions regarding emergency exits;

Fire-related entries in the staff Rule Book; and

The action plan for implementing recommendations of the National Transportation Safety Board.

(f) **LRPC 6:**
"Enforcement of the Underground Smoking Ban", report presented to LRPC's Information and Facilities Sub-Committee on 14/9/87.

"Enforcement of the Underground Smoking Ban", minute of discussion at meeting of LRPC's Information and Facilities Sub-Committee on 14/9/87.

Correspondence between LUL, LRPC and members of the public relating to the Underground smoking ban.

(g) **LRPC 7:**
Recommendation relating to fire precautions on underground railways overseas, viz;

"Fire Down Below" – article published in Railway Gazette International (1/86).

"Fire Safety in Metropolitan Railways" – report by the International Metropolitan Railways Committee of the UITP (1987).

"Vancouver Sky Train Fire Precautions" – note by the Special Adviser to the Chairman of BC Transit (22/11/87).

Note on fire and safety measures at stations of the Mass Rapid Transit System of Singapore (23/11/87).

Description of fire safety precautions in the Hong Kong Mass Transit Railway (7/12/87).

"Standard for fixed Guideway Transit Systems" – published by the National Fire Protection Association of the United States (1983).

"Empfehlungen fur betriebliche Brandschutz-massnahmen bei Schienenbahnen" (Recommendations for operational fire protection measures in railways) – published by the Verband Offentlicher Verkehrsbetriebe (Association of Public Transport Operators) of West Germany (4/82).

"De la Fumee sans Feu" (Smoke without Fire) – description of a fire evacuation exercise on part of the Paris metro system, published in "Entre les lignes", journal of the RATP (Paris Public Transport Authority) (6/86).

"Simulation d'Incendie dans le Tunnel du RER" (Fire Simulation in a Regional Express Network Tunnel) – report by the joint study group of the Paris Public Transport Authority and Paris Fire Brigade (19/11/86).

(h) **LRPC 8:**
"Emergency Evacuation Exercise", report presented to LRPC's Information and Facilities Sub-Committee on 16/5/88.

(i) **Other Documents:**
"Operating department – Handling of Major Incidents" – Briefing note circulated at LUL/Emergency Services Seminar held at White City Training Centre on 14/6/88.

"Environment and Safety Information Bill" – HL Bill 92, dated 17/5/88.

"Parliamentary Debates (Hansard) – House of Lords Official Report", 15/6/88, columns 347 and 355.

"Questions arising from LFB evidence to the King's Cross Fire Investigation" – letter of 8/6/88 to LFCDA from LRPC, and LFCDA response (undated).

15. **London Underground Limited**

(a) *"Interdepartmental Inquiry Report. Fire at King's Cross Station Wednesday 18th November 1987."*
14 January 1988

(b) **G. J. Duggan BA**
Senior Scientific Assistant (Development)
London Underground Ltd
"Critiques of expert testimony/Reports."
"Scheme for progress of fire."
"Qualitative aspects of toxic gas emission from materials under fire conditions."
All three undated.

(c) **I. J. Cockram CEng FIMechE FCIBSE FInstE**
Building Services Engineer
London Underground Ltd

"Fire detection system tests at Warren Street Station 15th/16th March 1988."
25 March 1988.

(d) **E. T. Osborne CEng BSc(Eng) ACGI MRAeS**
Scientific Adviser
London Underground Ltd

"Assessment of cellactite and other ceiling materials at the top of King's Cross Piccadilly Line escalator shaft."
20 June 1988

(e) **London Underground Limited**

"Review of the HASTAM Report on fire safety training and information in London Underground Limited."
June 1988

(f) **London Underground Limited**

"Formal Investigation into the King's Cross Underground Fire on 18 November 1987. List of Actions by London Underground Limited."
July 1988

(g) **London Underground Limited**

"Formal Investigation into the King's Cross Underground Fire on 18 November 1987. Response to the recommendations from other parties."
July 1988

(h) **London Underground Limited**

"King's Cross Fire – Final Comments on Scientific Investigation."
Compiled by E. T. Osborne, Scientific Adviser, London Underground Ltd.
23 August 1988

Appendix 1: H. S. Eisner BSc MSc PhD FIME
"King's Cross Underground Fire – Final Comments."
17 August 1988

Appendix 2: D. M. Tucker BSc MSc
"Comments on the meeting and fire test at HSE, Buxton on the 12 August 1988."
17 August 1988

Appendix 3: Professor D. J. Rasbash BSc ARCS DIC PhD CEng FIChemE FIFireE MSFPE MSFSE
"Fire dynamics of the King's Cross Fire."
22 August 1988

16. **London Transport Research Laboratory Reports**

    (a) *"Smoke emission testing of Prodorite B2 system: sample taken
         from King's Cross Station."*
         25 January 1988

    (b) *"Report on the examination of plywood samples from the
         Piccadilly line escalator balustrade and hoarding at King's Cross
         Station."*
         26 January 1988

    (c) *"Report on the examination of a coated asbestos ceiling tile from
         Staff Room 1 – King's Cross Station."*
         8 March 1988

    (d) *"Report on the examination of paint flakes from asbestos ceiling
         tiles – King's Cross Station."*
         15 March 1988

    (e) *"An investigation of escalator wheel track debris in connection
         with the Fire at King's Cross Station on 18 November 1987."*
         15 March 1988

    (f) *"Hydrogen cyanide generation from materials involved in the
         King's Cross Fire."*
         27 May 1988

    (g) *"Paint stability test monitoring of Prodorite paint samples from
         King's Cross escalator ceiling."*
         15 June 1988

17. **J. G. Marshall MA DPhil CChem FRSC**
    Consulting Scientist

    (a) *"Prodorite Ltd. Preliminary Report on certain aspects of the fire
         which occurred at King's Cross Underground Station on the 18th
         November 1987."*
         20 January 1988

    (b) *"Prodorite Ltd. Second Report on certain aspects of the fire which
         occurred at King's Cross Underground Station on the 18th
         November 1987."*
         26 February 1988

    (c) *"Comments of Dr J. G. Marshall on Harwell Report AERE-G-4677
         dated May 1988."*
         9 June 1988

    (d) *"Comments of Dr J. G. Marshall on Mr G. J. Duggan's statement
         LTS 11/E."*
         9 June 1988

(e) *"Comments on Professor Rasbash's further comments."*
10 June 1988

(f) *"Comments on Amendments to Professor Rasbash's Further
Comments."*
13 June 1988

(g) *"Air requirements and air velocities for fires of various outputs
in the escalator shaft."*
15 June 1988

(h) *"Comments on further studies in connection with the King's
Cross Fire carried out since the closing of the Inquiry."*
4 August 1988

18. **The Metropolitan Police**
"Kings Cross Fire, 18 November 1987. Factual Report."

19. **K. Pettett BSc**
Fire and Materials Limited

(a) *"Test Report on Heat and Visible Smoke release rates for
materials using an oxygen consumption calorimeter according
to E5 proposal P-190."*
9 March 1988

K. Pettett BSc
Queen Mary College Fire and Materials Centre

(b) *"Test Report on heat and visible smoke release rates for
materials using an oxygen consumption calorimeter according
to ASTM E5 proposal P-190."*
Three Reports all dated 3 June 1988

20. **P. B. Poulson MA CChem FRSC**
Technical Director of Prodorite Limited

*"King's Cross Fire Investigation. Comments on HSE ⅓ Scale Fire
Simulation Tests."*
25 August 1988

21. **M. W. Pullin BSc CPhys MInstP AIFireE MRSH**
London Scientific Services
Operational Fire and Safety Group

(a) *Preliminary Report into Fire at King's Cross Underground
Station on 18 November 1987."*
25 November 1987

(b) *"Fire at King's Cross Underground Station, 18 November 1987.
Examination of Stn. O. Townsley's Fire Gear and clothing."*
9 December 1987

(c) *"King's Cross Underground Fire, 18 November 1987. Scientists
meeting, 12 August 1988."*
25 August 1988

22. **P. D. Pugh BSc**
    R. B. Hawkins and Associates Limited
    Consulting Scientists
    (a) *"Report on Investigation into Fire at King's Cross Underground Station on 18 November 1987."*
    26 November 1987
    (b) **P. D. Pugh BSc and A. A. Muston BA**
    R. B. Hawkins and Associates Limited
    Consulting Scientists
    "A theoretical study of frictional heating on escalator number four King's Cross Underground Station."
    12 January 1988

23. **Professor D. J. Rasbash BSc ARCS DIC PhD CEng FIChemE FIFireE MSFPE MSFSE**
    (a) *"Some Comments on the growth of the King's Cross London Underground Fire."*
    17 May 1988
    (b) *"Further Comments on the Fire at King's Cross Station."* (Including amendment).
    8 June 1988
    (c) *"Calculation of correction of Cone Calorimeter Results on account of Hess's Law."*
    July 1988
    (d) *"Cone Calorimeter Test Information."*
    July 1988

24. **J. E. Ratcliffe HNC(Chem) and S. R. Huneyball BSc MSc MINSTP CPhys and G. E. Armstrong BSc CChem MRSC**
    British Coal Scientific Services
    "Report on the Analysis undertaken for the Fire Research Station at Cardington on 25 May 1988."
    3 June 1988

25. **S. Simcox BSc N. S. Wilkes BA DPhil and I. P. Jones BSc MSc PhD FIMA**
    Computer Science and Systems Division and Engineering Services Division
    Harwell
    (a) *"Fire at King's Cross Underground Station, 18 November 1987: Numerical Simulation of the bouyant flow and heat transfer."*
    AERE-G 4677
    May 1988
    (b) *"Fire at King's Cross Underground Station, 18 November 1987: Numerical simulation of the effect of train movements."*
    AERE-G 4782
    July 1988

26.   **Total Fire Protection Co. Ltd.**

  "King's Cross Fire Investigation. Report and observations on Escalators 4, 5 and 6 for the Piccadilly Line, King's Cross."
  18 March 1988

27.   **C. Towner**
The Gerald Honey Partnership

  "King's Cross Fire Investigation. Inspection of Piccadilly Line Escalators 4, 5 and 6 – Mechanical Condition."
  16 March 1988

28.   **Trades Union Congress**

  "TUC submission on the application of the control of major hazards to non-industrial undertakings."
  June 1988

29.   **D. M. Tucker BSc MSc**
Tucker Robinson Consulting Scientists

  (a)   *"Report on the Fire at King's Cross Underground Station on the 18th November 1987 for London Underground Limited."*
     19 January 1988

  (b)   *"Supplementary Report on the Fire at King's Cross Underground Station on the 18th November 1987 for London Underground Limited."*
     23 March 1988

  (c)   *"Comments on the Chementech Report dated 12 March 1988."*
     25 March 1988

  (d)   *"Comments on the Jagger and Moodie Report "Part 9: Fire Growth Calculations" dated 21 March 1988."*
     30 March 1988

30.   **A. H. Turney BSc(Econ)**
Home Office Fire and Emergency Planning Department

  "Investigation into the Fire at King's Cross Underground Station 18 November 1987. Memorandum of Evidence by the Home Office."
  January 1988

31.   **R. M. Warburton OBE BA**
Director General
The Royal Society for the Prevention of Accidents

  "Investigation into the King's Cross Underground Fire. Proof of Evidence – Safety Management Issues." With appendices.
  9 May 1988

Appendix H

Videos presented to the Court

1. Alucobond fire test. VHS copy of tape 45. London Underground Ltd Research Laboratory (archive material).

2. Crib test 52kg Crib on steel under a curved roof at 0° and 30° incline. VHS copy of tape 80B and tape 80C. London Underground Ltd Research Laboratory (archive material).

3. Computer 3D simulation of fire growth. Harwell.

4. Escalator Fire Growth Tests on 29 January 1988. Film and video unit, Health and Safety Executive.

5. Evening of 18 November 1987 at King's Cross. London Fire Brigade.

6. Green Park demonstration. London Regional Transport.

7. Ignition test on escalator 4 on 8 January 1988. Unedited, taken by Burgoyne and Partners and film and video unit, Health and Safety Executive.

8. Ignition test on escalator 4 on 8 January 1988. Edited version. Film and video unit, Health and Safety Executive.

9. Inclined channel U-matic small scale fire growth test. Film and video unit, Health and Safety Executive.

10. King's Cross ceiling lining test on 25 May 1988. Prod. no. 87/540 tape 4. Building Research Establishment.

11. Melaform gloss system test on 20 October 1984. VHS copy of tape 69. London Underground Ltd Research Laboratory (archive material).

12. Propane burner trials, inverted 'U' channel. Film and video unit, Health and Safety Executive.

13. Simulation of fire growth on a one-third scale model. Combined video record of Tests 1 and 2 on 25 July 1988 and 12 August 1988. Film and video unit, Health and Safety Executive.

14. Small scale flame growth tests held on 23 May 1988. Samples orientated at 0° and 30° incline. London Regional Transport.

15. Survey of damage to King's Cross Underground Station. British Transport Police.

Ventilation System at King's Cross Underground Station

1. The ventilation of the Underground system relies on two separate mechanisms. Whilst trains are running they ventilate the system and effectively change the air about four times an hour. The air is also changed by 130 cooling fans which operate continuously throughout the Underground.

2. At King's Cross station there are two exhaust ventilation fan shafts. One serves the Victoria Line (28.3 cubic metres per second) and the other serves the Northern and Piccadilly Lines (47.2 cubic metres per second). The Victoria Line fan draws air from a cross-passage between the running tunnels just to the south of the platforms. The Piccadilly and Northern Lines fan draws air from the concourse at the foot of the Piccadilly Line escalators and top of the Northern Line escalators. The fans are controlled from the station, although they may also be controlled individually by maintenance staff.

3. The draughts in the station caused by the movement of trains (commonly referred to as the "piston effect") are controlled by means of two large draught relief shafts. One of these shafts serves both the Victoria and Piccadilly Lines, and the other the Northern Line. An air velocity of 6.7 metres per second on escalators and stairways, and 4.5 metres per second in ticket halls is the maximum considered acceptable to passengers.

4. These effects are illustrated in the graph at Figure 17 showing the computed air velocities in the Piccadilly and Victoria Lines escalator shafts during the period 19:30 to 20:00 on 18 November 1987.

5. There is no ventilation equipment for the tube lines ticket hall, but heat may be removed from the escalator machine room by a supply and exhaust fan (4.7 cubic metres per second) which is operated manually from the upper machine room. There are small ventilation systems for the staff accommodation with controls also located in the upper machine room.

6. The Metropolitan and Circle Lines do not require artificial means of ventilation, being nearer to and sometimes at the surface. There are further exhaust tunnel cooling fans between King's Cross and Angel station on the Northern Line, between King's Cross and Caledonian Road station on the Piccadilly Line, and between King's Cross and Highbury and Islington station on the Victoria Line. These are so far away from King's Cross station that they are unlikely to have affected air flows in the passenger areas on the night of the fire.

Appendix J

A Review of Recent Serious Escalator Fires and the Oxford Circus Station Fire

1. Reports on 46 escalator fires on the Underground from 1956 to 1988 and detailed information on 13 of these were made available to the Investigation. Examination of these reports shows that the established or attributed cause of fire was:

   i)   smokers' materials in 32 instances;

   ii) electrical in 8 instances;

   iii) unknown or not stated in 5 instances; and

   iv) attributed to friction in 1 instance.

   Brief details of six of the recent more serious escalator fires are given in the following paragraphs. In addition, brief details are given of the major fire at Oxford Circus station on 23 November 1984, which did not involve an escalator but led to costs of over £5 million and the setting up of the Fire Safety Task Force, which still had not completed its work by 1987.

   22 December 1984 – Leicester Square Station
   Piccadilly Line MH escalator 1

2. Fire was noted at the top of escalator 1 at 08:00 and the escalator was stopped. Shortly afterwards flames could be seen through the hole in the newel post where the handrail returns. The water fog equipment and the handrail spray were turned on, and a carbon dioxide extinguisher was used. The fire was on the trailer wheel track which was well alight all the way down the shaft. The line controller was informed at 08:06 and requested the attendance of the London Fire Brigade and an ambulance. Thick smoke was coming from the escalator so, at 08:11, the line controller was requested to order Piccadilly and Northern Line trains not to stop at Leicester Square. The station inspector met the London Fire Brigade and advised them of the need for breathing apparatus. The Fire Brigade went to the machine room and used hoses to put out the fire, which was extinguished by 08:25 though it was not until 09:02 that the smoke had cleared. The station was closed to passengers for 50 minutes. A station inspector and a woman police constable were taken to hospital, and other police officers had later to attend hospital.

Damage was considerable but it was concentrated on the right-hand side looking up, where the flames were first seen.

3.   An internal inquiry held by London Underground concluded that the probable cause of the fire was a cigarette or match which ignited rubbish under the skirting board. It was recommended that there should be regular heavy cleaning of all wooden escalators, water fog controls should be located close to the machine room entrance, and staff instructed always to use the water fog when smoke or flames were observed.

25 January 1985 – Green Park Station
Piccadilly Line MH escalator 3

4.   A fire was noted two-thirds of the way up escalator 3 at 19:40. At 19:53 the Piccadilly Line controller was requested to summon the London Fire Brigade. While awaiting the arrival of the Fire Brigade, station staff attempted to control the fire with carbon dioxide extinguishers. The Fire Brigade, the Ambulance Service, and both the Metropolitan Police and British Transport Police attended the scene at 20:00. There was dense smoke and trains were ordered not to stop. All the passengers and some staff were evacuated from the station. The station was closed for 55 minutes. The fire was under control by 20:45. Escalator 3 was extensively damaged.

5.   The internal inquiry concluded that the fire might have been caused by friction in a fibre bush in a trailer wheel, or by a cigarette or lighted match, or by the filament in a broken light bulb adjacent to the main seat of the fire. It was noted that neither the station manager nor the station inspector was able to account for all their staff during the incident, and neither the water fog equipment, nor the water hydrant in the ticket hall had been used. The Scientific Adviser to London Underground noted that the plywood at Green Park was extremely flammable.

6.   It was recommended that:
    i)   a 'basement plan' of all sub-surface stations should be posted at station entrances for the benefit of the emergency services;

    ii)   consideration should be given to re-siting existing water fog controls outside the machine room chamber;

    iii)   smoke detectors should be installed on escalators, in machine rooms and other areas of risk; and

    iv)   each station should have a designated assembly point for staff in the event of evacuation.

7. The police recommended that London Underground should improve the procedure for calling the Fire Brigade and ensure they were met on arrival. They also recommended that London Regional Transport should be informed of the Fire Brigade's responsibility and powers.

31 May 1985 – Manor House Station
Piccadilly Line MH escalator 3

8. At 20:15 three passengers pointed out a fire at the bottom of the up escalator to a visiting station manager. The station manager tried to put out the fire with an extinguisher, but he quickly realised that he needed assistance. He contacted the line controller to summon the London Fire Brigade and to request that trains should not stop. Passengers were evacuated and the gates shut. The station manager and a station inspector re-started the escalator and turned on the water fog equipment, but before they could operate the handrail spray control they were driven from the machine room by dense smoke. The Fire Brigade arrived at 20:35 and at 22:04 the fire was fully extinguished. The station remained closed for 124 minutes. The damage was limited to a section of handrail, scorching of the skirting board and a burnt chain wheel.

9. The internal inquiry noted that this was the third fire on an MH escalator in six months. They noted that MH escalators have a considerable amount of wood and that the state of cleanliness under the escalator made it more difficult to contain the fire. Although smoking was prohibited beyond the ticket barrier, it was common to see smokers lighting up as they travelled up the escalator. Various recommendations were made about non-smoking signs, fitting smoke alarms to escalators, replacing wooden skirting boards and panels by metal ones, more thorough cleaning of escalators and more regular use of the water fog equipment to dampen down the parts of the escalator vulnerable to fires.

10. In response the lift and escalator engineer refuted the need to replace the wooden skirting boards and panels on the grounds of expense, noting that "the wood we use is chosen for its fire resistant properties". He noted that escalators were cleaned regularly at a frequency determined by station usage.

    Finally, he said that the escalator should not have been stopped when the fire was first observed and the water fog equipment should have been used immediately.

23 December 1985 – Holborn Station
MH escalator 7

11. At about 10:45 a passenger reported that the handrail of escalator 7 was on fire. When station staff arrived the part on fire had reached the lower landing. The escalator was immediately stopped, but the fire quickly engulfed the lower landing. Station staff requested both the Central and Piccadilly Line controllers to order trains not to stop and to summon the Fire Brigade. By 11:10 station staff had evacuated all passengers by train or to street level except for a single passenger who was found shortly afterwards. By 11:35 the fire on the escalator was under control, but fire spread to the roof of the lower landing and it was not until 13:20 that the whole area was declared safe. The station was closed for 210 minutes. Escalator 7 suffered considerable damage.

12. No internal inquiry was held by London Underground. The London Fire Brigade concluded that a discarded match was the probable cause of the fire.

12 June 1987 – Green Park Station
Piccadilly Line MH escalator 3

13. At 20:30 a passenger noticed that escalator 3 was on fire and she stopped the escalator and informed a member of staff. The booking clerk informed the station inspector, but as the smoke was getting thicker a member of staff asked that the booking clerk should contact the line controller. The station manager and station inspector arrived in the booking hall and went into the machine room and fought the fire with a carbon dioxide extinguisher, but with no success. They were unable to start up escalator 3 before operating the water fog equipment. On the instruction of the area manager over the telephone, they went back to the machine room to operate the water fog equipment, but the smoke was very dense. They opened one valve but it proved to be the control for the water sprays on escalator 1 and they did not succeed in turning it full on before they were forced out by the smoke. When they came out of the machine room the Fire Brigade had arrived and by 21:35 the fire had been contained.

14. Early on in the incident five off-duty staff from another station were passing through Green Park station when they noticed smoke in the ticket hall. They made their way to the Piccadilly Line platforms where, as the smoke was getting thicker, they decided to telephone the Piccadilly Line controller and asked for the Fire Brigade to be summoned. They then fought the fire with extinguishers and helped to evacuate passengers. The station was closed for 81 minutes. Escalator 3 was extensively damaged.

15. The internal inquiry concluded that the probable cause of the fire was a discarded cigarette end or a lighted match, and recommended that the controls for the water fog equipment should be relocated outside the escalator machine room. The same recommendation had been made after the previous fire on the same escalator at Green Park in 1985. The inquiry also recommended that there should be bulkhead lighting in the machine room, the introduction of adequate and up-to-date fire training for all operating staff, an emphasis on rendezvous points for staff in an emergency, practical training in the use of water fog, and suggested that consideration be given to the introduction of sprinkler systems in machine rooms.

30 August 1987 – Bank Station
Central Line MH escalator 3

16. A fire was detected on escalator 3 at 07:53. There was dense smoke on the Central Line platforms and in the ticket hall. Smoke issued from the steps and side panels for the whole length of the escalator. The station inspector operated the water fog equipment. The London Fire Brigade attended and used hoses, but they were unable to get at the site of the fire so they used foam extinguishers. The fire was extinguished by 09:50 and escalators 1 and 2 were returned to service. Trains were ordered not to stop and the station was closed for 157 minutes. Escalator 3 was badly damaged. Examination revealed sealed bags of cleaners' spoil, together with rags and clothes, lying around the site. The cause of the fire was believed to be ignition by a cigarette of grease and detritus on the running track.

17. No internal inquiry was held by London Underground.

23 November 1984 – Oxford Circus Station
Victoria Line Contractor's Storage Area

18. At 21:50 a passenger reported smoke on the northbound Victoria Line platform. The station inspector found the contractor's storage area ablaze at the south end of the platform. Flames were already licking the frieze and ceiling. At 22:00 the line controller was requested to call the London Fire Brigade and to order trains not to stop, although in fact the Fire Brigade were first alerted at 22:02 by an employee at a fast food shop adjoining the platform in the station. Fire appliances arrived at 22:06 and ultimately thirty appliances were deployed. Attempts were made by the station inspector to attack the fire with extinguishers, but he was beaten back by dense black smoke which ultimately permeated the whole station and running tracks. Passengers had to be evacuated either to the surface or by trains. Staff and firemen trapped in the station operations room had to be rescued. Several trains on the Bakerloo, Victoria and Central Lines became stalled and as a result 720 passengers had to walk down tunnels to escape. The fire was under control at 01:43.

19.   Fourteen people were taken to hospital suffering from smoke inhalation, of whom four were passengers, one a woman police constable, and nine members of Underground staff.

20.   Very considerable damage was done to the northbound Victoria Line platform, passages to the concourse and the cross passage to the northbound Bakerloo Line platform, and there was smoke staining in much of the station. There was an asbestos problem which made it necessary to seal off the Victoria Line platform, and the Victoria Line was closed until 17 December 1984. The source of ignition was believed to be smokers' material and the spread was caused by the type of materials in the store, such as paint and acetone.

21.   The Oxford Circus fire provoked a report by the London Passenger Transport Research Group entitled 'Safety First', which was examined in detail by London Underground. It also led to the setting up of the Fire Safety Task Force, which continued to hold meetings until May 1987. This task force was involved in the implementation of many of the actions recommended as a result of the fire. Closer collaboration with the London Fire Brigade resulted. The prohibition of smoking was extended in February 1985 to all areas beyond the ticket barrier at all Underground stations wholly or partly below ground. Many of the actions recommended had not been adequately implemented by the time of the King's Cross fire.

Appendix K

Arson

1. The speed and extent of the fire was such that the police preserved the scene to investigate the possibility of arson. Enquiries were led by Detective Superintendent Clift of the British Transport Police. He, in his turn, invited Mr David Halliday, a Fire Investigator at the Metropolitan Police Forensic Science Laboratory, to examine the scene and within two days Mr Halliday had reached the preliminary conclusion that there was no evidence to suggest that the fire had been started deliberately. Police enquiries continued thereafter, but no evidence of arson came to light.

2. Notwithstanding the police view, London Underground indicated at the start of the Investigation that they remained concerned about the possibility of arson. It was suggested that evidence about a "man in blue overalls" seen at the entrance to the lower machine room of the Piccadilly Line escalator between 19:00 and 19:30 might give a clue to the culprit. Furthermore, Sir Keith Bright, who took a close personal interest in the arson theory, complained about the quality of the police investigations. And so all the relevant evidence was called before the Court and I was invited to consider the matter.

3. The evidence fell into three categories:

   a)   expert;

   b)   eyewitness;

   c)   remainder.

   I shall deal with each in turn, but before I do it is convenient to say a word about the background.

4. Although smoking had been banned on the Underground since 17 February 1985, it is clear that people continued to smoke and in particular to do so as they travelled up the escalator to leave the station. Mr Halliday discovered eight separate areas of burning on a single section of skirting taken from escalator 4, and expressed the view that they had been caused by a short period of flame contact followed by some residual smouldering. That theory gained added support from the matches he discovered in the running track underneath the escalator. No doubt they had fallen through the gap at the edge of the treads. Finally, it has to be borne in mind that there had been a series of fires on MH escalators as emerges in part from Appendix J.

5. The expert evidence came principally from Mr Halliday, the most experienced fire investigator at the Metropolitan Police Forensic Science Laboratory. He expressed the confident view that this was not a case of arson because amongst other reasons:

i) there was no evidence found at the scene to support the suggestion that the fire had been started deliberately;

ii) there was no evidence of the use of an accelerant;

iii) the accumulation of grease and detritus which formed the fire bed under the escalator was difficult to see and its inflammable qualities were not widely known even within London Underground.

iv) access to the machine room was difficult;

v) access to the escalator running track was difficult and physically dangerous.

He concluded by expressing the view that it was overwhelmingly likely that the fire had been caused by discarded smokers' materials.

6. The evidence about the "man in the blue overalls" came from three eye witnesses: Ilfray Mehmet, Dennis Hills and Paul Lane. I should say at the outset that I found each witness was attempting to help the Court and give a true account of what he had seen. But the fact is that each witness had had only a fleeting glance so that their evidence was of limited value.

7. Mr Mehmet said that as he was travelling up one of the escalators, some time between 19:00 and 19:30, he saw a man going underground at a point short of escalator 5 in the vicinity of three large panels. These panels can be seen in Plate 3. Mr Mehmet's view lasted for 10 or 20 seconds. In fact the panels which Mr Mehmet referred to could not be opened. There were further points of confusion in Mr Mehmet's evidence which led me to the conclusion that he was not a reliable witness.

8. Mr Hills, who had worked as a part-time employee of London Underground for a few months, recounted travelling down escalator 6 about 19:25 or 19:30 when he saw a man in blue overalls for a few seconds. The man was beside the wooden door in the side of the wall, just next to the metal handrail surrounding the trapdoor in the floor as seen in Plate 3. He never saw the trapdoor leading to the machine room in an open position. From his view Mr Hills provided a photo-fit of the suspected person to the police. It was wholly inconsistent with that provided by Mr Lane – to whom I come next.

9. Mr Lane said that having left the Northern Line platform at 19:20, he walked past the bottom of the Piccadilly Line escalators where he

saw a man positioned in the trapdoor leading to the machine room as seen in Plate 3. He saw the man for about 5 seconds. The man was facing Mr Lane but was visible only from the diaphragm upwards, presumably because he was standing on a ladder or something in the access chamber.

10. Mr Lane, a young graduate trainee bank clerk, was extremely confident in his evidence and utterly certain about what had happened and in particular the time. Unfortunately London Underground did not disclose the timings of the trains on the Northern Line until two weeks after the conclusion of his evidence with the result that this point could not be put to him in cross examination. But it is clear that Mr Lane's estimate of time cannot have been correct because it was totally at variance with the train logs. Furthermore the description he gave of the man's position in the access chamber was physically impossible because the ladder in the entrance was on the opposite side of the wall and accordingly it was impossible for Mr Lane to have seen the full front of the man, who would have been facing the wall as he emerged. Finally, the photofit he provided was totally different to that produced by Mr Hills.

11. In the face of the conflicts between Mr Lane's evidence and the established facts, I was driven to the conclusion that, however certain he was in his own mind, Mr Lane was not a reliable witness.

12. The remainder of the evidence also militated against the theory about arson. Mr Dwyer, a fitter's mate employed by London Underground, spoke of the danger of walking up the access way between moving escalators, and the same point was made by Mr Herbert, a station inspector employed at King's Cross Underground station. Likewise, it is difficult to see why an arsonist should want to start a fire half-way up the escalator when he could more easily have done so in the grease and detritus lower down. Furthermore, the point at which the fire began would have exposed any arsonist to physical danger which he could easily have avoided by choosing a more accessible point which was better lit.

13. While the hearing was in progress London Regional Transport carried out trials at Green Park station one night about midnight, to test various aspects of the arson theory. Mr Izienicki, the Maintenance Manager (Lifts and Escalators) of London Underground, gave evidence about the trials, but I did not find his evidence of particular help to me on this aspect. I observe in passing that it is a matter of regret that the police should not have been invited to attend these trials.

14. In my view the totality of this evidence failed to demonstrate any basis for an allegation of arson.

15. In view of the complaint made by Sir Keith Bright against the British Transport Police, as to the way in which they had investigated the possibility of arson, Cremer and Warner, as consultants to the Court, arranged to take the opinion of Mr Barry Pain, the former Chief Constable of Kent, upon the matter. Mr Pain expressed the view that the matter had been properly investigated. Mr Halliday expressed the same view. I agree.

Appendix L

Prodorite Limited

1. On 30 March 1988 at the conclusion of Part One of the Investigation, I was invited by Counsel for Prodorite, the manufacturers of the paint system used on the ceiling of the Piccadilly Line escalator shaft at King's Cross station, to give an indication as to whether their attendance would be required in Part Two of the Investigation. He put the matter in this way:

   > "As I explained yesterday, our presence before the Inquiry was to meet an allegation, which we regarded as serious, that our product substantially contributed to the flashover. That was an allegation which is, as you will appreciate, hotly contested. You have now heard the evidence on that issue. If you were to conclude that the product did not play a substantial part in the cause of the flashover, then the circumstances in which it came to be used in the London Underground are, I think it is agreed on all hands, of no importance so far as your Part Two is concerned, which obviously has much larger, wider and more important issues to address."

   I indicated that I wished to hear submissions upon the matter from all those concerned in Part Two and I received these on 11 April 1988.

2. After argument it was agreed that the relevant question for consideration by the Court was:

   > "... was the paint on the ceiling of the escalator shaft a substantial cause of the rapidity of the spread of flame from the shaft to the ticket hall, or did it only play a subsidiary role?"

3. Prodorite made the application in the light of the widespread publicity given to the suggestion that the paint system supplied by them had been a substantial cause of the flashover. Such an allegation was, of course, commercially extremely damaging.

4. Accordingly after a full consideration of the evidence then available, I delivered a provisional judgement on 15 April 1988 in these terms:

   > "Shortly after the fire at King's Cross, on 18 November 1987, rumours started and suggestions began to be made that the paint forming the top coat on the ceiling of the shaft housing escalators 4, 5 and 6 on the Piccadilly Line had been responsible in some way for the disaster. That paint had been manufactured by Prodorite and clearly a great cloud hung over their commercial reputation. To adapt the phrase of Mr Justice Sheen in the Zeebrugge Inquiry:

'The finger of blame was pointing at Prodorite'.

"Within a short time it became clear that the suspicion had crystallised into an accusation because the two experts engaged by London Underground Limited – Dr Eisner and Mr Tucker – in their separate reports of 19 January and 23 March 1988, and Mr Tucker's further reports of 25 and 30 March 1988, expressed the view that the Prodorite paint had been responsible to a substantial extent for the flashover. Not surprisingly, therefore, to protect their reputation Prodorite applied for leave to appear at the Investigation, and I granted such leave on 8 January 1988.

"By agreement between the parties, and to suit the convenience of the experts, I heard the scientific evidence on the twenty-eighth, twenty-ninth and thirtieth days of March 1988, which were days 38, 39 and 40 of the Investigation. Those days were chosen because they came at the end of Part One of the Investigation, during which all the eye-witness evidence had been given and when the overwhelming majority of relevant scientific tests had been completed.

"The scientific evidence comprised the work of a team led by Mr Keith Moodie of the Health and Safety Executive at the Explosion and Flame Laboratory at Buxton, who had undertaken a programme of research set out in the report issued on 8 December 1987, and subsequently reviewed at technical meetings under the chairmanship of Professor Bernard Crossland and attended by all experts engaged in the Investigation. Dr Marshall, a consultant scientist retained to advise Prodorite, gave evidence as well. The scientific evidence concluded with the evidence of Dr Eisner and Mr Tucker who had been instructed by London Underground Limited. The scientific evidence called by London Underground Limited had several unusual features. In the first place, London Underground Limited specifically said that they did not put it forward as the corporate view of London Underground Limited. Secondly, there was a divergence of opinion between Dr Eisner and Mr Tucker which became clear after they had given evidence. In short, Dr Eisner's position came much closer to that of Dr Marshall and Mr Moodie, whereas Mr Tucker remained firm in his view.

"After the scientific evidence was concluded, I was invited by Mr Simon Tuckey, leading counsel for Prodorite, to indicate whether I was able to make known the Court's view about the mechanism by which the fire spread up the escalator. That course was accepted by all parties, including London Underground Limited who said it could save a substantial amount of time at the Investigation.

"Accordingly, I heard argument about the matter on Monday, 11 April 1988, having first put the matter back until after the weekend at the request of leading counsel for London Underground Limited.

"It seems to me a cardinal principle of an Investigation like this that, as Mr Roger Henderson QC submitted on day 44 at page 71B:

'If it is practicable, consistent with proper and not hurried judgement, either to reach a final conclusion or a provisional conclusion, that those at whom the finger of blame may have been pointed should, either finally or provisionally, be acquitted of that finger of blame, then the sooner it is done the better'.

"Accordingly, after submissions, I was invited to answer the following question by Prodorite:

'Was the paint on the ceiling of the escalator shaft a substantial cause of the rapidity of the spread of flame from the shaft to the ticket hall, or did it only play a subsidiary role?'.

"Having originally accepted Prodorite's application for a ruling, London Underground Limited withdrew that support and opposed both the application and the form of the question. They said that the question was inappropriate and to answer it premature. On the latter point they said that further tests were under consideration but could give no indication whether they would or whether they would not be undertaken. They indicated that such tests as they might undertake were part of a general review of the fire performance of painted ceilings rather than a specific investigation aimed at resolving the events at King's Cross. This point is of importance because the scientific evidence clearly established that the fire performance of Prodorite B2 was greatly affected by its application to pre-existing paint up to about twelve layers in depth, varying from place to place. They could give me no indication as to when they would make a decision, although five months have now elapsed since the disaster.

"After forty-six days the time has now come, in my judgement, when I should attempt to answer the question posed by Prodorite. If I am content that there is sufficient satisfactory evidence available to be able to form a view, justice demands that I should.

"Bearing in mind that London Underground Limited have been unable to help me about the further tests, my decision must be a provisional one but I have reached the clear conclusion – as at present advised and on the basis of the evidence before this Investigation – that the paint on the ceiling of the escalator shaft was not a substantial cause of the rapidity of the flame spread from the shaft to the ticket hall.

"I should make it clear that I have given a provisional answer to a limited question. Fresh considerations must and will arise as far as Prodorite is concerned, but I take the view that having asked the question they are entitled to an answer which I now give. Since this is a provisional judgement I do not propose to give reasons. When I come to review my provisional judgement at the conclusion of the hearing, in the light of all the evidence, and including any further evidence which is adduced in Part Two, I will then set out detailed reasons for such conclusion as I finally reach."

5. I now set out my reasons for making this provisional judgement. My opinion at that time was based largely on the eye-witness evidence of the flashover which had by then been completed. This evidence is analysed in greater detail in the Report at Chapter 12, but in particular I found the evidence of P.C. Hanson and Mr Bates compelling when they spoke of the fire extending from escalator 4 into the ticket hall immediately before the flashover. Their evidence supported the view that the major fire development was on the escalator and contradicted the suggestion of major flame spread up the painted ceiling of the escalator shafts.

6. Other eye-witnesses described the development of the fire on the escalator at an earlier stage. That evidence was consistent with the existence of a well-established fire on the woodwork of escalator 4 shortly before the flashover.

7. In April 1988 the scientific evidence was incomplete and inconclusive. Mr Moodie had established a prima facie case in support of fire development on the woodwork on the escalator, but this contained various shortcomings. Others had argued in favour of rapid spread across the painted ceiling of the escalator shaft involving the Prodorite paint, but I found that evidence to be unconvincing and to be unsubstantiated.

8. I therefore made the provisional judgement which I have set out earlier.

9. With the benefit of further scientific investigation, I have reached the conclusions set out in Chapter 12. In my view this is consistent with the provisional judgement that I gave earlier.

Appendix M

Extracts from the transcript of evidence of Mr R.M. Warburton, OBE, BA, the Director General of The Royal Society for the Prevention of Accidents (RoSPA)

(i)   EXAMINED BY MR HENDERSON QC, COUNSEL TO THE COURT ON 3 JUNE 1988 [DAY 77 PAGES 2–8]

Q.   In coming to the conclusion which you set out in your short report you referred in paragraph 2 to the extensive reading of papers before receiving [the list of proposed actions by London Underground], and then proceed to say that in your view there had been a collective failure from the most senior management level downwards over many years to minimise the outbreak of fire, and more importantly to foresee and to plan for an uncontrolled outbreak of fire at an underground station with a real potential for large-scale loss of life. I want to ask you a few supplementary questions in relation to that opinion. First of all, having had the opportunity to read the transcripts of the evidence given by the witnesses since that report was made and supplied, have your views about that collective failure been fortified or reduced?

A.   I think fortified.

Q.   You speak of a failure from the most senior management level downwards to minimise the outbreak of fire. I would like to ask you a few questions about that, if I may. Do you draw a distinction between the need to minimise the outbreak of fire and any need to minimise the effects of an outbreak of fire?

A.   I think the primary reason is to minimise the outbreak of fire. The minimisation of effect is subsidiary.

Q.   Why is that so in your opinion?

A.   I think because of the aberrant nature of fire itself, that it can take many forms, that it can develop in so many different ways that the basis must be of any proactive programme to prevent the incident in the first instance.

230

Q. When you express that opinion, is that an opinion which you base upon your experience over the whole gamut of industry?

A. Yes.

Q. You speak of the aberrant nature – I think that was your adjective – of fire. We have heard and you will have seen in the transcript that the directors of London Underground Limited believed that there would always be the time and the opportunity to control an outbreak of fire. What do you have to say about plans for controlling an outbreak of fire once it occurs?

A. I think I addressed this one really by looking to see whether in fact there was a system built in which was based on experience, on inspection, on monitoring and on evaluation. And I looked very clearly at File Number 1 with the investigations of the whole range of fires that occurred between 1973 and 1987. I tried perhaps to generalise in a way as to what would be the common factors that came out of those. I think, looking broadly at them, it was the reiteration of the causative factors of smokers' materials, of friction, of the dust, grease, rubbish, that seemed to feature in most of the reports. I think that gave a clear pattern as to the way these fires occurred on escalators, and the characteristics seemed to be very much of a very rapid generation of smoke and, to some extent, either an entrapment of passengers, or that passengers had to be led away from areas of difficulty, and, because these were all MH escalators, in the investigations, wood skirting, balustrades and at times a spread of fire to the roof was apparent. I think the other thing was the importance of the very prompt fire-fighting. Where that was done very promptly, then the effect was minimised but the reports did also in many cases stress the limitation of training, an under-utilization of the waterfog and of where the controls were actually located. There was also in instances the problem of staff using hand extinguishers. I was very struck by a comment by a fire officer at the Holborn fire in 1985 where he commented in his own report that similarities were starting to appear. I think this question of passengers being in difficulty from smoke, and on occasion some members of staff had to be taken to hospital, struck me. The problem really I find in reading these reports was how limited the reports themselves are. All my training as an inspector was, in producing a report, to try to understand the causation because at the end of the day I think management can only make decisions if, in fact, the reports are in such a form that they are capable of management making a decision. So few of these reports in fact of the internal investigations really address themselves to the system within the London Underground and the contribution that organis-ation, management and indeed the staff could make. I think this is one of the main concerns I have for the future, that where investigations and reports are made, then they will have to be in a much broader context and they will have to provide management with very positive information that it can act upon.

Q. Now, you have dealt with many things in that answer, Mr Warburton. Can I try and make sure that we can understand the main components of what you have been saying? In the next sentence of paragraph 2 you went on to say:

> "It is my view that management had not learned from past incidents, from the evidence of their own inspections or from material supplied to them by outside bodies."

Coming to the first part of that sentence and the long answer you have given, when you read through File 1 and the history of escalator fires, did you see a learning by management of lessons from those past incidents?

A. No, I am afraid I did not. I think one of the problems there – and that was reinforced in the evidence of the directors – was how limited was the distribution of its information.

Q. I will come back to what lessons you learnt from them in a moment. Did you see evidence of a need of recognition of a need to minimise the outbreak of fire? I am not concerned with dealing with it for a moment but to minimise the outbreak?

A. No, I do not think that was ever really addressed. I think throughout the whole of the papers I have read there has been an assumption that fire is in fact an everyday happening and that, although such events could disrupt the service, and could cause damage, that in fact it was part of the everyday operation.

Q. Did you see any recognition that such an outbreak which could cause damage could also become uncontrolled?

A. No, and in fact again the directors were clear in their own minds, as I understand it, that, because of the very large number of incidents, one could draw a conclusion that that would not occur, and that there was also I sensed a sort of inherited wisdom in directors, that their predecessors equally had not seen that, and that, probably quite properly – that is not my area – the greatest perceived risk was in tunnels and Dr Ridley added a further one, the congestion of the system itself was a major problem.

Q. Is it a safe system, a safe approach, to base your planning for fire to proceed upon the premise that because there has been no loss of life, no serious multiple injury, as a result of fires, therefore it is unlikely to occur? Is that a safe premise from which to approach the question of dealing with fire?

A. No, I do not think so because, particularly given the environment within which these incidents occur, where large numbers of people are below ground, I think one would have looked for at least some one saying "what if" or some thinking as to "ought a case to be debated as to what in fact the worst possible consequence could be" and it was within that context that I was looking in effect at the system and the thinking behind the systems, and there were occasions at lower levels where I did find evidence of concern in that regard but broadly, no.

Q. Would you have expected to find within the documents some senior management questioning of "what if" and some questioning of potential major, uncontrolled outbreak of fire and its potential consequences?

A. I think one is always hoping that there will be the member of the awkward squad, if you like, who will ask a question. I think, given the deep conviction amongst senior management, I am not really surprised it was not.

Q. You have seen that all the directors who addressed this question have told the Court on oath that they genuinely believed that there was no risk to passengers because there would be the opportunity and the system to control an outbreak. Do you in any way doubt the genuineness of that belief from what you have seen?

A. No.

Q. Do you however believe that it is soundly based in the light of what you have read?

A. No, and I think the main reason for that is the lack of incisive information that was going to directors.

Q. Let me go to the second limb of that last sentence. "It is my view that management had not learnt from past incidents . . .". You go on, ". . . from the evidence of their own inspections". What is it that you had in mind there?

A. I think, looking at some of the work done by the safety department, and bearing in mind that good housekeeping and the cleanliness of the premises are factors that are always important in a positive fire prevention role, many of these inspections do from an internal point-of-view reveal that the Company had problems in controlling the potential combustible material that was within the premises.

Q. Did you discern in the papers you studied any success in reducing that problem over the years?

A. I think that is very difficult to answer because there was not to my mind any systematic evaluation as to where it was successful or not.

Q. What would you have expected to find or to see or hope to see in the sense of a systematic evaluation of those inspections?

A. I think the normal procedure would be that where an inspection revealed defects, firstly, those defects would be graded in order of importance, and then there would be a check system, there would be a follow-up, and over a period of time there would be an evaluation as to whether in fact the requirement not only had been achieved but was being maintained.

Q. Lastly, you referred to non-learning of lessons from materials supplied to them by outside bodies. Which particular materials did you have in mind there, Mr Warburton?

A. I was very impressed with the "Safety First" Report, and I understand that it was debated at very considerable length by senior members of management, but I cannot really find any evidence as to it being implemented.

Q. We know that as a result of the study of "Safety First" six additional tasks were added to the Oxford Circus Task Force List of some 60 tasks; but in relation to the "Safety First" Report, do you find that the reading of "Safety First" produced evidence that the lessons apparently being taught there were learned?

A. No; I have no evidence of that.

Q. Lastly, before leaving that matter, when you were looking at the documents did you look for evidence of a comprehensive review of fires and the assessment of risks?

A. Yes, I did.

Q. At what level would you have expected or hoped to find evidence of a comprehensive view of fires for the assessment of risk?

A. I would certainly think a director should have been involved in either chairing or setting terms of reference for such a study, bearing in mind that there had also been other expressions of concern – the APAU Report was one, the Railway Inspectorate was another – where the terms of reference would have been really within a context of the extent to which LUL's defences against fire were secure and comprehensive.

Q. We know – we have heard, and you will have read – that in the Summer of 1987 in the context of a fire at Green Park of the 12 June, a fire at Hampstead of the 27 July, and a fire at Bank of the 30 July, Mr Lawrence was concerned as to whether some pattern might be emerging, and therefore, together with others, called for a document which we have at page 372 of File III. It is the document of the Principal Civil Engineer of the 9 October, with which we are familiar. (*Same handed*). Mr Warburton, I just want to ask you one matter about that document. If you look at paragraph 2, the aim is stated to be, "to minimise the effects of fires and smoulderings in the operation of the underground". What do you have to say about that as an aim?

A.   I think it is an aim, but I think it perhaps encapsulates the problems we have discussed previously, that the assumption is that the fires will occur and therefore one has to minimise the effect rather than an aim or an objective perhaps being to reduce the number of fires.

(ii)   CROSS-EXAMINED BY MR READ QC, COUNSEL FOR LONDON REGIONAL TRANSPORT AND LONDON UNDERGROUND LIMITED ON 3 JUNE 1988 [DAY 77 PAGES 49–51]

Q.   I have one or two matters of generality before I take you to a few matters in particular. I am in this part of the questions addressing the subject of performance in the past but at no great length. You referred to the fact that it appeared to you from the documents that you had read and the transcripts of evidence that you had read that the occurrence of fires on stations apparently had been regarded as – I use your language – an every day event?

A.   Yes.

Q.   That needs some thought, does it not, Mr Warburton, because in the first place whatever reasonable efforts may be made, a fire somewhere on some part of any of 270 underground stations has to be in reality an every day event, does it not?

A.   No, I do not think it does.

Q.   What proposal do you suggest that the Underground should have in order to remove a fire somewhere on some of any of 270 stations from being an event which occurs every day?

A.   I think they have to have a lot more information about the cause of fires, their actual location, and determine whether it is practical or not to seek a reduction in certain areas. What concerned me was essentially that I could not find a great deal of evidence that that data if it existed was brought to the attention of the directors or senior management.

Q.   We are, are we, being sure that in that part of your evidence you are referring to fires in stations in general as opposed to a fire involving an escalator or an escalator machine chamber in particular?

A.   Both in a way, because of the ones that I have seen on escalators and the inquiries that were conducted on them I could not trace any evidence as to where those reports ultimately went, if anywhere.

Q.   That is another point, if I may say so. You, of course, remember the evidence that one of the shortcomings that is unequivocally accepted is a failure to report adequately, to follow up the reports, and indeed to analyse the implications of the reports.

A.   Yes.

Q.   I understand and there is no ambiguity about that acceptance. But all that having been said, I was simply wishing, with due respect, to take you up on a proposition, if it be a proposition, that a fire somewhere on one of 270 underground stations in practical terms is an event which happens every day of the week.

A.   Yes, it may be, but the implication of my comment was does it have to be an every day event?

Q.   It has to be unless you can find some practical means of avoiding it.

A.   Yes, but I was looking for evidence that someone had addressed the problem of what practical means could be applied.

Q.   You appreciate, do you, that there is not anything in core bundle 1 which is addressed to the general question of the problem of fires in stations generally as opposed to fires on escalators in particular?

A.   No, but repeatedly in the papers I read in general terms people referred to the frequency of fires, full stop. Perhaps I was wrong in interpreting that as a general considerable outbreak of fire over time.

Q.   I am only concerned, no more than that, simply to invite you to think that it is a little unfair to suggest that the Underground – and I include all levels of management and indeed the staff – have not made reasonable endeavours to minimise the outbreak of fires on stations generally, as opposed to the accepted shortcomings in relation to escalators in particular. That is all, since the subject, frankly, has hardly been touched. That is why I raised the point. So that you see the context of the point that I am respectfully putting to you, has your reading embraced core bundle 2, Mr Warburton?

A.   I do not know.

Q.   That is a good answer.

THE INSPECTOR: The point that has been worrying me and I think may be at the back of Mr Warburton's mind, is the answer that Dr Ridley gave on Day 73, page 30, letter G when I said:

> *"You cannot regard fire as an acceptable hazard, can you? A fire is not an occupational hazard, is it?"*

The answer from Dr Ridley was:

> *"There are, and have been, fires – or to use the euphamism, smoulderings – on London Underground year in and year out. They are part of the nature of the oldest, most extensive, most complex underground railway in the world. Anyone who believes that it is possible so to act that there are no fires ever, is, I fear, misguided."*

MR READ: I well remember that, Sir, and I well remember Sir Keith making a not dissimilar point, and it is, with due respect, a point which in my submission the Court and the Assessors must accept.

Q. That is quite a different thing from concluding there from that one should not make practical efforts in order to reduce the number of fires.

A. In all of the papers I was provided with I did not see any analytical work which said that there are X numbers of fires each year and we'll do this, that, and the other, with them. So perhaps it was a negative.

Appendix N

The opinion of Counsel to the Court on Fire Certification

Opinion

1. The object of this Advice is to assist the Court with a review and interpretation of the legislative regime which applies to King's Cross Underground Station in the context of fire precautions and safety at work. The relevant legislative provisions are contained in the Health and Safety at Work etc Act 1974 ("the HSWA 1974"); the Fire Precautions Act 1971, as amended ("the FPA 1971"), and statutory instruments made thereunder; and the Offices, Shops and Railway Premises Act 1963 ("the OSRPA 1963"). Although reference will be made to the manner in which the relevant law has been construed and applied by the appropriate enforcing authorities, namely the Railway Inspectorate ("the RI") and the London Fire and Civil Defence Authority ("the LFCDA"), it is not the purpose of this Advice to proffer critical comments.

2. **The Health and Safety at Work etc Act 1974**

    Part 1 of the HSWA 1974 is concerned, in general terms, with the health, safety and welfare of employees and others in connection with places of work. Section 2 imposes general duties upon employers to their emloyees: the specific matters to which these duties extend are set out in subsection (2). In particular, every employer is charged with the responsibility to ensure and maintain a work environment, systems of work and procedures of instruction and supervision which are adequate and safe, so far as is reasonably practicable. In the context of the London Underground system, the authority endowed with the powers and duties to enforce Part 1 of the HSWA 1974 is the Railway Inspectorate. The Railway Inspectorate does so pursuant to an agreement made on 1 May 1981 between the Health and Safety Commission, the Health and Safety Executive and the Secretary of State for Transport under section 13. The Railway Inspectorate has power to enter and inspect the underground railway for the purposes of investigation and enforcement (section 20), and may achieve compliance by issuing improvement notices (section 21) and prohibition notices (section 22). Prosecution for infringement of the statutory duties previously adumbrated may be made under section 33.

Except under section 1(1)(c), the HSWA 1974 is not specifically concerned with risk to the health, safety and welfare of employees and others created by, or in consequence of fire.

Section 1(1)(c) provides:

"The provisions of this Part [namely, Part 1] shall have effect with a view to–

(c)   controlling the keeping and use of explosive or highly flammable or other dangerous substances, and generally preventing the unlawful acquisition, possession and use of such substances".

Plainly, however, the general health and safety matters set out in section 2 of the HSWA 1974 entail the reduction of risk from fire, insofar as it is reasonably practicable, in the context of, for example, systems of work and the maintenance and provision of a working environment. Thus, the RI does have a significant enforcing role as regards the activities of London Underground Limited *qua* employer in relation to fire risks generally. Such a role would appear to exist irrespective of whether the local fire authority may have a greater and more specific superintending and enforcing responsibility under the relevant provisions of the FPA 1971. The interrelationship between the overlapping responsibilities of the RI and the LFCDA will be addressed at the end of this Advice.

3.   **The Fire Precautions Act 1971**
The FPA 1971 creates, so far as is relevant for present purposes, two distinct levels of control, both of which are administered by the local fire authority, the LFCDA (see section 27 of the Local Government Act 1985). First, particular categories of premises which are put to a "designated use" require a fire certificate. The consequences of certification have been helpfully summarised at paragraph 16 to the *Memorandum of evidence by the Home Office* submitted to the Committee of Investigation. Broadly speaking, the fire certificate may impose requirements for securing that the means of escape are adequate to meet the circumstances of the case, and are properly maintained and kept free from obstruction; that firefighting equipment is sufficient and satisfactorily maintained (Article 6 of the Fire Precautions (Non-certificated Factory, Office, Shop and Railway premises) Regulations 1976, S.I. 1976 No. 2010); that employees are appropriately trained to deal with fire and its consequences. The scope of the FPA 1971, and the circumstances in which certification becomes a mandatory requirement, will be discussed in the succeeding paragraphs. The second level of control is that contained in section 10 of the

FPA 1971. Specifically, this provision applies to "any premises which are being or are proposed to be put to a use (whether designated or not) which falls within at least one of the classes of use mentioned in section 1(2) of this Act...". Section 1(2) sets out six classes of "designated use", including "use as a place of work" (see section 1(2)(f) as added by the HSWA 1974, s.78(1)(2)). Section 10(2) provides:

> "If as regards any premises to which this section applies the fire authority are satisfied that the risk to persons in case of fire is so serious that, until steps have been taken to reduce the risk to a reasonable level, the use of the premises ought to be prohibited or restricted, the authority may make a complaint [to a Magistrates' Court]".

Plainly, the LFCDA's section 10 powers are capable of being applied to any underground station, given that the criterion of designated use as a place of work is satisfied. In our opinion these summary powers are applicable irrespective of whether or not the same underground station requires a fire certificate under section 1. In any event, it does not appear that the LFCDA would, or should, have exercised its section 10 jurisdiction in relation to King's Cross before 18 November 1987.

4. **Certification**

King's Cross Underground Station is not the subject of a fire certificate; nor has application for one been made or required under section 5 of the FPA 1971. Whether or not London Underground Limited, or its predecessors, *should* have applied for a fire certificate turns, in the final analysis, on the classification of King's Cross as a "building" rather than a "structure". In our opinion, *any* underground station (that is to say, including stations above and below ground level) is a "building", and is required to be certified as railway premises under the Fire Precautions (Factories, Offices, Shops and Railway Premises) Order 1976, S.I. 1976 No. 2009 ("the Fire Precautions Order"). The reasoning in support of our conclusions is as follows.

5. Section 1(1) of the FPA 1971 provides that a fire certificate shall be required "in respect of any premises which are put to a use for the time being designated under this section". Section 1(2) empowers the Secretary of State to designate by statutory instrument particular uses or premises for the purposes of certification. Plainly, railway premises are capable of being so classified because they are used as a place of work (section 1(2)(f)). Under the Fire Precautions Order, which came

into operation on 1 January 1977, "railway premises" have been designated for the purposes of section 1 of the FPA 1971. By Article 2(1), railway premises mean "premises to which the Offices, Shops and Railway Premises Act 1963 applies and premises which are deemed to be such premises for the purposes of that Act". Under Article 4(1), a fire certificate is *not* required for railway premises in which not more than twenty persons are employed to work at any one time, or not more than ten persons are so employed elsewhere than on the ground floor. Given that King's Cross exceeds these employment thresholds, it follows that a fire certificate is required – provided that the Underground Station constitutes "railway premises" as defined in the OSRPA 1963. It should be observed that a significant number of smaller underground stations would fall outside the ambit of section 1 of the FPA 1971, owing to the employment limits not being satisfied.

6. In section 1(4) of the OSRPA 1963, "railway premises" means "a building occupied by railway undertakers for the purposes of the railway undertaking carried on by them and situated in the immediate vicinity of the permanent way". By section 90(1), "except in section 1(4) of this Act, 'building' includes structure". Thus, for the purposes of defining "railway premises", "building" and "structure" are mutually exclusive. Accordingly, the issue to be resolved is whether King's Cross Underground Station, or discrete parts of it, constitute a building in this context.

7. Neither "building" nor "structure" is defined in the OSRPA 1963. According to the Oxford English Dictionary, the terms are synonymous. Thus, the mutual exclusivity posited by section 90(1) would appear to defy the ordinary meaning of the words. It has been suggested that assistance may be derived from the interpretation sections of the FPA 1971 (by section 43(1), " 'building' includes a temporary or movable building and also includes any permanent structure and any temporary structure other than a movable one") and the Building Act 1984 (by section 121(1), " 'building' . . . means any permanent or temporary building, and, unless the context otherwise requires, it includes any other structure or erection of whatever kind or nature (whether permanent or temporary)". In our view, however, these later provisions cannot assist in drawing the dividing line between "building" and "structure" expressly created by section 90(1) of the OSRPA 1963 because they presuppose that a structure may often be a building. In any event, by well known canons of statutory construction it is trite law that a particular statutory provision may not be interpreted by reference to subsequent legislation. Furthermore, although it may seem somewhat anomalous, the Fire Precautions

Order 1976 expressly does not apply the definition of building laid down in the FPA 1971 itself, but refers back to earlier legislation. In differentiating between these two closely-related terms in the context of railway premises, it is sought to draw a distinction which is capable of sensible, systematic and pragmatic application without doing any violence to the parliamentary language.

8. The case law shows that what is a "building" must always be a question of degree governed by all relevant circumstances. Its "ordinary and usual meaning is, a block of brick or stone work, covered in by a roof" (per Lord Esher MR in *Moir -v- Williams* (1892)1 QB 264). In different circumstances, however, it has been held under Factory Acts legislation that it is quite possible for a structure to be a building notwithstanding that it is not enclosed by walls and a roof and is not one of the ordinary forms of building (see *McGuire -v- Power Gas* (1961) 2AER 544 and *Paddington Corporation -v- AG* (1906) AC1). An ordinary railway embankment with a railway upon it is a breach of a covenant not to erect "any erection or building of any kind, except a fence wall not more than two feet high": "If it be necessary to say that a railway embankment is covered by the word 'building', I see no inconsistency in saying so. The term 'building' is not, necessarily, limited to bricks and mortar and to houses. One may build an embankment, and one may build a railway" (per Collins MR in *Long Eaton -v- Midland Railway (1902) 2KB 574*).

9. "Structure" is also a term of uncertain meaning whose precise definition depends upon the context of its application. Its natural and ordinary meaning is:

> "something which is constructed. It is not everything which is 'constructed' that would ordinarily be called a building, but every building is a structure" (per Lord Goddard CJ in *Mills & Rockleys Limited -v- Leicester City Council (1946) 1 AER 424*).

Perhaps the most helpful definition is to be found in *Almond -v- Birmingham Royal Institute for the Blind (1967) 2 AER 317*, a decision of the House of Lords:

> "Structure is a word which is wide enough to cover every kind of building as well as hoardings and erections of various kinds which could properly be described as buildings . . . the sole surviving qualifying concept seems to be that a 'structure' must be an adjunct of, or ancillary to, a main building in some way . . . " (Per Lord Hodson at page 321).

10. In our view, the imprecision of the statutory language has the consequence that "railway premises" in section 1(4) of the OSRPA 1963 is capable of two possible constructions in the context of underground stations. First (and we believe the better view), an underground railway is a "building", or series of buildings, of substantial size and construction in the immediate vicinity of the permanent way. On this interpretation, escalators, shafts and passageways would require to be certified as integral parts of the "railway premises" of which the building is constituted. The term "structure" would be apt to accommodate only those erections and hoardings, for example, which were adjuncts of or ancillary to the building itself: namely, platform signs, signal gantries, revolving train timetables etc. The permanent way itself (i.e. the track) would also probably be outside the ambit of "building". Secondly (and we believe an arguable construction, albeit erroneous), an underground station taken as a whole is not a building because it can only properly be classified as a series of passages, shafts and stairways, being a collection of interlocking structures: certification under the Fire Precautions Order 1976 is only necessary if a distinct building or part of a building may be identified, such as a room or set of rooms within the railway system itself. Once identified, that particular unit – which may be an office, shop or railway premises, depending upon the circumstances – may contain passages and stairways; but the Fire Precautions Order 1976 and OSRPA 1963 are not to be regarded as applying directly to underground passages and stairways in their own right.

11. Given the obvious difficulty in differentiating between "building" and "structure", the second construction which we have sought to set out has considerable force. It might be said to strain the natural and ordinary meaning of "building", according to Lord Esher's definition for example, to contend that the term properly embraces a complex of tunnels, shafts and passageways, none of which are covered by an identifiable roof. Moreover, on the first construction previously propounded there would appear to be little reason to exclude the permanent way itself, and the tunnels linking the stations; whereas s1(4) of the OSRPA 1963 refers to "a building . . . situated in the immediate vicinity of the permanent way", thereby specifically excluding the track. Even so, in our opinion the first construction is to be preferred. The key to the problem of statutory construction posed by section 90(1) of the OSRPA 1963 is to recognise that the draftsman has undoubtedly given the term "building" a particularly wide meaning, and that "structure" represents a residual category of artifacts which are not recognisable as buildings in any proper sense. If a railway embankment is a building, there appears to be no reason why an underground station should not be equally so. Given the size,

permanence and nature of construction of King's Cross Underground Station, it would be straining the parliamentary language overmuch to suggest that the constituent passageways, escalator shafts and ticket halls may only be classified as structures and therefore fall outside the purview of section 1(4) of the OSRPA 1963. On this basis, the term "structure" would be apt to comprehend those erections and hoardings which are adjuncts of, or ancillary to, the main building: platform signs, fences, signals, timetables, hoardings, erections (temporary or permanent) on platforms, etc. Furthermore, the tunnels linking underground stations would appear to be more accurately described as "structures" rather than "buildings" in that they are not occupied by railway undertakers and have not been built up and constructed in a manner similar to the passageways and shafts comprising the railway premises themselves.

12. **Certification in practice**

For many years the RI had taken the view that the OSRPA 1963 did not apply to underground railway stations, unless individual offices, shops or workrooms could be identified. Once specified, an escalator leading to such a distinct building would be itself a "building" if it were the sole or normal means of access to the particular office, shop or workroom. This approach was articulated in a Memorandum from HM Factory Inspectorate to HM Inspectors of Factories dated 1 April 1968 (when the fire precautions provisions of section 28-41 of the OSRPA 1963 were still in force, before their repeal in 1971), and in an Office Note prepared by Mr J Seager of the Department of Transport dated 7 May 1980. A shift in approach was prompted by the construction of two underground stations at Heathrow in the late 1970's: the RI were originally of the view that fire certification was not necessary, but encountered opposition from the Greater London Council. The debate developed in correspondence in the following way.

13. On 26 October 1977, London Transport Executive applied for a fire certificate under section 5 of the FPA 1971 in respect of Heathrow Central Station. On 19 April 1979, the GLC set out various works which were required to be carried out before a fire certificate could be granted: these works specified the steps to be taken in connection with the means of escape and for giving warning in case of fire, and the means for fighting fire. The London Transport Executive forwarded the GLC's recommendations for additional fire facilities at Heathrow Central Station to the RI who wrote to the Chief Officer of the London Fire Brigade on 25 June 1979 in the following terms:

> ". . . The station platforms and main passenger access passages do not require a fire certificate as the OSRPA 1963 was not applicable to them . . ."

The GLC replied on 31 October 1979, setting out the alternative construction of sections 1(4) and 90(1) of the OSRPA 1963 which we believe, on balance, to be the correct one:

> ". . . the Director of Legal Services takes the view that the station platforms and main passenger access ways are integral parts of the building of the underground railway station and should not, therefore, be excluded from certification".

It seems, however, that the RI were not persuaded by the force of this argument because on 12 December 1979 response was made to the GLC's letter and the following points emphasised:

(1)   the FPA 1971 does not apply to underground railway stations, in that as a class of premises they have not been designated under s1(2)(e) of the Act;

(2)   the safety of the public using an underground railway lies within the responsibility of the RI, although since 1908 the GLC (and its predecessors) has carried out annual inspections of LTE's underground stations on the Department's behalf to ensure a continuing high standard of 'housekeeping'.

Following meetings which took place between the GLC and the RI in the spring of 1980, the GLC reiterated its position by letter dated 9 December 1980:

(1)   Heathrow underground station is an underground building in which persons are employed to work. Its use falls within a class of use contained in section 1 of the FPA 1971, namely use as a place of work (s1(2)(f));

(2)   the underground building contains railway premises as defined in s1(4) of the OSRPA 1963;

(3)   all other parts of the same building require certification under the FPA 1971 because s1(8) provides: ". . . where premises consisting of a part of a building are put to a designated use, any other part of the building which is occupied together with those premises in connection with that use of them shall . . . be treated as forming part of the premises put to that use". Thus, the main passenger access routes and platforms are brought within the ambit of certification.

14. This exchange of correspondence excited further meetings between the London Fire Brigade, the London Transport Executive and the Department in 1981. A possibility canvassed by the GLC was that an arrangement under section 18(2) of the FPA 1971 might be made between the GLC and the Health and Safety Commission which would allow the RI (as agent for the HSC) to discharge the GLC's function as fire authority. An internal memorandum by Major Rose of the RI dated 21 July 1981 recognised the force of the GLC's arguments to the effect that the FPA 1971 probably did apply to the whole of Heathrow Central Station, but counselled against the RI taking over full responsibility as the fire authority:

> "I think that the question of whether anything further should be done at Heathrow and, if so, what, will have to be sorted out between the GLC and LT. Our contribution can be to point out that, in our view, the investment necessary to provide everything that LFB have requested at Heathrow would be better used putting right some of the shortcomings in safety (including fire precautions) on the older parts of the Underground".

On 30 July 1981 the RI wrote to the chief officer of the London Fire Brigade proposing this form of compromise:

> ". . . There are obviously differences of opinion as to the exact status of Heathrow Central Station *vis-a-vis* the 1971 Act, especially the public areas such as the platforms and passageways. However, I do not regard these differences as particularly important, since even if these areas were ruled to be outside the Act the Inspectorate would not wish to see a situation where the Fire Brigade were dissatisfied as to the standard of fire precautions in the station as a whole. Put another way, even if the Inspectorate became the fire authority we would still wish to seek advice from the Fire Brigade and would not accept as permanent a situation in which we were in disagreement with the Brigade over what the latter regarded as the *essential* fire precautions at Heathrow Central".

Even so, the RI also pointed out that the considerable investment that would be needed to provide everything that the LFB had requested would be better deployed elsewhere. In the result, these issues were to be resolved between the GLC and the LTE in the context of the latter's outstanding application for a fire certificate.

15. Finally, on 18 June 1982 the RI wrote to the LTE suggesting a *modus vivendi* as regards future action on the following lines:

    (i) for reconstruction of existing stations not involving significant changes in the existing layout, no formal approval from the GLC was necessary;

(ii)   for the new stations and major reconstruction of existing stations, the fire authority had to be approached and be generally satisfied with the proposals before the works were carried out: in the event of significant disagreement, the RI was to act as adjudicator. This procedure was to apply whether or not a fire certificate was formally required.

16.   Accordingly, the view has been taken that older underground stations such as King's Cross do not require a fire certificate; although substantial works of reconstruction involving changes in the physical layout of the station would need the imprimatur of the LFCDA. In the absence of such works, the LFCDA continues to act in an advisory capacity and purportedly outwith the strict scope of the FPA 1971, pursuant to an informal arrangement made with the RI some eighty years ago. Clearly, the responsibility for enforcement remains entirely with the RI acting pursuant to its HSWA 1974 powers and duties: the LFCDA, on the law as currently applied, has no enforcing powers under sections 18 and 19 of the FPA 1971, but may only advise the RI.

17.   Although it is not suggested that the question of certification necessarily affected the course of events leading up to the disaster on 18 November 1987, it is our view that King's Cross Underground Station requires to be the subject of a certificate under section 1 of the FPA 1971 and the Fire Precautions Order 1976, for reasons previously outlined. In those circumstances, sections 9A and 5 of the FPA 1971 are of direct relevance. Under section 9A, all railway premises are required to be provided "with such means of escape in case of fire for the persons employed to work therein as may reasonably be required in the circumstances of the case". The overall circumstances include the number of visitors who may reasonably be expected to be resorting to the premises at any time (section 9A(3)). In our view, this subsection applies irrespective of whether the employment thresholds as provided by Article 4 of the Fire Precautions Order 1976 are satisfied. Under section 5, application for a fire certificate has to be made to the fire authority in the prescribed form, whereupon the authority may grant the certificate if being satisfied of the matters specified in section 5(3): for example, the means of escape in the event of fire being safely and effectively used at all times; the means for fighting fire being adequate, etc. Once granted, the fire authority may enforce compliance with the terms of the certificate by inspecting premises on reasonable notice (section 19): contravention of its terms constitutes an offence under section 7.

18.   Under existing arrangements as previously outlined, the RI is charged with the legal responsibility of enforcing all matters germane to fire precautions in the context of its wider powers under the HSWA 1974; the LFCDA acts in an advisory capacity alone. If, as we suggest is appropriate, London Underground Limited were to apply for, and receive, a fire certificate in respect of its designated use of King's Cross Underground Station as a place of work, no anomalous or unworkable situation would thereby be created. The RI would continue to be responsible for enforcing the relevant provisions of the HSWA 1974 : such responsibility would include fire safety. In practice, however, the LFCDA would enjoy greater and more specific powers in this sphere, in the exercise of its inspecting and enforcing role under the detailed provisions of the FPA 1971. In the event of any disagreement, it would seem appropriate that the views of the LFCDA should prevail. On this basis, therefore, the HSWA 1974 and FPA 1971 would be easily and effectively applied.

Roger Henderson QC
Robert Jay
15 March 1988

Printed in the United Kingdom for Her Majesty's Stationery Office
Dd 0503085,   11/88   C80,   Ord 8406095